Rhythm of the Spirit

One child's inner strength to overcome illness and multiple disabilities

Lisa Marie Anderson

Order this book online at www.trafford.com or email orders@trafford.com
Most Trafford titles are also available at major online book retailers.

The design drawing is the original work of the author.
Cover design by Joni Anderson and D.Elaine Photography.
Cover photo and author photo courtesy of James and Doris Casselton

Printed in Victoria, BC, Canada.

ISBN: 978-1-4269-2280-0 (sc)

*Our mission is to efficiently provide the world's finest, most
comprehensive book publishing service, enabling every author to
experience success. To find out how to publish your book, your way,
and have it available worldwide, visit us online at www.trafford.com*

Trafford rev. 1/14/2010

www.trafford.com

North America & international
toll-free: 1 888 232 4444 (USA & Canada)
phone: 250 383 6864 ♦ fax: 812 355 4082

For my sons Giovanni and Kenneth

"No pessimist ever discovered the secret of the stars, or sailed an uncharted land, or opened a new doorway for the human spirit."

Helen Keller (1880-1968)

Acknowledgements

Although raising a child with multiple disabilities is often a challenge, the rewards I reap are well worth the effort. There is no doubt that I could not meet these numerous challenges alone. It is humbling to me just how many people have shown an interest and love for Giovanni in his young life. I am very thankful for all the kind, generous, hardworking people who have helped Giovanni to grow and thrive.

In many books, authors give credit to the many people who make the book possible. In this case, I give credit to the many people who make Giovanni's growth possible.

Because of privacy issues, I have changed many names in the manuscript. However, I believe the people that have been most helpful in Giovanni's life will be able to see themselves in the story.

I want to thank my mid-wife and her assistants for their compassion and support during my pregnancy and birth. Thank you also to Giovanni's aunt who, despite the break-up of the family, was present to assist with Giovanni's birth.

During those first stressful weeks of Giovanni's life, which were spent in the hospital, there are so many people to thank. Thank you to the doctors and nursing staff at Kaiser Hospital in Santa Rosa, for responding quickly and calmly to help stabilize Giovanni for transport to the San Francisco Kaiser NICU. I am grateful also for the kindness and empathy given by members of the transport team who brought Giovanni from Santa Rosa to San Francisco.

I am so grateful to the doctors and nursing staff at the San Francisco Kaiser Neonatal Intensive Care Unit (NICU), who have the difficult task in caring for critically ill children on a daily basis. I am sure that being witness to so much heartache can have psychological effects. I want these wonderful people to know that their sacrifices do not go unnoticed. The pediatricians did the best they could in providing answers to my never ending questions. The nurses not only cared for Giovanni, but for me also. I believe it takes a special person with a special mental constitution to be able to handle the intensity of a job in the NICU.

A special thank you to the neurologists on staff whose job it is to be "detectives" of the very complex human brain. These doctors have daily challenges in providing prognoses through reading a variety of brain scans, blood tests, and clinical observations. They were very kind and always tried to remain positive.

Thank you to Deborah Jansen, the nurse case manager for Giovanni's neurologists. Even though Giovanni changed neurologists four times with Kaiser, Deborah has always remained a constant voice of encouragement. She has been more than an assistant to the neurologist. She has been a confidant and a source of compassion even during the sad and depressing times.

Thank you to Giovanni's current neurologist, who is always friendly and welcoming when we attend appointments. She has also been very supportive in my exploration of alternative medicines and therapies. I am grateful for a doctor who believes in my ability as a parent to be the best advocate and caretaker for my son.

Thank you to the alternative healers, who have influenced Giovanni's development in very dramatic and positive ways. Giovanni's chiropractor, Dr. Alex Day, was responsible for placing Giovanni's central nervous system into alignment, which likely cured a chronic condition. Thank you also to Dr. Katherine Picoulin BSN, ND, who has recommended remedies to improve Giovanni's multiple disabilities.

During Giovanni's first three years, he received support and compassion from the staff at Alta Regional Center, First Steps Infant Program, and the Children's Therapy Center. Thank you also to Giovanni's vision specialist, who drove from Placerville to see him every month. Her valuable advice helped me to understand Giovanni's cortical visual impairment. I was always encouraged about her positive attitude in what Giovanni could accomplish.

I am blessed to be working with such a supportive and compassionate group of people. Thank you to the Fairfield Police Officer's Association and the Manager's Association for their monetary contributions during the most vulnerable time of my life.

Thank you to all my friends and co-workers at the Fairfield Police Department dispatch center. They have been a constant source of encouragement and support over the past four years. Moreover, they placed my needs (and Giovanni's needs) first when developing a unit work schedule.

I am grateful for the hard work and dedication of the staff of the Woodland Prairie Special Pre-School. Giovanni has grown and developed so well since he began pre-school. No doubt, the love and attention of his teacher, Belinda Halonen, and aides have influenced that growth. Additionally, the representatives of the Yolo County Office of Education have been very receptive to Giovanni's needs and my concerns.

Thank you to James and Doris Casselton, who provided the beautiful cover photo for the book. Their kindness of spirit helped put Giovanni at ease.

Thank you to Mary Moeller, who was a friend of my in-laws and became a friend and supporter of mine also. She gave me that final "push" to write this book.

I would still be in a pit of depression if it was not for the love and support of my family.

I want to give special recognition to my parents, Jim and Joni, who agreed to the task of editing my "great masterpiece." They provided a fresh perspective that helped me to narrow the focus of my book.

I have much love and respect for my family who have provided love, encouragement, and childcare for the past several years.

I want to acknowledge Giovanni's brother, my very special "little man" Kenneth. His love and compassion have helped me survive my darkest days. He continues to be Giovanni's biggest motivator. Kenneth is very sensitive to Giovanni's special needs. At times, he treats Giovanni like a typical little brother when he tries to stir up mischief with him. However, he never raises his voice to him, never instigates fights with him, and never shows any jealousy for the extra attention that Giovanni requires.

Thank you for the helpful and friendly staff at Trafford Publishing in their assistance with publishing my book.

Finally, thank you to all of you readers who have shown an interest in my book and have decided to read it.

Introduction

This is a story about a special child. Let me rephrase that, as every child is a special creation of God. This child is a different kind of special, as he was born with a unique set of challenges that most people do not even think about.

This special set of challenges is so unique that he does not even quite fit in with typical "special needs" children, never mind the "typical" children without disabilities.

This child was given the label of "severely developmentally delayed." Although this label may be accurate, it is a general term for a condition that is influenced by many other neurological impairments. This list includes cortical visual impairment, epilepsy, motor planning delay, sensory integration or processing disorder, and speech delay.

Some conditions that appeared evident in the first few months of life, like cerebral palsy and total blindness, turned out not to be the case. Other conditions, like the epilepsy and sensory issues, appeared later in both infancy and in toddler hood. No one doctor has been able to diagnose a permanent medical or neurological condition, aside from the epilepsy as this was manifested in behavior that we could witness. However, the one thing everyone may agree upon is the uniqueness of this individual child.

This child's name is Giovanni.

Although we do not know what Giovanni sees through his big brown eyes, we do know that what he "sees" or perceives is from a point of view that is difficult to understand unless we really try to imagine ourselves living his life.

My family and I searched in vain for stories of children like Giovanni. I have been searching for stories of hope, encouragement and inspiration while getting a little education in the process. I know I am only one of many parents who face daily struggles in caring for a child with special needs. In addition to those struggles are the struggles of dealing with relationships and life in general. Raising a child with special needs is a challenge even under the best of circumstances with two willing and self-sacrificing parents. These challenges can sometimes become overwhelming when one parent decides to reject his responsibilities and walk away from the situation.

Since Giovanni cannot yet speak to share his point of view, I hope that in sharing my experiences with others, I can provide encouragement to parents going through the feelings of shock, denial, pain, guilt, anger, desperation, and loneliness. I hope I can show that even under the most daunting of circumstances— a family falling apart in the wake of the birth of a special needs child—that there is an eventual acceptance of the situation, a restructuring of life, and hope for the future.

I would like to share my point of view as a single parent of a disabled child, one who has a variety of labels that can sometimes be overwhelming. With the love and support of friends and family, I know that I am not alone in the daily struggle of doing the best that I can for my child. Being the best advocate for him that I can be is important for him to reach his full potential.

In learning about life, we learn about ourselves. As Giovanni lives his life and continues to overcome his physical and neurological challenges—all with a smile on his face—perhaps we can learn something about life, also. Many people have said that life is a journey, and Giovanni's journey, while leading us to question our own life's purpose, is an inspirational one.

Chapter 1

I believe that God has a special plan for each of us. Sometimes His purpose takes years to unfold. Sometimes, one reaches a point in life where reflection of one's path in life gives enlightenment of what God's purpose is.

I have always had faith, and I always felt like God had a special plan for me.

Even as a little girl, I felt that God had a plan for me that was out of the ordinary, perhaps extraordinary. My friends laughed at me for my belief that my life had some higher purpose. Even my churchgoing friends brushed off this belief. I felt like I was living in a box, and allowing everyone around me to influence whom I was and what I did.

I felt like an outsider. As a teenager, I did not seem to fit in to any one group of people. That changed after high school. I went off to college and joined the Army ROTC. For the first time I felt like I belonged to something bigger than myself. Through some very strenuous training, I bonded with my peers. I was going to be an Army officer. I felt that was my calling.

I was commissioned as a Second Lieutenant two months before the outbreak of Desert Storm, the first Gulf war. I felt that I needed to be there with my fellow soldiers. At that time, I was in the mandatory military police professional training at Fort McClellan, Alabama. Before I could catch up to my military police unit, the war was over.

Years later, I talked to colleagues who deployed in that conflict. Many were suffering from undefined physical ailments. What a blessing that I was not able to deploy, as I realized the potential problems I may have had during a pregnancy. Apparently, God had some other plan for me.

I got a job as a police dispatcher and began to work toward my master's degree in Education, having already earned a bachelors degree in English. I was going to be a teacher.

I remember in one class—about special education—I thought that maybe I should specialize in special education. At the time, I was unmarried and had no children. I remember justifying to myself if I ever needed special education training, I'd know where to get it, and I would cross that bridge then. Little did I know that bridge would need to be crossed about eight years later.

I began my master's course work with excitement as I now felt pretty strongly that being a teacher was my calling. At the time, I did not realize my true calling went beyond being a teacher in the classroom. In fact, by the time I had finished the course work, I had decided that being in the classroom was not really what I wanted. When I had children I planned to use my training to home school them.

After I earned my masters degree, I was promoted to super-vising dispatcher at work. I had attained all my educational and professional goals. Deep inside, however, I felt there was something missing. Although some people were impressed with my accom-plishments, I was not fulfilled.

I thought I had found fulfillment when, in 1999, after dating five years, I married my now ex-husband, Jude, in an extravagant ceremony. The reception was on a yacht on the San Francisco bay. Guests talked about that reception for years (and still do). I was not worried about finances then. At that point in my life, this big "show" of our "great love" was important to me, and to my husband. Little did we know that our priorities would change a few years later, and extravagant events and luxuries and expensive toys really did not bring true satisfaction. I was on top of the world and I was so happy. At this point in my life, I am not sure if I knew what true happiness was, as everything really turned out to be superficial. Yet, for all the love I felt for my husband, I felt inside that something was still missing.

After nine months of trying, I finally became pregnant and gave birth to my first son, Kenneth, in 2001. I was more excited than I had ever been in my life. My husband was excited also. The birth took place in a hospital and was all natural. I was able to walk around the room and spend most of early labor in the shower. The nurse came in periodically to hook me up to a monitor to check on the baby. I felt everything, from the first pains of early labor, to the exhaustion of heavy labor and then the elation of delivery.

Without the constant attention by doctors and nurses, I had the privacy to videotape a message to my son. Later, Kenneth, at age six, was excited to see how he was in my "tummy" and I was talking to him. He really enjoyed watching the video of my message to him. He watched all the video after the birth, but the birth itself did not interest him.

Even though I was excited about the birth, I was not pleased with the experience in the hospital. The nurse was rarely in the room and the doctor only came in once or twice to check on the progress of labor. Thankfully, my sister-in-law Diana was there to help me though the process. She was very knowledgeable as she was a nurse mid-wife.

As I started pushing, the nurse told me that I would be pushing for a while as this was my first child. She did not stay in the room. Diana helped me through labor while my husband videotaped it. The nurse did not believe Diana when she told the nurse the baby was crowning. As I pushed Kenneth out in just five minutes, Diana was there to catch him as he came out. Had she not been there, Kenneth would have landed on the floor. In watching the videotape years later, I can still hear the nurse screaming, "Doctor Patterson, get in here!" as she pushed Diana out of the way to grab Kenneth. He was two weeks early, yet weighed 7 pounds 1 ounce.

Within three hours, at about 5 a.m., I was ready to walk out of the hospital. To my dismay, the nurse told me I had to stay until daylight so the pediatrician could examine Kenneth. A nurse told my husband they would call Child Protective Services if we asked to leave "against medical advice." I felt trapped. I didn't even have a room to myself. My husband had to leave because it was not visiting hours. I had a roommate who was recovering from a C-section and her child was crying a lot.

I resolved that I would never have this experience again.

Within a few months, I had given up full-time work and was working part-time. This was all with my husband's blessing, although I do not think he realized what a major financial change this would bring. I had also resigned my supervisory position, so I was making about 40 percent of my prior salary. Still, my husband received a decent salary as a police officer. With proper budgeting, we would be okay.

Now I was a mother. I finally realized that THIS was my calling. Though I would have been happy with just Kenneth, I soon wanted more. I was bursting with love and I knew I wanted more children. Jude and I had discussed having two or three more children.

When Kenneth turned one year old, we began trying for our second child. I thought nine months was a long time to try to conceive, but this time it took eighteen months. I was so thrilled and thankful that we were finally successful. I remember the night that I told Jude, because I remember feeling so disappointed that he did not seem to share my excitement. I found out later that Jude had already made the decision that he did not want to be married anymore. He was only staying in the marriage for Kenneth, and now we were going to have a second child.

I started home schooling Kenneth at about the time he turned one year of age. His learning style was amazingly similar to mine, so it was not too difficult to tailor his pre-school curriculum to his needs. In retrospect, I believe that I was so busy focusing on Kenneth that I probably neglected to nurture my marriage.

One area I felt I was lacking in educating Kenneth was sign language. At the time Kenneth was born, it was common for parents to teach their infants baby sign language as a precursor to spoken language. I taught Kenneth some basic signs for milk, hungry, thirsty, mommy, daddy and grandma, but I did not stay focused to teach much more. I was determined that I would not make the same mistake with my second child. I was determined that child #2 would learn sign language.

Like most parents, I made mistakes with my first child and learned lessons along the way. I erroneously assumed that what I knew and learned about raising children would translate to any other child I would raise.

One day, shortly before I became pregnant with #2, a thought flashed through my mind as I was driving through a Java City coffee drive-thru. I thought maybe I should learn Braille, too. At the time I thought that it would be good for my own enrichment. I have always been eager to "learn more", as if it would bring some sort of fulfillment. Again, I got distracted from following through with this goal.

Once I became pregnant, I was determined to stay healthy. I was diagnosed with gestational diabetes with my first pregnancy. It was likely I would be diagnosed with the same condition again. Instead of putting myself through the agony of the required fasting and blood testing, I decided to consider myself a "gestational diabetic" and adjust my diet accordingly.

I had a blood glucose monitor from my first pregnancy and I did well keeping normal blood sugar levels throughout my second pregnancy. I did not gain as much weight either during this pregnancy. Then again, I began this pregnancy heavier.

As the pregnancy progressed, I decided to find myself a midwife. My OBGYN concurred. She worked at the hospital clinic. Unfortunately, she did not actually deliver the babies. Otherwise, my entire experience the first time around would have probably been more pleasant and less stressful.

At any rate, I was determined to have a positive natural child-birth this time around. With Diana's help in screening midwives, I quickly found one that made me feel comfortable. Her name was Lily. I would have all my prenatal visits at her home, and then she would come to my home for the delivery.

My son Kenneth was excited as my tummy began expanding. He was 2 ½ years old during the summer that I was feeling nauseous and tired. By that time, he had memorized several phone numbers and would call his "Nonna and Papa" (my parents), or my sister or occasionally his Grandma Esther. He would make these phone calls while I rested. One time, he called my sister and spent the entire time on the phone with her while I took a nap.

All was going well as I continued to see the midwife with Kenneth by my side. He was her little "assistant" and would hand her instruments from her medical bag. My husband, however, did not show much interest in attending any of the early appointments. In fact, by this time, he had grown emotionally distant from me and even from Kenneth.

Kenneth was my "little buddy" throughout the entire pregnancy. He was with me during the one scare that I had during an otherwise uneventful pregnancy (aside from marital concerns). When I was about 3 ½ months pregnant, Kenneth got a minor case of chicken pox. I became very anxious. I was extremely concerned because of the susceptibility of the fetus.

I went straight to my OBGYN, who tried to calm my fears. Since I had already had the chicken pox as a child, I was supposedly "immune", and so therefore the fetus was "immune." This did not fully make sense to me as I had known people who had acquired chicken pox more than once in their life. Also, I knew that shingles was a condition related to chicken pox that occurred later in life.

In my mind, what difference did it make that I was "immune" from chicken pox? My baby was a separate individual with his own immune system. I did not understand how my immunity could "transfer" to him. How could we have the same immunity when it was possible that we did not even have the same blood type? The doctor insisted that everything was fine. However, I never could shake the feeling that something was not quite right.

Furthermore, the doctor must have had some concern since she was upset that I had brought Kenneth into the clinic with me. She was concerned that he would be contagious to "other patients." Why was I so different that it was okay for me to be exposed? I was confused. I tried to trust in the doctor's opinion and tried not to worry.

By the time Kenneth turned three years of age in October, I was at a loss as to what to do to help the marriage. Whenever I asked my husband what I could do better, he would say, "Nothing, you're doing fine." He would continue to deny any problems. The pregnancy was going well. My son and I were excited, but I was still feeling stress about the state of our marriage. I held on to the hope that Jude would "come around" by the time the baby was born. After all, every marriage has bumps.

On November 4, 2004, my husband was more depressed than usual. When I pushed too hard with too many questions, he finally blurted out that he was not happy in the marriage. He said he did not think he loved me anymore, and that he was staying in the marriage for our son. He felt stressed about the second child and even said that it was a "mistake to get pregnant again." When I asked why he allowed us to try for so long, or why he did not try to prevent it, he was silent. After all, it was not that long ago that we had talked about having three children.

On that day, I think I was remarkably strong for a woman with raging hormones whose marriage was falling apart. Actually, it probably was not so much falling as it was already fallen. Unfortunately, I had kept blinders on, even through the "red flags." Since I was in denial, I was blind to these signs.

I was suffering some physical effects of the stress of the marital situation. I had lost my appetite. But, I was concerned about my health, for the baby's sake, so I really tried to eat something. Diana was around to make sure I took care of myself. I spent some time at my in-laws home, still believing there was some hope to save the marriage. Needless to say, I was not in the best emotional and physical state to be working, so I began my maternity leave on November 5.

My tendency to be controlling in stressful situations did not help matters I am sure. I was desperate to fix things and suggested counseling, which Jude refused. He said the "feeling was gone." I was confused as I did not believe love was just an emotional high that could just disappear. He also said that he felt like he was "forced" to get married because of other peoples' expectations. I suppose that after dating five years, he felt it was the "right thing to do" to get married. He claimed that he had been thinking about leaving the marriage for years. Even after stating that the second pregnancy was a "mistake", he maintained that he wanted to stick around for a few months to "bond" with the baby.

Now that his true feelings were out in the open, he felt freer to disappear and leave the house. However, he did decide to attend one pre-natal visit. On that night, I was sick, but I managed to make the 50 miles round trip for the appointment. I was really hoping the experience would be a bonding one for us and maybe could be the first step in repairing the relationship.

Sadly, my husband did not participate much during the appointment. Later, the midwife expressed her concern about how Jude would react during the actual birth since he seemed so distant and detached during the appointment.

When we got home that night, my husband decided that I could take care of Kenneth, despite being sick, while he left town to have dinner with a friend's family.

Perhaps I should add that his friend lived over 50 miles away, since our individual perceptions of distance would later return to haunt us. Rather, it would return to haunt me.

Needless to say, I was not feeling like a very loving wife that evening. For Kenneth's sake, I tried to stay positive as he kept questioning, "why does Daddy have to leave?" I felt abandoned, and I felt sorry for myself and especially felt sorry for Kenneth. I was still determined to fix the marriage, because I was a "control freak" (which in this case was a weakness) and because I still loved my husband. I believed I could fix anything if I put my mind to it and worked diligently at it.

Well, I learned that fixing a marriage takes two people, and I had no control over my husband's desires. I would later come to realize that there was a lot more in life that I had no control over. That fact would cause me agony and frustration until I could learn to accept it.

What I did not have control over was the position of the baby in the womb. By 36 weeks, the midwife found that the baby was in the breach position. This meant that his head was high and his bottom was low.

The OBGYN confirmed this with an ultrasound. Her suggestion was that I do an "inversion" to get the baby's head down. She said it would be uncomfortable and painful for me. Furthermore, the baby still had time to roll back into breech position.

Indeed, the doctor said the baby still had time and room to roll into the breach position again before the birth. Therefore, the entire procedure could turn out to be useless anyway.

If the baby had enough room to roll from head down to breach, then he had enough time and room to roll from breach to head down without help. I declined the procedure and within two weeks the baby had turned on his own.

I did have control over myself and what decisions I could make for the benefit of the children. I knew that with a separation or divorce would also come the need for me to go back to work full-time. There was no way I could go back full-time. I could barely handle it for four months with one child, so there was no way it would happen with two children. At this point, we never imagined the possibility of having a child with special needs. At least my husband and I were in agreement that we did not want our children in childcare.

We were living in Petaluma, CA and I was working my part-time job 45 miles away in Fairfield. My mother-in-law, who lived in Fairfield, watched Kenneth while I worked. However, she was terminally ill with cancer and I could not expect her to care for both children. My shift work made it more tiring for her. My own family support was over 100 miles away.

My husband's solution for a separation was that I would live upstairs with the children and he would live downstairs. He wanted to have his own life apart from us. We were living in a tri-level condominium and the downstairs room was isolated and private. Right or wrong, I personally did not feel it was emotionally healthy for the children to be in an environment where the parents lived as roommates and tried to co-exist while living separate lives. The tension in the house would be too high. My husband would still make reasons to be out of the house, and there would be no bonding between him and the baby anyway. In addition, Kenneth would be witness to this behavior and would learn unhealthy ideas of what it meant to be a father.

I requested my husband to decide whether he wanted to fix the marriage or whether he wanted out. If he wanted out, he needed to just "cut the cord" and separate so that we could all go through the grieving process and heal. I did not want to cause Kenneth any more confusion and heartache. I also wanted some certainty, one way or the other, over the state of the family. This was not just for my own emotional well-being, but for Kenneth's also.

My husband made it clear through several conversations that he really wanted out of the marriage. Financially, he wanted us to "take away from the marriage what we each brought into it." What he seemed to forget was that I brought nearly everything into the marriage, including the financing for our first home. However, his main concern was my claim to his law enforcement retirement. I came up with a deal. If he gave me the deed to the house so that I had security for the children, I would not touch his retirement. I gave him until Christmas to make a final decision—which gave him about six weeks. I was still hanging on to some hope that he would change his mind.

His decision was that the marriage was definitely over and he signed over the house to me. I listed the home for sale the day after Christmas. My desire was to sell the home and take the equity and by a less expensive home near my family so that I could still work part-time.

The housing market at the end of 2004 was still good and I got an offer within one week. The housing market was so active that my buyer, Jane, offered $15,000 over the asking price. My mother found an affordable home in a nice neighborhood in Woodland, about 80 miles away. It was one block from the elementary school and a five-minute walk to my sister's house. Little did I know then what a blessing it was to be in this location.

In the midst selling one home and purchasing a new one, I was trying to maintain some normalcy for Kenneth. The new year of 2005 was the saddest in my life as I spent it at home with Kenneth— alone and very pregnant—while my husband went to a New Year's celebration in San Francisco.

In the years since the separation, I came to fully accept my role in the breakup of the marriage and family. Therefore, this chapter was not meant to illicit sympathy or pity, but to give a full picture of what situation into which Giovanni was born.

I do believe that there is a meaning and purpose to the events in our lives, even if it takes years to become clear to us. We do not exist in a vacuum. We all influence and are influenced by the circumstances surrounding our births. I do not believe it was mere coincidence that Giovanni was born in the midst of family change and upheaval.

Chapter 2

After a depressing New Years, I was more than ready to meet my son. Even though my due date was January 6, I felt maybe he would be early since his older brother had been two weeks early. So, I was actually expecting him around Christmas. Of course, this was something else I had no control over.

In the meantime, we needed to get the birthing tub set up. We actually had a perfect room for it. The first floor of the tri-level condominium consisted only of a bedroom attached bathroom, and a door to a small outside patio. The main living area was on the second floor and the main bedrooms were on the third floor. This afforded me plenty of privacy for the birth, even with other family in the house.

Lily, the midwife, had given me the tub the week prior and my husband and father-in-law set it up. As I watched the assembly of the birthing tub, I grew even more excited about the birth. I could not wait to have this amazing birth just the way I had planned. I only wished that Jude had taken an interest in the planning so as to share my excitement. As he assembled the tub, he acted as if it was more of a chore rather than a "labor of love."

Once the tub was assembled, I waited anxiously for my water to break. I had to wait over a week. When it happened, on January 10, it occurred in the mid-morning, just like the first time. Just like the first time, I did not feel any immediate labor pains. So, I was already mentally prepared for labor that would be similar to the first time.

I went downstairs to our "birthing room" to let my husband know. After he had decided on our separation, he had decided to sleep in the downstairs bedroom. He was asleep and showed no interest in waking up. He generally worked nights, so he was tired and not ready to get up. On the other hand, I was wide-awake and making calls to my midwife, my sister-in-law and even to my friends. All my friends at work were aware of my domestic situation and were concerned about the children and me. I called to let them know we were okay and that I would call when the baby was born.

Although Lily did not think she needed to come right away because I was not having contractions, my sister-in-law Diana headed to my house to help me prepare. When Diana arrived, she helped me to wake up Jude to and sent him upstairs. My water broke about 9:30 a.m., but I did not have any major contractions until afternoon time. In fact, Lily and her assistants came around noon and decided to get lunch because I was not progressing quickly. They thought it would be several more hours before they were needed.

Diana stayed in the room with me, providing a nice massage and a relaxing environment with candles and music. Jude stayed upstairs.

When I started heavy labor just before 3:00 p.m., Diana ran upstairs to call Lily. In the two or three minutes she was gone I had two very painful contractions. When Diana came downstairs, she could not believe it. It appeared the birth was imminent. We were not sure when the midwives would return. No one expected the pace of labor to change so dramatically. Obviously, I had no control of the situation—a tough thing for a "control freak" like me. Mentally, I was not prepared for labor to progress so fast. I had a "plan" in my head about how labor would progress based on what happened the first time.

However, every labor is different, and I could barely keep up with this one. I felt like I was on an express train.

My mother-in-law, Esther, and Kenneth had barely finished filling the tub when I was begging to get in. The warm water helped to relax me, as much as I can be relaxed in labor. By this time, the contractions were almost constant. Kenneth was getting anxious to meet his brother.

My husband was in the room while I was in labor. This was not for any moral support as much as it was to videotape the birth because there was no one else there to do it. I was hoping for some words of encouragement, or even a smile, but there was none. The sour look on his face just gave me more stress, so I averted my eyes.

By the time Lily had arrived, I was in the latter stage of labor and Diana was coaching me in the tub. Lily was there in case we needed her, but Diana provided most of the directions.

I remember being in so much pain that I was begging the midwife to "please help me." Even as I spoke the words, I realized how silly it sounded, since it was MY body going through the labor. I did not realize until later that Lily had an oxygen tank with her in case I needed it.

When it was time to push, I could feel it. The human body is amazing, as it knows exactly what to do, even with the presence or absence of medical personnel. I pushed three times and Giovanni was born. He floated to the surface and appeared so calm. He also appeared to me to be so small. He measured a long 21 inches, but only weighed six pounds nine ounces. I felt that was too small. However, Diana and Lily did not seem worried. Diana said six pounds nine ounces was within "normal weight limits," but I just felt something was not right with this weight.

Again, I was comparing this child with my first child. Kenneth was over two weeks earlier than Giovanni and was three inches shorter, but he weighed a half pound more. Since I was a gestational diabetic, albeit controlled, the doctor and I expected to welcome a baby weighing between eight and nine pounds.

In addition, when Giovanni opened his eyes, they seemed "confused" and were unfocused, even more so than for a typical baby. Diana and Lily did not seem worried. If they were worried, they did not let on.

Giovanni and I relaxed in the water for about twenty minutes. Three-year-old Kenneth helped his dad cut the cord. He was so excited that he could take part in his brother's birth. When Kenneth spoke, Giovanni responded and looked for his brother. I know that Giovanni recognized Kenneth's voice due to the many conversations between Kenneth and his brother during my pregnancy. Since he turned his eyes to "look" at his brother, no one would have suspected that he could not actually "see" his brother. On the other hand, Giovanni did not respond at all to his father's voice. I felt like it could be due to the fact that Jude never talked to him while I was pregnant with him.

Even after the birth, Jude did not show much interest in Giovanni. I was so excited, I started making phone calls to let family and friends know that Giovanni had arrived. I told Jude he could call his "best friend" to let him know because I knew his friend wanted a phone call. Jude's response was, "I'm too tired. I'll call later." With that, he went upstairs, presumably to go back to sleep.

As Lily was taking down Giovanni's APGAR scores and temperature, I could not shake the feeling that something was not right. APGAR is an acronym representing activity, pulse, grimace, appearance, and respiration. This is the test that midwife or doctor uses to judge the health of the newborn.

However, I was going through a lot of stress and depression with the separation and my husband's lack of involvement that I attributed my feelings to general sadness because of the breakup. Lily expressed some concern over the difficulty of keeping Giovanni's body temperature high.

After the midwives left, Kenneth held his brother for the first time. Kenneth was so sweet and gentle. He was already bonding with his brother so I knew he was going to be a great big brother. I was thankful for that because I was having a growing feeling that the family I'd hoped for was just going to be me and the two children. Kenneth lay in bed next to Giovanni and told Giovanni that he loved him.

Based on what Jude had said in November about Giovanni being a "mistake," I was afraid for Giovanni's future relationship with his father. Even if the comment was made in some emotional state, I believed there was still some meaning to it, if only subconsciously. In other words, the thought was somewhere inside him.

As for Jude's dad, Grandpa Jude Sr., he was happy and thanked me for "giving" him a "beautiful grandson." I do not recall if Grandpa ever held Giovanni for long. When Kenneth was born, he held him in the hospital. I could tell that his relationship with his second grandson was going to be much different. Jude and his father were similar in what I perceived as difficulty in connecting emotionally with others.

Grandma was excited. Even in her condition with the cancer, she was a great help in keeping the house in order just before, during, and after the birth. It was not long before she would be a bigger help.

During the first 24 hours, Jude took advantage of holding his son in the baby sling upstairs while I showered downstairs. Giovanni needed to be bundled up constantly since he continued to have difficulty keeping his body temperature up. What I did not know then was that difficulty in regulating body temperature is a sign of a fever in an infant.

Since Giovanni was born in the afternoon, it was too late for my mother and grandmother to make the 125-mile trip from their home in Shingle Springs. They came the next day to visit. I was so upset and distracted that I barely even remember the visit. My mother told me that both she and my grandmother were concerned about Giovanni. They believed, as I did, that he just seemed "too small." They were concerned about his weight.

They also noticed his twitching eye movements, most prominent in the left eye. Since they were not sure of the significance of this, they did not mention it to me so as not to alarm me. In hindsight, it is likely these eye twitches were actually seizures. My mother and grandmother were the first to notice this behavior, even before lethargy had set in.

Giovanni was a great nurser—the first day. He latched on quickly and was efficient. Unfortunately, this only lasted less than 48 hours. He continued having problems maintaining a proper body temperature, even while he was sleeping next to me. By the second day, he was also becoming lethargic. In addition, he had a lot more "jerky" movements and twitches than I remembered Kenneth ever having. Again, these were probably signs of his seizures. I had never seen infant seizures. He was declining to nurse, and not showing any energy to wake up.

On the morning of January 13, he was very lethargic and didn't really want to wake up. Every time, he opened his eyes, they appeared dazed and unfocused. On this morning I witnessed a behavior that definitely was not normal. As I was holding him, he "startled," his eyes grew wide and I heard him "gasp". It seemed as if he was holding his breath for a few seconds.

I believe now that this was the second such episode I had witnessed. The first one occurred when I was half-asleep, and I did not understand then what it meant. But this time, Diana was there to witness it. I was so sad about the breakup of the marriage I was not trusting in my motherly instincts that were yelling at me that something was amiss with Giovanni. Indeed, he appeared sick to me. Diana was concerned enough to get a second opinion. She ran upstairs to call the midwife. Lily agreed with our assessment and told us to take Giovanni to the hospital.

I was still in a daze—very physically and emotionally exhausted. We ran upstairs to the third floor to wake Jude and Grandma. Jude was upset to have been awakened and seemed a little "put out" to have to get dressed to drive to the hospital. His mom woke up to care for Kenneth.

The weather was overcast and gloomy, which matched my emotional state. Jude did not drive as if he was in any hurry to get to the hospital. I sat in the back seat near Giovanni, trying to hide my increasing fear. The drive from Petaluma to Santa Rosa was less than 25 miles, but the traffic was the weekday morning commute. However, once we got to the hospital, we were the only ones in the emergency room.

Because Giovanni was a home birth, there was a delay in checking him in. If he had been born in the hospital, he would have immediately been issued a medical record number. Since I had not yet called Kaiser to report the birth, we had to fill out paperwork and answer questions about the birth before hospital staff admitted him. When they weighed Giovanni he only weighed in at five pounds fifteen ounces. This was disconcerting because he had lost over half a pound in two days.

As the nurses recorded all his vitals, they appeared unfazed by his condition. He was not running a traditional "temperature". In fact, it was slightly lower than normal. I did not have unusual concern about it because my body temperature is routinely one to one and a half degrees less than "normal." I thought it might just be hereditary. These nurses were not that concerned about his symptoms. No one was able to tell me what could be Giovanni's issue. None of the staff felt they had enough information even to pronounce him "sick."

There were no answers. Little did I know that this was a phrase, which would become as familiar to me as to actually be descriptive of Giovanni. There were "no answers" and there "are no definitive answers now."

As nobody could determine the actual problem, the doctors decided that maybe they should admit Giovanni for "observation." It was not long after that when Giovanni would give us the big clue that there was something wrong—very, very wrong.

Chapter 3

Before I could finish the admission paperwork, Giovanni's condition changed from an uncertain "bad" to an obvious "worse". He had a seizure in which he stopped breathing. The doctor and nurses were calmly surrounding him and "bagging" him with oxygen.

At this point, I was feeling disoriented and confused. When the nurse calmly told me that he had stopped breathing, I went into shock. Much of what happened after that was a blur. Although I was in the emergency room as the staff worked on Giovanni, I was not allowed to be close enough to touch him. Diana stood beside me and tried to keep me calm. Jude stood in the back of the room, eerily calm and quiet.

Immediately, I began to pray to God to save my baby. I knew that Jude was leaving the family and that was devastating enough. I could not imagine losing a child, and I was worried about the ramifications for Kenneth also. He was three years old. How would he deal with losing his father and his brother? I did not even know how I would survive. This statement may sound a little melodramatic now, but at the time, that is how I felt.

My mind was in a panic and my most prominent thought was "I want my mommy." I was 37 years old, but this was the first time in my life that I could remember that I felt so helpless. I momentarily left the ER to call my mom, who was over 130 miles away.

Imagine her panic and concern upon hearing that her grandson was in the hospital and there was no prognosis or diagnosis. To

19

make matters worse, my father was working for the United States government in Iraq. My mom had to drive out by herself, probably imagining the worst for several hours before she could get to the hospital. This was one reason why I disliked living so far from my own family.

I was too overwhelmed to make any other phone calls. My mom called my sister and my sister's partner, who were both ready to make the long trip out. My mom told them to wait until we knew more information, since there was not much they could do at this point. She also advised my dad in Iraq and my brother in Afghanistan.

My family was literally scattered thousands of miles away from each other. On the other hand, all of Jude's family, aside from Jude, lived together in the same home. I wished my family could have gathered around me for moral support. I learned through this experience that it is not the proximity or distance from each other that makes a "family." It is all about love, sacrifice and sticking together. It was not long before I would find out just what a strong bond my family did have.

While my mom was en route, Giovanni's condition worsened. No one knew yet what the underlying issue was that was causing the seizures. They did know that the seizures were more frequent and severe. Giovanni would stop breathing, freeze and stiffen during his seizure episodes.

The first "knowledgeable" opinion we got was a nurse who stated Giovanni's blood sugar was low. She believed his seizures were related to this condition. In addition, she said it was not uncommon for a newborn to have blood sugar problems. I do remember that Kenneth's blood sugar was erratic for the first two days, so I was not unusually concerned with the nurse's observation. I am not sure if this was supposed to make me feel better or not. When your child stops breathing, it is a physical and emotional pain that is difficult to describe.

The nurse said that the condition appeared to be easily correctable. As his blood sugar balance improved, so would his condition. His temperature was still low, and no one told me what that meant.

Unfortunately, the blood tests the nurse took on Giovanni were unsuccessful on three occasions because the blood platelets kept "breaking down." I was not sure what this meant, but a nurse said it indicated some type of infection. The nurses could not isolate the strain because they could never get a good blood sample. Therefore, they immediately began treatment with antibiotics. Giovanni was given three different antibiotics, among them was amoxicillin.

I was still walking around in a daze. Giovanni was still not diagnosed with any specific illness, but his seizures appeared to be getting worse. The medical personnel worked to bring the seizures under control. To that end, they brought him to a private room, where they shut the door and closed the blinds.

I collapsed outside the room. Now I was totally separated from my baby. I had no idea what was going on inside the room. The doctor came out at one point and told me of a waiting area where I could sit in a chair instead of sitting on the floor, and wait for news. I told her that I was going to be sitting on the floor right outside the door. I was not leaving Giovanni.

Diana was right next to me. She was trying very hard to get me focused on something more positive. She had a breast pump and told me that I needed to pump for Giovanni because he was sick and he needed my milk. She told me that this was something I could actively do to help my baby. Although I felt weak, sad and tired, I tried to pump. Here, at least, I had some control.

The doctor offered to show me to another room for more privacy. I did not care about privacy and I certainly did not want to leave Giovanni. I sat down near a water fountain and pumped. We were near Giovanni's window. It had the shades shut, but we could still see just a little bit inside.

I am not sure where Jude was at this point. I do not remember him being there, but then I was highly emotional and my brain had shut down. I am sure he probably called his mother, who was taking care of Kenneth.

During my stay in the hallway, I remember the nurses coming to get me for blood tests. I believe they were still trying to isolate what kind of illness Giovanni had and whether I may have any infections.

After blood tests, I returned to the hallway outside Giovanni's room. I did not want to be far away from him. Lily, the midwife, arrived with a care package and moral support. At one point we had a conversation about Giovanni's birth, and if any of us had realized how sick he was at birth. I also asked Lily about her experiences with extremely sick newborns. Of the hundreds of home births that Lily had attended, she said that Giovanni was the first baby to become this sick.

Eventually, the primary doctor came out to the hallway to ask me questions about the birth. I explained that the pregnancy was normal, and the birth was normal. I told her that Giovanni was calm when he was born. For the first of many times, I reassured the doctor that Giovanni did not stop breathing at any time during his birth.

At one point, the doctor came out and told me they were having difficulty in giving Giovanni some medications because he was being resistant. On the positive side, he was strong, and he had a mind of his own. He extubated himself three times before the doctors were successful. Eventually, the doctor was able to administer enough of the Phenobarbital to bring some of the seizures under control.

My mother arrived in the late afternoon. By this time, the doctor had made the decision that Giovanni would need to be transferred to a higher care facility. However, he could not be transported until his seizures were under control and his condition was stable.

The ambulance transport crew arrived that afternoon and prepared to transfer Giovanni from Kaiser in Santa Rosa to the Kaiser facility in San Francisco. The doctor and nurse assigned to the crew were kind and patient. The doctor explained to me and my mother that once the brain is "wired" for the seizures, it takes time and sometimes a lot of medication, to "calm" the brain down. The doctor was confident that the seizures could be brought under control.

I became distressed again when I was told that I would meet the ambulance in San Francisco. Meet the ambulance? I wanted to be in the ambulance! Apparently, there was no room in the ambulance for riders aside from the crew. Again, I felt shaky and anxious about being away from my baby.

It was dark outside when the doctors told me that Giovanni had stabilized and was ready for transport. Jude and Diana took his car back home to Petaluma and my mother and I followed in her car. Traffic was miserable because it was rush hour. We fought our way through traffic. It seemed like an eternity to get back home to Petaluma.

We had to go home so that we could pack for the night. I anticipated I would have to spend at least one or two nights in San Francisco. I was packed and ready to go within minutes. However, Jude felt the need to take a shower and freshen up before we left. I took this opportunity to call my best friend to let her know what was happening. I also briefed my mother-in-law. In addition, I tried to keep my composure for Kenneth.

Believe me, it was not easy to keep calm and composed as I sat helpless, waiting for my husband to "look nice" so that we could go to San Francisco. I really wish I could have left when I was ready, but I had to wait for the group.

My mother offered to stay with Kenneth at the house so that Grandma Esther could come to San Francisco with us. The house was in disarray since Jude was in the process of moving out. He had found a luxury condominium about two miles away. Even knowing his children and I were moving 80 miles away, he chose not to find an apartment closer to his children, but to stay in a town alone. After several years, he is still unable to say why he made this choice.

On the way to San Francisco, we had to stop to get gas. I was stressed and upset and every minute just seemed to drag by. The traffic was not that bad, though, since by the time we got on the road it was rather late in the evening.

Once we got to the City, there was added stress of trying to find the hospital. Jude was driving. First, we were turned around and confused on a one-way street. When we finally found the area, there was a Kaiser Hospital clinic that had a different address than what we were looking for. Consequently, we drove farther, and eventually found the correct hospital on the corner. The lobby was closed.

We found a parking space and walked up a hill to get to the emergency room. My poor mother-in-law had to struggle to walk up the hill. She was out of breath when we got to the emergency room. True to form, she did not complain once.

As I walked through the halls of the hospital, making my way to the NICU on the third floor, I was not sure what to expect. When I had left him in Santa Rosa, hours before, Giovanni was stable and preparing for transport. I was really hoping that I would walk in and find a happy smiling child who had been "cured" of whatever mysterious illness had afflicted him.

I did have some worry, however, about what type of illness caused Giovanni to have so many uncontrolled seizures. By now, I was very emotionally and physically drained. I had just given birth about 72 hours before from which I had not fully recovered. I was fortunate to have my in-laws Diana and Esther for moral support, because my husband had pretty much shutdown emotionally. It is difficult to have your husband and father of your children ignore your emotional needs. Jude gave no physical affection and expressed no concern for me.

I realized that I had my faults in causing the breakdown of the marriage, but I did not feel that it warranted this treatment.

The previous day's events had nearly overwhelmed me, but I managed to survive. I was feeling fragile and I did not know if I could handle any more distress.

When I finally entered the NICU, I could not get to Giovanni fast enough. He was lying in his bed with IV tubes and an oxygen bag next to him. He appeared so pale and fragile. When he looked up at me, he did not react at all. The first time I saw him there, his eyes were quivering. The nurse said that was because he was having a seizure. The nurse then started "bagging" him with the oxygen bag. She explained that Giovanni stopped breathing during the seizure and she was giving him oxygen.

I really was feeling sick to my stomach and I was ready to pass out.

My fears about Giovanni were confirmed when the nurse told me that the uncontrolled seizures resumed while he was being transported to San Francisco. Oh how I wished I had been in the transport ambulance to at least give my son love and support and to let him know he was not alone. Although the staff was compassionate, it did not change the fact that my son was dangerously ill and suffering in the company of strangers.

The seizures apparently had become worse as he arrived in San Francisco. In fact, he was having almost constant seizures. The nurse said they were administering Phenobarbital in increasing doses in attempts to control the seizures. His dose was getting high and the nurse said if he did not respond soon, they would have to start giving him Dilantin. The nurse said that this was a very powerful medication and one that they preferred not to use on newborns.

During the time that Giovanni was adjusting to medication, one of the experienced nurses, Seth, spoke to Diana and me about his opinion of the situation. Seth was optimistic as he stated that he believed Giovanni had sepsis which would clear up as soon as the antibiotics took effect. Diana also provided her input as she had dealt with infants with sepsis.

At that time, sepsis was explained to me as an infection that has spread throughout the entire body through the blood stream.

With this explanation and with how calm Seth was about it, I did calm down a bit. I felt that once the seizures were under control and the antibiotics cured the infection, that Giovanni would be all right. Shortly thereafter, Giovanni's seizures came under control of the medication. Seth was relieved also, as he told me that the next step was to start the Dilantin. Giovanni was on the highest possible dosage of Phenobarbital that his body could handle. I was so thankful that the seizures were finally under control that I did not even think of the possible side effects of the medication. After all, survival comes first.

The next problem that Giovanni faced was the need for a "picc" line to provide intravenous fluids. Unfortunately, aside from being a tiny newborn, it appeared he had inherited my tiny veins. Seth had no luck in getting a line into his ankles or his wrists. Seth was going to try Giovanni's head next. The procedure was not easy. Seth needed to get the tiny picc line into the tiny vein in the head and then thread it through the veins to his chest. I could not even imagine the patience and steady hands he needed for it to be successful.

As it happened, I was told that Seth was the most experienced of all the NICU nurses in this type of procedure. How fortunate we were that he was on duty that night! Indeed, he was successful and Giovanni looked so sick with the line sticking out of his head. Seth said it was not painful for Giovanni. It was good that the line went into the head because the next location would have been the neck. There were more inherent risks with the neck since the carotid artery was the major artery to the heart.

So, I breathed a sigh of relief that Giovanni was finally hooked up to a steady stream of antibiotics and fluids. Meanwhile, I was trying the best I could to keep myself hydrated so that I could pump milk for Giovanni when he needed it.

One of the benefits of being confined in the hospital was that I had nothing else to do but to drink water and pump. I had never been a big water drinker, but with Diana monitoring me, I had a 2-liter container next to me at all times. I was pumping every two to three hours. Over the first couple of days, I managed to pump eight to ten ounces every time I pumped. This was exciting to me since I always had trouble when I pumped for Kenneth. I struggled to pump just two ounces each session for Kenneth. I realized then than it really made a difference in how much water I drank.

After I pumped, I would label the bottles and place them in the refrigerator/freezer in the NICU where all the mothers put their milk. I found that after a few days, I had three to four times the amount of milk the other mothers had. After several days, the nurses asked me to start taking some home for storage. My bottles had taken over most of the storage space in the refrigerator.

As a parent with a child in the NICU, and entrusting all of his care with the hospital staff, I was feeling helpless. As I stated before, the controlling part of my personality found it difficult to "let go" and let others help. Pumping milk for Giovanni was the one area where I felt that I could contribute, and I had some control in, Giovanni's recovery. I am sure that Diana knew this as she played "mother hen" and tried to keep me focused. She knew my personality and realized the importance of keeping me busy. Although, I am sure this advice would apply to almost any parent in my situation. Every parent wants to feel empowered to care for his or her child.

I had some privacy for pumping in the "parents' room" adjacent to the NICU. It had a couple of chairs, a television and a bathroom. I would become all too familiar with this place as it became my home away from home for 19 days. As I was trying to relax in the room, Seth came in to discuss Giovanni. With his years of experience, it was his opinion that Giovanni indeed had sepsis.

Diana concurred. Giovanni was very sick. She and Seth exchanged knowing looks as they discussed sick babies, as they both had significant experience with them. Aside from hearing them talk about their experience with sepsis, I had no clue to the meaning of what they were saying.

Since that time I have researched the illness and discovered that it was best I did not know the seriousness of the situation. I do not know how well I would have handled it. I feel certain now that both

Seth and Diana were probably trying to protect my feelings in not sharing the serious facts about the illness.

Sepsis is also called "SIRS" or systematic inflammatory response syndrome. It is a severe illness that is caused by an overwhelming infection of the blood stream by toxin-producing bacteria. The toxins can quickly cause life-threatening conditions in the body.

Sepsis, most commonly manifests itself in the kidneys, liver, gall bladder, bowels, skin and lungs. It can also be caused by a fungus, parasite or virus attacking the abdomen, lungs, central nervous system, skin, and urinary tract. I believe now that Giovanni had a virus attack his brain, which spread throughout his entire nervous system. I am more convinced now that the virus was varicella, or chicken pox—the same virus I was exposed to when Giovanni was in utero. Of course I have no empirical evidence of this. This will be discussed in a later chapter.

The following are symptoms of sepsis: drop in blood pressure, hyperventilation, rapid heartbeat, fever, chills, shaking, warm skin, decreased urine, confusion, high or low white cell count, low platelet count, acidosis, blood culture, and abnormal kidney and liver function. This could lead to organ failure.

Sepsis can be diagnosed by a blood test. Because the nurses were not able to get a good blood sample to test for infection when Giovanni was in Santa Rosa, there was no way to officially diagnose sepsis. In Santa Rosa, he was given antibiotics under the assumption that he did have a severe infection of some kind. Doctors in San Francisco assured me that this was the proper procedure. However, the downside was that there was never a good sample, or "proof", obtained. By the time the doctors had obtained a good sample in San Francisco many hours later, the antibiotics had taken effect and the infection could neither be traced nor identified with any certainty.

It was a mystery. I had lingering questions about the origins of Giovanni's illness—but there were no answers.

I tried to focus on the positive—that the doctors in Santa Rosa acted quickly enough to save his life. Now the staff in San Francisco needed to treat Giovanni's condition, even without knowing the cause. At this point, the doctors could not even make a prognosis. There were many more tests to complete before they could provide a definitive answer—if there even was one.

Chapter 4

On Giovanni's first full day at the hospital, he continued to struggle and fight the mysterious illness. In the morning, he continued to have episodes of apnea lasting 45-60 seconds each. Each episode was frightening, as I imagined the worst case scenario—that his breathing would stop permanently. Every time he would stop breathing, the nurse would "bag" him with oxygen and I would hold my breath too, until Giovanni started breathing again.

There were still so many tests to be done. Once Giovanni's seizures were controlled and his IV line was stable, the doctors could then do their myriad of tests. Each morning during his stay in the hospital, Giovanni had his blood drawn. The lab checked for common viral infections such as nasopharynx, conjunctiva and herpes. All of these tests came back negative.

One of the tests done on Giovanni was a spinal tap, and the doctor told me at this point that the white cell count indicated a possible meningitis infection. The cell count was "borderline" so the doctor could not draw any conclusive results.

Earlier, I explained the initial treatment with antibiotics had been started so quickly, any proof of the origins of the illness was eradicated. However, the doctors could do tests for what I called "damage assessment." To that end, Giovanni was given a head ultrasound the first morning of his stay. I was hoping that the ultrasound would provide a clear picture of the brain so that the doctors could make a diagnosis.

Dr. Roth met with me and Jude in order to provide us with all the information about the testing process. The social worker was there also, which made me nervous. Coming from a law enforcement perspective, I was distrusting and concerned that the social worker would be looking for something "wrong" with the birth or to lay blame. I did not realize that the social worker was there to provide support for the parents and the family of the patient. She was very warm and friendly.

In our meeting, we discussed the circumstances around Giovanni's birth—again. We talked extensively about stressors, about our family situation, and about pending tests. The social worker suggested we might want to stay at the Ronald McDonald house when a room became available.

The Ronald McDonald house is a place for parents of critically ill children to stay so that they can return frequently and conveniently to the hospital. My concern was that it was a few miles away and I would have to leave Giovanni's bedside.

The ultrasound tests were available after lunch and Dr. Roth took my husband and me aside to give us the somber results. It appeared that Giovanni had bleeding in the brain or possibly a brain tumor. The doctor said that the picture showed a "compression of the left ventricle including the occipital horn." They needed to run more tests to get a clear picture of the brain. The ultrasound was a useful tool for obtaining initial brain information, but the picture was "fuzzy." I am sure they began with the least invasive, and least expensive, test.

The neurologist wanted to get a better look at the brain than what the ultrasound provided, so she ordered an MRI. An MRI, or Magnetic Resonance Imaging, provides a more detailed look at the brain structure, but requires sedation. I was stressed as Giovanni was given the anesthesia and wheeled away to the lab where I could not be with him.

By the time Giovanni returned almost three hours later, a friend of Jude's father—the pastor at their church—had arrived to pray over Giovanni.

Giovanni was still unconscious and on oxygen. The nurse told me that the neurologist wanted Giovanni to stay on the oxygen as long as possible. The MRI showed significant brain swelling, so much that the doctor could not yet make a prognosis. However, the only treatment for brain swelling was to provide oxygen.

At some point during this process, the senior pediatrician provided his initial view about the MRI. He was the one concerned about a tumor or brain bleed, so he was pleased that the MRI showed that neither condition existed. In fact, he said that Giovanni's brain appeared "asymmetrical," which described his brain structure and not any type of illness.

The pediatrician said that the brain structure was not a concern to him. He was pleased that there appeared to be no brain damage. Although I was excited about that news, I still had many questions for the doctor about the brain structure, and what it meant. I do not remember the questions I asked, but they must have been very specific because the social worker who was there as my advocate asked if I was in the medical field. I told her I was not— that I am just a very analytical person.

Again, I had to tell the pediatrician the circumstances around the birth. Again, I explained that Giovanni AT NO TIME suffered from lack of oxygen. The doctor said that they were classifying the injury as a hypoxic-ischemic injury—which meant that the brain had suffered from lack of oxygen.

I believe that the medical staff settled with this explanation because they could find no other explanation. In addition, this was one explanation they could not rule out because there was "no proof" to the contrary. There was no medical doctor present at the birth to record the birth and delivery. They were apparently uncomfortable on taking the word of four midwives, the child's mother, father, and grandmother regarding Giovanni's condition. I have also watched the video of the birth, which showed a perfectly normal birth. Upon viewing it now, however, and hindsight being 20/20, Giovanni did show signs of illness and lethargy even at birth. Perhaps I just know so much more now that my memory may be clouded.

Consequently, I figuratively threw up my hands and gave up trying to seek clarification where there obviously was none. The doctors seemed to be running in circles trying to define a condition for which there was no evidence. I focused instead upon the resulting injury and what we could do to help Giovanni.

Although Jude was present for this meeting, he gave no verbal input. I am not sure if he even understood what was going on since he continued to have a "glazed" look and seemed constantly overwhelmed.

After the meeting, I spread the news to family and friends that there was no brain damage. When my father called from Iraq, I tried to tell him that there was "no brain damage," but with the poor connection, all he heard was "'brain damage." He went silent and seemed very upset, until I reiterated "no" brain damage. Members of my family and Jude's family went to the cafeteria to celebrate the good news and to have dinner.

Our reprieve was short-lived, however, as I was pulled aside by the pediatrician on duty that evening. Apparently, the original pediatrician made an error in reading the scan, and had talked to me prior to clearing it with the neurologist. She said that there was indeed some brain damage.

What the pediatrician did not see, which the neurologist saw with her trained eye, was encephalitis.

Encephalitis is an acute infection and inflammation of the brain itself. This meant, that whatever illness infected Giovanni had actually infected the brain. Generally, the illness is viral. The most common viruses are cold sores, mumps, measles, and chicken pox. Here again, I saw that chicken pox appeared as a suspect in the mystery.

Severe case symptoms of encephalitis include seizures, muscle weakness, paralysis, memory loss, impaired judgment, and poor responsiveness. In addition, Giovanni appeared to have cerebral edema, which is an accumulation of excessive fluid in the substance of the brain.

The only treatment for encephalitis is symptom relief, including hydration with IV fluids, providing anticonvulsants and monitoring brain swelling.

I had to call my father and retract what I had told him earlier. After all the excitement and thankfulness that there was no brain damage, I had to tell him about the doctor's misdiagnosis and that the actual expert believed there was brain damage. I hated having to put my father on this emotional roller coaster. It was hard for me, and he was thousands of miles away with no control or ability to help. He asked me if I wanted him to come home. He was ready and willing to return. However, it would take several days to get the clearance and then travel home. As much as I really wanted him with me, I did not want him to leave if there was nothing he could physically do for me at the hospital. Besides, I was hoping that maybe Giovanni would be "cured" within the next several days.

It was incredibly frustrating to be given a diagnosis by a doctor, in whom we placed so much trust, and find him be completely wrong. This incident was significant in that it eroded a lot of blind trust I had placed in doctors. Just because they had an education and experience did not make them 100 percent accurate. In fact, I place much more trust in doctors who readily admit they do not have answers. Jumping to quick conclusions for the sake of providing a diagnosis is not a good thing for anxious parents.

Over the past four years, I have had contact with many doctors, nurses, and therapists. Those I respect the most are the ones that readily admit to having "no answers." Honesty and humility go a long way with me.

Although the doctor that read Giovanni's MRI was not sure what was going on with Giovanni, the nurse assigned to him seemed to have her own opinion about Giovanni's condition. She was not allowed to articulate her opinion, since she was not the doctor. My mother got the impression by what the nurse had told her that there was some concern over Giovanni's condition, even though the pediatrician seemed to have no concern.

I was so heartbroken about the MRI results, I could barely move. I remained constantly by Giovanni's bedside. As Giovanni lay still and quiet, the pastor prayed over him with me. Giovanni looked so helpless with the picc lines and the tube connected to him.

The pastor also met with my in-laws and may have talked to my husband about the separation/divorce. This pastor happened to be the same pastor who had provided my husband and me with pre-marital counseling and had married us. He also had provided marriage counseling when I was seeking it two months prior, right after the separation. I knew that he was upset about the separation. Since Jude never showed interest in counseling, I imagined that the pastor probably spoke to him about it.

Within an hour after the pastor left, Giovanni woke up—and he was feisty. He pulled out the oxygen tubes and decided he would breath on his own. His nurse was amazed. She said that as long as he was breathing on his own, there was no need to have him hooked up to an oxygen tube. We all believed that this was a good sign. Giovanni was showing his spirit and his inner strength to beat the illness and to fight on his own terms.

I was anxious to speak to the neurologist to find out more about the MRI results, but I was told she would not be in until morning. Jude and I retired to the parents' room adjacent to the NICU to spend the night on the pullout chairs. This was one of the few nights that Jude stayed at the hospital. We both wanted to hear what the neurologist had to say.

I was restless that night and did not sleep. However, Jude slept so soundly that the nurses on the floor could hear him snoring. I kept getting up to either pump or to go sit by Giovanni's bedside. By morning, I was so exhausted and I still wanted answers. After sleeping for ten hours, Jude awoke and stated he was tired and did not sleep well on the chair. We were awake and ready—and we waited. And we waited.

We were finally told that the neurologist was sick and would not be able to come in that day. Jude decided to leave because he was packing his belongings and moving out of the house. Later, however, the pediatrician on duty agreed to sit down and provide me with some information. I remember that we sat next to Giovanni's bed as we discussed the results.

The doctor stated that it did "not look very good." I will never forget that one of the first comments he made was, "We don't know how well he'll do in regular school." I think my jaw dropped. The child was one week old, and almost died, and they were ALREADY concerned about school? Where were their priorities? Even I was not thinking about future school as I was home schooling Kenneth and had intended to do the same with Giovanni. I was more concerned with Giovanni's survival.

The doctor assured me that survivability was not an issue and so I assured him that schooling was not either. I had years ahead of me before I would have to worry about that. I was trying to focus moment to moment.

Although the doctor was not a neurologist, he said he could see significant damage to some parts of the brain. He explained that the brain had swollen and had probably placed pressure on the blood vessels within the brain. Perhaps this is where the hypoxic-ischemic (lack of oxygen) theory came in. The brain had suffered lack of oxygen, but it was not from the birth but rather from the illness. However, no doctor made that connection, at least not to me. I could not find any reference to it in Giovanni's medical records.

Moreover, the swelling caused a few areas of the brain to atrophy. Atrophy is a term used to describe the deterioration of a tissue or organ form lack of oxygen or lack of use. Giovanni's brain suffered from lack of oxygen as the brain was too swollen to allow enough oxygen to circulate. In addition, it suffered from lack of use because he was so sick. The doctor made it sound like brain atrophy was some sort of permanent condition. I knew enough about the brain to know it is constantly growing and changing. Brain synapses are constantly making new connections, even around damaged tissue. In fact, when researching "atrophy" the information usually related to Alzheimer's disease or stroke.

As the doctor explained what parts of the brain were affected, I tried to think of what functions might be impacted. I told the doctor I was aware that specific areas of the brain were responsible for specific activities. So, I asked, what functions would be affected by this traumatic brain injury? His answer was that the areas controlling "eating, speech and walking" would be affected, but only time would tell the severity of the damage. Part of me was thankful that there was no long-term prognosis, because then there was hope. Still, part of me was fearful. I have always strived to keep my brain active through learning. Giovanni's situation certainly had given me a completely new set of information to digest. Even though I did not have a medical background, I intended to learn as much as I could about Giovanni's illness and how his brain worked.

The doctor had given me so much information, and I was so emotionally drained that I couldn't even imagine how I was going to make any sense of this to explain to Jude, who had already left, and to my family.

Although I did not yet know how Giovanni's mind would work, I did know how mine worked. I wanted to find an answer for everything, so that I could put all the pieces of the puzzle together in order to make a comprehensive and understandable—and hopeful—picture. My mind did not feel "in balance" around so many unknown variables, so I set out to search for some answers.

If I wanted to understand Giovanni's brain and how it worked, I had to first understand the physical layout of the brain. I learned some neuroscience terms. I found the brain could be divided down the middle lengthwise into two halves called the cerebral hemispheres. Each hemisphere of the cerebral cortex is divided into four lobes: the frontal lobe, the parietal lobe, the temporal lobe, and the occipital lobe.

The sulci and gyri are the grooves and bumps that divide the brain into the four lobes. I found out that although most people have the same patterns of sulci and gyri on the cerebral cortex, no two brains are exactly alike. This made sense to me. I figured that if no two brains were exactly alike in the physical aspect, then every brain also reacted to illness in a different way. Following that, I believed that providing treatment for the brain should be considered on an individual basis. However, I was not a doctor.

The frontal lobe is located in the front part of the brain and is concerned with reasoning, planning, parts of speech and movement, emotions and problem solving. The motor cortex is in this area. The parietal lobe is located behind the central sulcus and is concerned with perception of stimuli related to touch, pressure, temperature, and pain. The temporal lobe is located below the lateral sulcus and is concerned with perception and recognition of auditory stimuli and memory. Finally, the occipital lobe is located in the back of the brain and is concerned primarily with vision.

Over time, I would realize what parts of Giovanni's brain were actually injured by the way he acted. I find it very interesting that while the doctor's would come to the conclusion that he had injury in areas controlling walking, talking and eating (the motor cortex), they never mentioned a link between the damage to the occipital lobe to a potential vision problem. I wonder how an MRI could show all that damage every other place, but not in the place that controls vision?

Again, I was not a doctor, so I was not in the position to say what was or was not shown on the MRI. I would have liked to have seen the actual picture of my son's brain, but no one ever showed me anything except their own sketches of the brain.

In between pumping and being near Giovanni, I searched out answers everywhere. I "interviewed" every nurse and doctor that cared for Giovanni. After all, there was a wealth of information to be gleaned from all the experience of the staff in the NICU.

Until I could talk one-on-one with the neurologist, I had to satisfy my inquisitive nature by speaking to everyone who cared for Giovanni. It turns out that I had all weekend to do it. Although I questioned every nurse and doctor that worked that weekend, no one could provide any insight as to what Giovanni's diagnosis or prognosis could be.

Chapter 5

A s I was adjusting to the stress of the hospital, I still could not forget that I was also in the process of a domestic separation. The escrow process with the buyer turned out to be a bigger stressor than I could have imagined.

The "saga" of my escrow process was a story unto itself.

While I was in the hospital, my mom did all the hard work of coordinating with my real estate agents in Petaluma and Woodland to work through the escrow processes. She evaluated the various real estate markets from Fairfield to Woodland, enlisted the assistance of a real estate agent in Woodland, evaluated homes that may suit me and finally presented me with a recommended home. I trusted my mom completely to make that decision. Kenneth approved of his new home—so I had my mom make the offer on the house, sight unseen.

It turns out the buyer of my home was not the sweet young lady that I had first met. When I met Jane, she presented herself as a sweet, hardworking single lady whose mother had just passed away and left her some insurance money. She wanted to invest in some property and buy herself a home. I felt bad for her. When it came time to choose between her and another offer I had received, I choose her. She also outbid the other person by $15,000, which was $15,000 over the asking price. With my stated income, this amount of money made the difference for me to qualify for a mortgage for my new house.

I was a responsible buyer and did not ask a loan amount that I could not afford. The "new" house I was moving into was in an older established 20-year-old neighborhood in Woodland. The house was a modest three bedroom two bathroom home with 1400 square feet.

After I accepted Jane's offer, her personality changed. She became more elitist and demanding. She knew I was pregnant and going through a separation and that I really wanted to sell my home. She also knew I intended to have the birth at home. Still, she was difficult when coordinating times for inspections. She seemed to expect to have things done on her own terms.

The escrow moved along with only a few bumps, until Giovanni was born. Through her agent, Jane made requests to enter the home the day after Giovanni was born, while I was still recovering.

Then Giovanni was admitted to the hospital. According to my in-laws who were at the home while I was in the hospital, Jane came over and made negative comments about the decor in the residence. In my sister-in-law's opinion, she walked around as if she already owned the place, and she was not very friendly to my family.

I am sure Jane was well aware that I was in the hospital with a sick baby. If my family did not tell her, I am sure that her real estate agent did. My agent was aware of the circumstances and tried to keep in touch with me through my mom.

When Jane realized I was in the hospital with a sick baby, she started to balk at the purchase. After the home inspection revealed some work that needed to be done, which was information already disclosed to her. Jane reduced her offer by $15,000 while threatening to withdraw her offer.

I could not believe this was the same polite and demure 23-year-old girl who acted so friendly when we met in person. I could not believe I chose her offer instead of the other woman who was much older, probably much wiser, and I am quite sure more mature.

Although my mom was concerned about her grandson, my dad who was in Iraq, and her son in Afghanistan, she steadfastly represented me with my real estate agent and with Jane's real estate agent. Eventually, I had to make the decision whether to accept $15,000 less—which would then affect the loan approval for the purchase of my house in Woodland—or to begin the process again, and place my home back on the market.

Patty, my realtor, felt confident that she could market the house and get another offer quickly. I was not so sure. My mom, who had real estate experience, believed that the housing market was about to enter a decline and home values would be much lower. At any rate, if I lost this buyer, then I would lose my house in Woodland and I would have to start the process all over again. I was in the bottom of an emotional dark pit, with a sick child and soon-to-be ex-husband, and I just knew I could never go back to the home in Petaluma. Even if I was fortunate to get another buyer within a month, all the costs associated with waiting and searching for a new house, would cost me the $15,000 anyway.

I remember sitting in the corner near the NICU elevator (the only place I could use my cell phone) and telling my mom to tell Patty to "...just accept the lower offer. I need to be out of that house now. I can never go back. I need to just be done with this." I place this in quotes because this is one of the significant events in my life that I recall with clarity.

By this time, we were within two weeks of closing escrow. I was so disappointed that Jane wanted to play games. I could not help but feel she was trying to take advantage of my situation. For several days, there was some issue with her loan and her funding and she seemed to be dragging her feet at every turn. It appeared she had gotten herself into one of those "can't beat" low rate adjustable rate mortgages, which allowed her to purchase more of a home than she could realistically afford.

I was not the only frustrated one in this mess. My mom was upset and Patty was upset. It turns out that Jane's own agent got so frustrated with her that he asked to be removed as her representative. He told Peggy that he had also found her to be too difficult and unreasonable.

The house escrow closed on January 30, 2005. In retrospect, it was a wise move to continue with the sale, even at a $15,000 "loss." In March, Patty told my mom that after my house closed in January, the market softened in the San Francisco bay area. My home was one of the last that she sold at an inflated price before the housing market "bubble burst."

Even though Jude was upset with me for moving out of the area, he was cooperative in that he did not object to signing his community property interest in the home to me. He also had quickly found his own "luxury condo" (advertised as such) and he had moved into his new residence before Giovanni was released from the hospital.

My parents were able to loan me the capital I needed to secure the mortgage for the home in Woodland. I am thankful that I have a home in Woodland to raise my sons. I am also blessed to have a family who has the resources to help me and the trust that I will repay the loan.

Within two years after the sale of the Petaluma residence, I learned that Jane had to sell the home, presumably because she had a variable rate mortgage which escalated in 2007. She sold the home for $15,000 over what she had paid me—which ironically was her original offer to me. The principal difference was that it had been two years and she was required to pay selling costs. Another irony was that when Jane had purchased the home she was "in the business" as she worked for a mortgage company. So, presumably, she should have known better. At any rate, I believe that you "reap what you sow", and she reaped nothing because she gave nothing.

Chapter 6

The weekend seemed long, as I waited for Monday to arrive in hopes of getting some answers from the neurologist. The stress was wearing on me, and I was feeling depressed.

Jude spent most of the time away from the hospital, so I felt very alone. I also was sleeping on a pull out chair in the parents' room. All the medical "beeps", "buzzes", and alarms were keeping me up through the night. Every time I heard an alarm, I had to get up and check to see if it was Giovanni's monitor. It usually was not.

Every child in the NICU obviously had some severe issues. One child, "Pablo", was several months old and had severe brain trauma. He was going through a series of brain surgeries. I felt bad that his parents both had to work and could constantly be there. I imagine, however, that there comes a point where parents have to accept reality and are not able to spend every minute at the hospital. They have to go on with life and its responsibilities. I had not reached that point yet.

"Sammy" was also several months old. He was born with part of his intestines outside his body, so he was going through a series of operations. I also was able to witness his physical therapy. I did not know anything about physical therapy at this point. I did not realize how much I would come to know about that particular subject.

"Zachary" also was a long-term patient. He had some type of rare nerve issue that could not be diagnosed. It appeared it might have been a terminal condition. He even had to be fed through a tube. He was so cute! His parents were so nice. I felt so bad for them because they had to deal with the "unknown" of their son's condition. His mom was trying very hard to continue pumping milk, but she was having problems with her milk supply. At this time, I did not fathom what living with the "unknown" really meant.

Then there was "Anna", who was brought in after Giovanni. She was born with breathing problems and oxygen deficiency. It was apparent quickly that she was going to have a brain trauma. I remember this child because I sat in the waiting room with her father on the very day I found out that Giovanni did not—then did—have a brain injury. As I listened to the father and felt so bad for him, I was secretly thankful that my child, as sick as he was, "at least did not have a brain injury." Within a few hours, I had found out otherwise. So, again, I found that I had a "kinship" with other parents, who were suffering through some of the came concerns and fears that I was having.

Throughout our stay, I met several parents with their children who were more "transitory." They were there for short periods of time after the birth of their children to address specific issues, like jaundice. In fact, I felt somewhat useful in helping the parents of a jaundiced child to be able to ask the right questions in order to get a breast pump.

Even as I talked to all the nursing staff throughout the weekend, I was also talking with other parents and meeting other children. I did feel as if I was part of a larger, special, community.

On that first Saturday, I was able to hold Giovanni. He was still having problems with his body temperature, so he was still sleeping in a bed with a warmer. He had some periods of alertness and I spent as much time as I could holding him. Thankfully he had no clinical seizures. Clinical seizures were outward seizures that were visible to us. Sub-clinical seizures occurred within the brain that could be recorded with an EEG. I hoped this pattern continued.

On Sunday, Jude visited in the afternoon. He was still spending most of the day moving his items across town. He usually came to visit after dinnertime. This was even during his "parental time off" from work. I could not understand why he would spend so much time away from the hospital. I was thankful that Kenneth did not have to be around so much. I am sure he could feel the stress and sadness.

After the weekend, I anticipated speaking to the neurologist. She was difficult to reach! Apparently there were only two neurologists at Kaiser. They had to make the rounds of the NICU, and also handle their regular caseload. I found that the neurologists would come in early in the morning and then disappear to their office. Then I would have to wait until they had time to come back across the street to the main hospital to meet with me.

Even though the neurologist came in to examine Giovanni on Saturday morning, I did not speak to her that day, or for several days afterwards. I honestly cannot remember if and when I ever spoke to her that first week. I had to be content to ask opinions of the pediatricians who were in charge for the day. However, they were not neurological experts and could not properly interpret any of the scans or the MRI. None of them were very hopeful with a prognosis.

In reading the neurologist's inpatient consultation report, I can see now how uncertain the doctors were that first week.

In her report, the neurologist described the MRI as "quite concerning" with "cerebral edema, but this does not quite seem to match the clinical picture, so it is difficult to determine its significance." She also stated that "cerebral edema to this degree is usually secondary to significant anoxia (oxygen deprivation), which does not appear to be the case either based on history or based on the child's clinical exam."

She tried to extrapolate other causes. She stated that "herpes infection can give a diffuse change in gray matter signal in the neonate (child), but it is often more patchy." Then, "hyperammonemia can give diffuse cerebral edema, but his ammonias have been stable."

So this is what the expert had to say? How could I draw a conclusion about Giovanni's condition or prognosis if she was not able to come to a conclusion?

The neurologist's recommendations for Giovanni when he was 5 days old was to, first and foremost, control the seizures because they could make the edema worse. She prescribed a high dosage of Phenobarbital to keep the seizures under control.

She also recommended an EEG to determine if there was any background or subclinical seizures. Subclinical seizures are those that are not visible in a clinical setting, but are occurring in the brain. She wanted to continue a full course of antibiotics under the assumption that he did have sepsis. She also wanted blood and urine samples to be sent for metabolic tests.

Finally, after all her recommendations, her prognosis at this point was "unclear" and that she needed to follow the "clinical course." In other words, we had to wait until Giovanni recovered from his initial illness/sepsis before we could determine what the full effect would be on brain function.

Of course, all this information I find out only years later, after obtaining official medical records.

On Tuesday, the social worker returned to follow up with me. I told her that I was feeling a little better, because Giovanni was doing better. She offered Ronald McDonald house again. By this time, I felt no need to go off the hospital grounds. I had become used to sleeping on a chair and I was ready at any moment to nurse Giovanni whenever he was ready to try.

Tuesday January 18 also happened to be Jude's 31st birthday. When he came in that evening with his family, they brought in a cake. We "celebrated" Jude's birthday in the parents' room. I cannot even remember if Giovanni was in there. Needless to say, I was distracted. It was hard for me to try to get on with "normal" life, when my week-old son was still seriously ill in the hospital.

At least, with Jude there for his birthday, he also had the opportunity to visit Giovanni, take his temperature, and change his diaper.

I am not sure how long he held him that day or how much bonding took place. I wonder how confused little Kenneth was—with a birthday celebration occurring while his brother was in the hospital. He was probably sensing my stress.

By Wednesday, there was discussion of possibly transporting Giovanni back to Santa Rosa, but only if he was weaned off the Phenobarbital and was able to eat. As it turned out, this never happened. However, the good news was that an EEG showed that there was no subclinical seizure activity.

That evening, Giovanni had episodes of low resting heart rates of 84-95. These set off the infant monitoring alarms, which made me anxious and I was unable to sleep that night. I sat by Giovanni's bedside and stared at the monitor as if that would somehow help. The nurses put a warm blanket on Giovanni and allowed me to try to nurse him. I was disappointed because he was making very poor attempts to nurse.

The next two days was a matter of waiting. I spent the days either pumping or trying to nurse Giovanni without much success. By the end of the week, another CT scan was done to assess Giovanni's neurological progress. This was another hard day, as I had to digest more sad news.

The CT scan was done to "assess the evolution of the diffuse cerebral edema." The scan now showed "atrophy" with "laminar necrosis." The diffuse cerebral edema had evolved into "significant atrophy and brain injury."

Like the assessment the prior week, the neurologist maintained that the source of the problem was "unclear." She again hypothesized. However, "it is hard to hypothesize a severe enough hypoxic injury to cause such complete and diffuse damage without compatible history." She stated that a "prolonged apnea event would lead to other organ damage." Then, "encephalitis typically gives more patchy, less homogenous distribution." Finally, that "metabolic disorders typically don't give diffuse cerebral edema."

Therefore, a week later, there was still confusion and uncertainly over what was going on with Giovanni. Except, the last line in her evaluation was, "prognosis for normal development and motor functioning is very poor."

It seemed that there was so much bad news. I wanted to be able to have hope for the future that Giovanni would start behaving "normally." On Monday, I got a glimpse of "normal" as he got his first bath. The nurse did it in the middle of the night when he was quiet.

He responded positively to his bath. It was obvious that he loved the water. He was calm throughout the process. I was excited that Giovanni finally was able to experience something besides being "poked at" and examined. I was excited that Giovanni was the cleanest he had been in almost two weeks. It also was somewhat symbolic. In being washed, I felt he was being "washed clean" of all the sickness.

There was also reason to be thankful this night as Giovanni continued to gain weight. He had been nursing very little, but I was able to "gavage" feed him breast milk, which means to feed him through a finger tube. I knew that gaining weight was a main sign that he was getting better, and perhaps he would be released to the Santa Rosa Kaiser facility or be able to go home.

The next day, I was more excited as I was allowed to take Giovanni outside the NICU and into the parents' room where I could nurse more privately. He really was trying, but he seemed to have more difficulty with latching on than he did when he was born. The advantage of being in the parent room was that I could keep him for longer periods, without being approached by nurses for one thing or another.

The social worker met with me again to check in on my well-bring. We spoke about my frustration in waiting for Dr. Shayne, the neurologist. I was anxious to get more information about a long-term prognosis, although I was fearful about the content of it.

Jude missed this meeting, as it occurred during the day. By this week, he had moved into his new condominium and was back at work. He did come in on Tuesday night, the 25th, in anticipation of Dr. Shayne coming in the next day.

The next day, Dr. Shayne was not able to come in. Jude left, while I stayed and took care of Giovanni. I did all his diaper changing and checking his temperature. I also took care of all his feedings. I am sure this pleased the nurses as it relieved them of some burden. The NICU is stressful enough, so I am sure that not having responsibility of all Giovanni's care was a relief.

Providing care for Giovanni gave me some control while living in chaos. It also helped distract me from the fact that the doctors were not as responsive as I would have hoped. I do not blame them because they had many other responsibilities aside from my son.

On Thursday the 27th, I had a lengthy discussion with a doctor from the neurogenetics clinic. I suppose these physicians were adept at "playing detective" as they tried to map out Giovanni's history. The doctor literally drew a graph with everyone in Giovanni's family, making marks of what hereditary issues existed within the family.

Still, the neurogeneticist, and her supervisor, could find no link between Giovanni's illness and his genetics. I did learn that these results were forwarded to Johns Hopkins Medical Center. This was where all of Giovanni's test results were being forwarded for review.

I imagined that the master detectives of neurological issues were quite busy at putting all the pieces of the puzzle together. At least, I hoped they were busy with it and would arrive at the answer.

Dr. Shayne came in during the afternoon. Jude was not able to be there. I listened to Dr. Shayne as she tried to remain positive in her outlook. I appreciated that she tried to describe Giovanni's condition in a positive, rather than negative, way.

Dr. Shayne was pleased that Giovanni appeared to have normal tone. She noted that he moved all extremities "well and with force." In addition, there was some improvement in his encephalopathy, which indicated the condition of his brain. There still was no answer as to an origin, since there were no ongoing symptoms. The diffuse nature of the injury ruled out every other explanation the doctors could offer.

Dr. Shayne's final prognosis was that she anticipated motor and cognitive deficits. When I asked her what parts of the brain were affected, she echoed several other doctors when she stated the "parts that control walking, talking and eating." In other words, the motor cortex was severely damaged.

In my eagerness to anticipate the future, ostensibly so that I could "control it", I tried to pin her down on specifics. She chose to speak in more general terms, stating that we would have to "take one day at a time." She reminded me that "every child is unique." Giovanni, in particular, had this unique set of circumstances that medical doctors could not even label.

Dr. Shayne tried to remain positive. She told me that she had seen children recover from some of the most desperate circumstances. However, she did remain realistic when she told me that in her opinion, chances were very low that Giovanni would completely recover from his illness without serious long lasting effects.

Chances of Giovanni living a "normal" life were not impossible, but highly unlikely. I was determined that I would take on that "impossible" challenge and help Giovanni beat the odds.

After spending several hours adjusting to my new reality, at least the way Dr. Shayne saw it, I was instructed by a nurse how to administer Phenobarbital through a bottle. Apparently, the Pheno-barbital had a very strong taste, which could not be hidden in breast milk. Giovanni's reaction was highly negative.

At any rate, by this time, I had a bigger worry than giving Giovanni his medication. Giovanni's weight had dropped signifi-cantly over a 2-day period, because he was not nursing well. Once Giovanni had started nursing a few days before, my intent was to get him away from gavage feeding or bottle feeding, in order to avoid "nipple confusion."

Unfortunately, Giovanni lost more weight in two days than he had gained in the five days prior to that. The doctors said he would not be released until he gained the weight back. I was so upset because for several days I had hoped he would be released before the weekend. Well, it was now Friday, and it appeared Giovanni and I would be stuck at the hospital for a third weekend.

I was desperate to do anything to help Giovanni gain weight. I was even willing to supplement with a bottle—with breast milk of course. However, I met with resistance from Jude and Diana. They were both overly concerned about nipple confusion.

I could not believe what I was hearing. By this time, I had been confined (by my own will to be with my son) in the hospital for over 16 days. I was being told what to do by these people who had no idea of the situation. They were not around but every other day.

I also knew that these same people were not going to be around to help me with the daily struggle of caring for Giovanni—feeding him or otherwise.

So, I just snapped.

I told my soon-to-be-ex husband and his sister that, although I am sure they meant well, this was my decision to make because it would be me who would be doing all of Giovanni's feedings. We were not even talking about the alternative of formula feeding. We were talking about a bottle—a bottle of my breast milk. Who cares how it got into his tummy as long as it got there!

I assured everyone that I intended to breast-feed Giovanni, especially because of his neurological issues. I reminded them the most important objective was to get Giovanni to gain weight, so I could get him home, so that I could then nurse at my leisure—all day if necessary.

Needless to say, when confronted with angry "momma bear," they backed down.

Thankfully, milk supply was not an issue for me. I had been fortunate when it came to providing Giovanni with breast milk. Unlike the other mothers, I had the "luxury" of being able to stay in the hospital with my son and to be able to pump every few hours, for over two weeks. The NICU freezer was full of breast milk that was mostly mine. In addition, I had dozens of bottles in the freezer at home, or rather, Jude's home.

In fact, breast-feeding was a high priority around the NICU. I think that Diana thought that the nurses unwittingly promoted formula feeding, when in fact the opposite was true. Though some individual nurses were not as "militant" about breast-feeding as others, there was a policy within the NICU that all mothers needed to pump milk to help their sick babies. There was an understanding within that community of medical professionals that breast milk was the best food for babies' brains.

Shortly after our conversation about "The Bottle", Jude and Diana departed that evening. Indeed, it was me that was awake throughout the night, "stuffing" Giovanni with as much breast milk as he would suck down from the bottle.

I spent all weekend trying to "pump up" Giovanni. At the nurses' insistence, however, I did leave for one night. I went to Jude's new condominium to try to sleep in a real bed and to take a real bath. I felt so guilty leaving Giovanni behind.

Since the condominium really was Jude's new home, I felt uncomfortable having to spend the night there. With the closing of escrow at the end of January, we had to be out of the house in Petaluma by mid-January. I had nowhere else to go. Because of the separation, my financial position was uncertain and I did not want to spend several hundred dollars to stay at a hotel in San Francisco. In hindsight, it probably would have given me more peace of mind if I had done so.

While traveling from San Francisco to Petaluma, I had the opportunity to think about the current situation in my life. It was easier at the hospital to try to "hide" from the stress of a marital separation. But when I reached Jude's condominium, reality hit me like ice water in the face.

The condominium was a two bedroom and two bathroom, luxury condominium. I only state that it was "luxury" because that is how the management advertised it. It had as much living space as the house I was moving into with my two boys. I realized that Jude was prepared, probably more than I was, to move on with his life.

I found it odd that everything appeared to be unpacked and organized. I am sure Jude's mother had helped quite a bit. Still, I could not comprehend how he had the time to set up a home when he claimed he did not have the time to come to the hospital.

Anyway, it was difficult staying the night there. I do not even think I spent the whole night there. I took a bath and left for San Francisco while it was still dark outside. I cried all the way to San Francisco trying to grasp the idea that my marriage was over. I essentially was a single mom, and my ex-husband was already using my move to Woodland as an excuse not to bond with Giovanni.

My mood changed when I got to the hospital. The nurse excitedly told me that Giovanni had gained 140 grams. In total, he had gained 460 grams since he was admitted, so 140 grams represented 30% of that gain in just 1 day. This was the biggest single weight gain in two weeks. I had renewed hope that he might be released that day.

As the night shift nurses briefed the day shift nurses, I waited anxiously for the pediatrician of the day to talk to me. He eventually did speak to me and he was pleased with Giovanni's weight progress. There was no need for Giovanni to remain in the hospital, as he had completed his antibiotics treatments and was no longer ill.

The doctor did give me stern advice about continuing to feed Giovanni from the bottle so that he would continue to gain weight. He said that Giovanni would need to continue 14 milligrams daily of Phenobarbital, until such time as he could have a follow up EEG to determine if he truly had epilepsy. At this point, doctors believed that the seizures were related to the sepsis and brain injury. There was no indication that Giovanni had a permanent seizure disorder, or epilepsy.

Giovanni was discharged at 2:25 pm. As I walked outside with him for the first time in 19 days, I felt alone and a little scared. For as stressed and fearful as I was in the hospital, I always had nurses available to help me care for Giovanni's needs. There was always someone there to help me, 24 hours a day every day. Now, for the first time since his birth, I was going to be Giovanni's primary care giver.

As excited as I was about being able to go home and care for Giovanni in my own way, I also felt sadness and emptiness in thinking about my poor child and the difficulties that lay ahead for him. I was feeling sorry for myself, and for Giovanni.

I walked out of the hospital with a child who had been "cured" of whatever physical ailments he had, but with no answers about the underlying causes of his illness. After 19 days, there were still no answers and no firm prognosis.

It was two months later when doctors finally noted on an exit report what terms they had used to classify Giovanni.

His diagnosis during hospital admittance was "convulsions." These were treated with Phenobarbital.

His principal diagnosis during his hospital stay was "sepsis of newborn." This was treated with antibiotics.

His secondary diagnoses included: convulsions in newborn, feeding problems in newborn, hypersmolity or hypernatremia, neonatal hypoglycemia, birth trauma, primary apnea of newborn, UNSPECIFIED encephalopathy, and UNSPECIFIED bacterial infection of UNSPECIFIED site.

After 19 days, dozens of tests, contact with dozens of doctors and nurses and specialists, the only clarity I had was that there was none.

Chapter 7

My intent in documenting the daily activities of Giovanni's hospital stay over the last few chapters is twofold. First, I wanted to give the reader an idea of just how much was going on during the hospital stay. Second, I wanted to give myself the opportunity to "relive" the events as they unfolded, so that I could make some sense out of them. I needed to be able to file them away in my long term memory, where they would not cause me distress. Part of the purpose of this book is to help me to heal from the emotional trauma.

To write those chapters, I had to digest over 350 pages of hospital records and documentation. All these pages were solely specific to Giovanni's 19-day hospital stay. There was so much material that my head hurt just trying to make some sense of the information. I was able to analyze the day-to-day data and I organized it to make sense to me. As overwhelming as this was for me, it is Giovanni who will learn to live within his physical limitations.

In reflecting over those difficult days in the hospital, I was heartened by all the support that I received while I was there. Indeed, there was an outpouring of love and support for Giovanni from so many people that did not even yet know him.

Of course, among the first people to arrive at the hospital were my family members. Since my mother was helping with selling my home and buying a new one, she was not able to be with me every day. She was traveling back and forth from Petaluma to Woodland to Shingle Springs to San Francisco. I know she really wanted to be there for Giovanni, but she also knew the best thing she could do for the boys and me at that point, was to take care of my affairs. It was due to her ability to set aside her stress and sadness and focus on helping me that I am where I am today. I certainly did not have the mental capacity at the time to deal with anything, as my plate was already full.

My 79 year-old grandmother wanted to be there, but she could only come with my mom. Therefore, she only was able to visit Giovanni on a couple of occasions.

My sister Gina and her partner Traci were able to come the first week. Gina swore that Giovanni smiled at her when she held him and talked to him. None of us knew at that time how great a role that Gina and Traci would play in the boys' lives. They were family and would be neighbors, as soon as I moved into the Woodland house that was three blocks away from their house.

Unfortunately, my father was in Iraq and my brother was in Afghanistan. My brother James was a Chinook helicopter pilot in the war in that country. Both my dad and brother had access to computers and my dad had a cell phone. My mom kept them updated. According to mom, James had faith in Giovanni even in the beginning, saying he was going to "show those doctors" and get better.

Jude's family and family friends arrived the first few days also. Aside from the pastor who came to pray over Giovanni, there were some other family friends who came to offer their support. I know they continued to pray for Giovanni, even though they were not able to visit in the hospital.

I understood that many people had to work. Jude and I were the only ones who had time off from work because of Giovanni's birth. That was probably why we got most visitors on the weekends, especially the first one.

Giovanni's aunts Diana and Olivia visited as often as they could. However, they both had to work and Olivia did not have her own car so she could only come with other family members. More often than not, my sisters in law came to the hospital only with their brother. I am sure that our separation cast a cloud over the family relationship.

Aside from my dad and mom, who placed the blame for the separation on BOTH me and Jude, all the other family members, including mine, seemed to take sides. It was heartbreaking for me, since I spent a decade as a part of Jude's family. I know that Jude's family did place blame on me for leaving, as their belief was that I should be a good Christian woman and stay in the same house as Jude. That way, he could have the children there when it was convenient, while sleeping downstairs and living his own life.

Most family members seemed to want us to work things out, even if it was only for the kids. The only one who did not want the marriage to work was Jude. In hindsight, I believe what we did in our separation was for the best. I see now how Jude and I were responsible for a negative and toxic environment in the household. I believed the boys were better off emotionally having one constant positive parent than two unhappy negative ones.

Jude's mom Esther tried to support both Jude and me. She helped Jude pack his belongings and helped to move him across town. She also packed my clothes and food the first several days I was in the hospital. Though she was ill, she never complained and she was very stoic. Mostly, she tried to keep things calm and normal for Kenneth. She came in during evening visiting hours when Jude drove in to San Francisco. When Jude had to go back to work, she was not able to come as often. She stayed at Jude's new condominium and kept up house there for a while.

Aside from concerns I had for Giovanni, I had separate and pressing concerns about Kenneth. He had so many life-changing events occurring simultaneously in his young life. Having a new baby brother in the family was a major change for him, but one that he seemed to enjoy. I knew that he was struggling with the stress in the house that existed because of the separation. Like me, he had been dealing with that stressor for two months.

Shortly before the separation, Jude and I had an argument where we raised our voices for the first time, in front of Kenneth. He also knew that his dad was sleeping downstairs and that we were both on edge. One afternoon, at his dad's request, he went downstairs to wake him. His dad woke up and got angry with us for waking him. Although Jude's anger was directed at me for waking him up, poor Kenneth was standing there fully knowing that he was the one who asked his dad to wake up. This was probably the first incident that really affected Kenneth, since he remembered it and continued to mention it occasionally for two years afterwards.

I do not claim that I was totally blameless in all of my interactions with my husband. I am quite sure that the negative aspects of my personality probably had in impact on Kenneth. We are all affected by things that our parents say and do.

I digress from the story to mention these incidents, because it was influential in what Kenneth's state of mind was during the birth and hospitalization of his little brother. A positive side effect came from the stress that Kenneth suffered. When Kenneth was sad and upset and insecure, because of the pending separation of his parents, he became clingy. Although he was three years old, he had a desire to nurse again. His personality was already the clingy type in that he never self-weaned. I had to literally turn him away and force him to wean before he was three years old.

I still do not know what the side effects of this forced weaning would have on Kenneth. Indeed, some people thought I was strange for nursing a toddler to almost three years old. I was so upset and depressed over the separation myself, and felt badly for what Kenneth was going through. When he was crying for milk and begging to nurse again, I allowed him to, hoping that the bonding experience would give him some confidence in dealing with the separation.

The positive side to this was that, through nursing, my milk came in much sooner. I had an overabundance of milk while Giovanni was in the hospital. My body was producing milk for a toddler and for a newborn, so I was able to pump more milk for Giovanni than I ever thought possible. In addition, since the health and brain benefits of breast milk are so well documented, it was very comforting for me to know that Giovanni was getting the best "brain food" on God's Earth.

Kenneth first saw his brother in the hospital while Giovanni was in his bed with tubes and monitors protruding from all over his small body. I am not sure what effect that had on Kenneth. He did seem sad that he could not hold his brother, since he was one of the first to hold Giovanni after his birth.

I do remember that Kenneth was particular about keeping his hands clean. Every time he came into the NICU, he used the hand sanitizer that was on the wall. He would sometimes go back to the dispenser and ask to be given another squirt of soap.

As I mentioned before, Kenneth came to visit almost every night that his father came to visit. A few times, he was able to stay home with Grandma Esther, while other family members visited. He was at the hospital during his father's birthday celebration. He was usually with Grandma Esther when he was not at the hospital.

One night Kenneth did get to stay the night at the hospital with me. Diana had made it clear one day that Kenneth was really missing me and that he needed his mom. But of course I knew that. I felt guilty that I was not able to be around every day for his needs. These were extraordinary circumstances and Kenneth's brother needed my presence more desperately than Kenneth did at the time. I was convinced that Kenneth would understand and forgive me for not being there for him for a few weeks. I wanted Kenneth to know that his mom loved her kids so much that she would be by their side when they were ill.

I was emotional at that time, and perhaps I took things too personally. I was particularly sensitive to the people who even with good intentions would try to direct me in how to be a mother, or what priorities I should be having. This was not the way to provide encouragement in this crisis. There obviously was some resentment which I carried around, that I needed to address and overcome. It would take years for me to overcome some of these destructive feelings. I would first have to take responsibility for my own shortcomings and ask for forgiveness to enable me to move on.

Kenneth was only three years old, but he was perceptive (as many kids are) and sensitive. Though I worried that he might feel "abandoned", I also knew that he was well cared for by his Grandma and other family members. He had plenty of love around him. Giovanni needed that same constant love to help him get through his illness. Four years after the fact, Kenneth still remembers bits and pieces of Giovanni's hospital stay. He remembers sleeping next to me on the pull out chair. He has no recollection of ever feeling sad or abandoned.

Giovanni, on the other hand, needed all the love and support he could get to give him strength. Giovanni was not diagnosed with a visual impairment, or "cortical blindness" until he was almost four months old, so it was not until much later that I realized how confused and frightened he must have been in the hospital. I imagine since his brain was so sick at that time, that he was not processing his vision at all, and may have very well been living in the dark. The fact that he would occasionally smile at the nurses, even while he was so sick, was even more encouraging, given the fact that he was blind.

Since most of Jude's friends were in the Bay Area, within 20-30 minutes of the hospital, I assumed that his friends would rally around him during his time of crisis. Only two of his friends came to visit. They were both female officers and they expressed their concern and support for Giovanni and me.

They told me that after they found out about me being pregnant, Jude was initially excited and often talked about the baby and me. Sometime before the end of summer, he had lost his excitement and no one knew the reason. I found some circumstantial evidence that Jude was involved with another woman, at least on an emotional level. No one believed that Jude ever was, or would ever be, unfaithful.

Jude had always been adamant that there was "never anyone else" involved. He claimed our problems were between us and he just did not feel "in love" with me anymore. I was emotional and very pregnant at the time, so I did not want to believe that he could be unfaithful. However, I could not help but feel uncertain when I looked more closely through our cell phone records. We had excessive charges in September and October. There literally were hundreds of dollars in extra charges. I had found one phone number that was recurrent dozens of times—at all times of the day and night. Many calls occurred during the times when Jude was supposedly "asleep" downstairs.

My fear and insecurity was aroused even more when Jude's own mother asked if he was being unfaithful. I was hoping that my hormones were just making me paranoid about the circumstances. I wanted people to tell me that I was wrong. If Jude's own mother could question his faithfulness, I really was concerned it may be true.

As for Jude's employer, they allowed him two weeks of family sick time, to be with the baby. However, he spent most of his days moving his belongings out of the house. He would visit Giovanni in the evening for a couple of hours.

I was disappointed that Jude spent so much time away from the hospital. I was present when Jude called his supervisor at the end of the first week. He said he did not feel ready to go back to work so soon. He wanted another week to "be with his son." I held out some hope when I heard that. Instead, it turned out that Jude felt the need to move, unpack, and sleep before he could be with his son. I am not sure why he did not just hire a moving company to do the moving for him.

One of Jude's closest friends, Simon, probably would have come out to see Giovanni. Because Simon's father suddenly passed away on January 21st during surgery, Simon was not able to visit. He called me to congratulate me. I apologized to him for not being able to leave the hospital to attend his father's memorial service. I remember that he told me that he understood and that my place was with my child. He was a new father himself, and he said that he would be by his child's bedside if he were in my position. After having a male friend say that, I really was confused when I found out that Jude left town with Kenneth and his family to attend the memorial for Simon's father, leaving me alone in the hospital with Giovanni.

Ah, priorities! This was the first time, of many, when I realized that Jude and I really did have different priorities in our lives. I do not think it was just a difference between a woman's view and a man's view. I believe that we had different ideas of what it meant to be a parent and what it meant to be part of a family.

In the years since Giovanni's birth, there have been many instances where I have found I believed that parents truly sacrificed for their children, while Jude believed that as long as he paid child support, he was a "father." In actuality, if anything required inconvenience or sacrifice, Jude was nowhere to be found.

There are other instances that I recall in Giovanni's young life, in which his father was not around for him (or for Kenneth). Those details will emerge throughout this book.

I am sure, there will be people who read this book and think I am painting Jude out to be a "villain." Again, let me reiterate, that I also had my own faults and shortcomings. I had to "own up" to my responsibilities. I simply want to state facts, with my feelings, and perceptions. The reader can make any judgment about Jude, or about me.

My friends, and those with who I work, really came through in their support for me. The Police Officers Association for my department sent me a check (on behalf of Giovanni) for $500. The Manager's Association for my department followed shortly after with a $500 check of their own. I was so touched and humbled by the support. I truly needed all the help I could get, now that I would be a single parent. The financial support given to me by my department was more than the child support I received from Jude for the first three months of our separation.

As thankful as I was for the financial support, I also received an abundance of emotional support and friendship. As a police dispatcher, I belong to a unique group of individuals. Though we may have our differences, we are also a family and there is always a lot of strong support for anyone going through a hardship. From the very first night of the hospital stay, I was in contact with my friends in dispatch. I would call them with daily updates on Giovanni's progress. The other dispatchers would post the information on the wall in dispatch and let other employees know of Giovanni's status.

During one night I was at the hospital, one of the officers named Chrissy called to lend her support. Her now-adult son had a brain injury after a lack of oxygen at his birth. She explained how he had learning disabilities and some processing delays, but he was still able to function normally. She gave me hope that someday Giovanni would overcome his challenges.

Giovanni's first presents while he was in the hospital were toys from my friend Krystal. They were a set of colorful tactile building blocks. I still have them to this day, because not only were they Giovanni's first present, but the bright colors still stimulate his vision.

My friend Lisa came to the hospital and took some of the first pictures of Giovanni. He was a week old when she got a picture of me feeding Giovanni with a bottle. She enlarged the picture and hung it in the dispatch area as an "inside joke." Most of my friends knew how "anti" formula I was, and I did not like the idea of bottles. Well, in Giovanni's case, it was necessary to get him fed with breast milk in any way possible to get him to gain weight. Some of the dispatchers probably got a laugh out of "anti-bottle" mom, feeding her child with a bottle.

Other friends stopped by to offer support. Suzanne came to visit Giovanni when her family was in San Francisco. Sally visited me to get me out of the hospital and to take me to lunch. She gave me some moral support in dealing with my separation, since she had been through a divorce herself. My friend Dawn came to take me to lunch, to give me an opportunity to vent my anger at Jude and to express my fears and frustrations about Giovanni.

In trying times, it helps the heart and soul to have friends and family around to lend moral support. I know that I gained strength from the support given to me. Therefore, Giovanni and Kenneth were able to benefit from the strength as well.

I cannot reiterate enough how much friends and family helped in my recovery, and the boys' recovery, during and after the hospital stay. Circumstances truly laid bare people's true nature and I really found who my true friends were and who my family was. The strength in my own family, I believe, is unmatched. Future challenges would prove this statement true.

Chapter 8

Having had four years to analyze and adapt to all that happened just before and just after Giovanni's birth, I have realized that I experienced an actual process that led to my healing. Although Giovanni did not actually die, I believe the best way to describe my experiences is through the framework of the grieving process.

I realize that most grieving process models specifically address the loss of a loved one or dealing with death. There is a big difference between dealing with the death of a person and dealing with the "death" of preconceived ideas, hopes and dreams. In reading a couple of different models, I found one in which my experiences seem to fit.

When a parent is anticipating the birth of a child, the parent usually has feelings of love and elation. I think every parent expects to have a normal birth either in the hospital or at home. The parents expect to greet the happy smiling face of the new life they helped to create. I do not think any parent allows himself or herself to think the unthinkable—having a child born with severe developmental issues.

Parents need to go through a process of grieving and healing as they say goodbye to all their pre-conceived ideas of how their baby will be or look, or act. Not only is this grieving necessary for the emotional well-being of the parents, but it is also necessary for the child in question. A child born with special needs requires the love and support of his or her parents, family, and friends in order to become the most independent and productive individual he or she can be in society.

The grieving model I will use in describing my experiences contains seven stages. I found that progress through these stages is not necessarily linear. In fact, "progress" sometimes means "One step forward and two steps backward." There were days I thought I had made it through one stage only to find myself regress again. It is only because I feel I have reached the seventh stage that I am able to compile my memories into a book that I hope will be encouraging to others who feel alone in their struggle.

As I worked through my feelings, emotions, and grief for Giovanni, I realized that I was simultaneously experiencing feelings, emotions, and grief over the end of my marriage. Overwhelmed is an understatement to what I felt as I grieved over both situations. It became apparent to me, almost from the beginning that the gravity of what I was experiencing with Giovanni's situation actually helped me to "get over" the marriage more quickly.

Knowing the seven stages of grief probably will not make your journey any less painful as you progress through the stages. Realizing that they exist may help you to know that your emotions and feelings are valid and normal. More importantly, you will know that there is an eventual adjustment to your new reality. Knowing this will give you hope for happiness in the future.

The grief one experiences with the loss of a loved one is different from the grief experienced in a traumatic situation. The first requires adjustment to a permanent situation. A traumatic situation, although requiring adjustment and acceptance of a new reality, is distinct in that the parameters of the situation can change over time. There is always hope. Additionally, while the loss of a loved one may take months or years to grieve through, I found that grieving through a traumatic event might only take weeks or months. The word "only" belies the fact that every moment of that time is a struggle.

The first stage of the grief process is shock and denial. In this stage, there is a numb disbelief and a denial of reality at some level in order to avoid the pain. Shock is the body's mechanism to protect it from being overwhelmed all at once.

I could make the argument that I was in a minor state of shock even from the moment of Giovanni's birth. Reality hit. I had a second child and a husband who was progressively disassociating himself from us. The utter sadness I was feeling then probably clouded my brain. Obviously, the main state of shock for me occurred when Giovanni stopped breathing in the Santa Rosa Kaiser emergency room. This is when I fell on the floor and could barely move or breathe. I remember feeling the physical symptoms of shock—pale, cool, and moist skin. I felt a pressure in my chest that made it difficult to breath.

As I was experiencing shock there in the emergency room, Jude also was experiencing shock in his own way. He appeared aloof and stood off in the corner. I am sure he was experiencing his own pain. We are two very different people from two very different backgrounds. Our coping mechanisms for stress and trauma were certainly different also. I saw him as cold, even though I am sure he was not uncaring. I believe now that he probably had his own internal struggle over the guilt of having decided to leave the marriage.

I was in a state of shock for at least the first several days in the hospital. It was difficult to function. Then, I resolved to be strong for both my sons. I knew that Kenneth was watching his parents and learning about coping strategies by observing us.

I do not think I ever experienced denial about Giovanni, as I really believed that facing reality head-on was the best way to conquer the fear and uncertainty over his future. I needed to be strong and "in control" so that I could help him. I was more in denial of the marriage being over. Sadly, I believe that Jude and I had both been going through denial regarding the marriage for at least a year or more. With both husband and wife in denial, there was no hope of improvement.

With Giovanni in the hospital in his serious condition, I felt that this would be the true "test" of our marriage. Either Jude was going to realize that he really wanted his family, or he was going to walk away for good. I hoped, as did some of my friends that Jude would see what he was giving up, realize that he really did love me, and change his mind. Unfortunately, this did not turn out to be the case.

In fact, I think that Jude was going through his own version of denial. Although it was the first stage of grief, it was a stage that Jude appeared stuck in for a long period. It was probably in part due to denial that allowed Jude to be able to be away from the hospital, and his son, for so long. In talking with other fathers, I was assured that most men would not want to leave their son's side. However, we do all have our own ways of coping. It was probably that denial that prevented Jude from asking the questions that would help him to understand Giovanni's condition better.

While my denial about the end of our relationship and the marriage lasted for at least a year after Giovanni's birth, Jude's denial about Giovanni's condition lasted just as long or longer. Even now, over four years later, I still question if Jude has ever really accepted the reality of Giovanni's condition. What was concerning to me, however, was that Jude's denial of Giovanni's condition seemed to morph into a denial of Giovanni himself.

A very telling conversation occurred between Jude and me several days prior to Giovanni's first birthday. While we were meeting to exchange Kenneth, I tried to engage Jude in a conversation about Giovanni. He made no attempts to interact with Giovanni, which by that time was his normal behavior. When I tried to volunteer positive information about Giovanni's neurology appointment, Jude simply stated, "Well, we love him, even though there is nothing we can do for him." This simple statement would reverberate for years in my head as it really set the tone for Jude's relationship with his son. Clearly, Jude did not, and does not, have the inner drive to try to search for opportunities to promote Giovanni's physical and emotional growth. It fed on my fears that if something happened to me, Giovanni would not receive the care, encouragement, therapy, love and HOPE from his father.

Denial is powerful. In essence, it allows a person to relinquish responsibility for his or her own life and future consequences. It can lead to stress and distress. More importantly, it can prevent a person from moving forward in a positive way. In my inner circle, I have called it "ostrich syndrome." Since my ex-husband and I do not talk much in relation to the children, all I can judge is his actions toward Giovanni. If those are any indication, he is still in denial even four years later. The reason why I mention Jude's denial is only that it has affected his relationship with Giovanni and with Kenneth.

As shock wears off, it leads to the second stage of grief, which includes pain and guilt. This is the phase where life feels chaotic and frightening because there is so much suffering and pain. Part of the pain for me was the guilt that I was feeling. I was the one who gave birth to this child, so I started questioning if there was something that I did or failed to do, causing him to become so sick.

My mind would race over the possibilities. I was upset thinking about the potential that my stress over the divorce, when I was eight months pregnant, may have caused him to become sick. The doctors all agreed that Giovanni's sickness was nothing that I caused or could have prevented. Although medical doctors never would agree on just what the causal factor was, there were indicators later that the illness probably originated with chicken pox exposure.

In any case, as a mother, I constantly questioned myself throughout Giovanni's hospital stay, and beyond, if there was anything I could have done to prevent what happened. After years of soul-searching, I had to conclude that everything happens for a reason, and I do not have much control over anything outside of myself.

The third stage of grief is one that includes both anger and bargaining with God. The guilt that I was feeling within myself eventually transformed into anger. Some of this anger was internal as I was struggling to deal with the frustration of having no control over certain events in my life. A great deal of anger began to build up and spill over towards Jude.

This third stage was a difficult and a very long stage for me. Part of this stage also involved bargaining with God. In actuality, I was beyond the bargaining aspect as I prayed to God from the beginning to save Giovanni. The bargain that I promised God was that if Giovanni lived, I would do everything within my power to help him have a full and happy life. I promised to give him all my love. I also promised to do whatever I could to seek out every possibility to help Giovanni to succeed, no matter what the naysayers may say.

Although I did not feel a need to bargain further with God, as I believed he placed Giovanni in my care for a very special reason, I did struggle for years with the anger issues. Even though one characteristic of this stage is to place "blame" on others, I never ever placed "blame" on God. I never did have any anger at God. In fact, I reached out more than ever to God to help me through the crisis. The love and support I felt from Him in the beginning, and up through now, has only grown stronger and more comforting. It's only through God's love and grace that I can hope to get over the anger issues.

I do not know if I ever really "graduated" from the anger stage, especially as it pertains to Jude. Even though I progressed through all seven stages of grief at some point through the past several years, it was the anger that stayed with me, through each stage. I did not feel it was fair to place blame on Jude for what happened to Giovanni, but I did place a lot of blame on him for the disintegration of the marriage and the family. Of course, as I have said, I had my faults that contributed to the eventual outcome. One thing that remains true in my mind, though, was that when I KNEW things weren't right in the marriage and I confronted Jude, he denied it. I realize now that Jude is really an expert in denial. Regardless of my contributions to the downfall of the marriage, he should have been up front and honest about his feelings, instead of disappearing and running to other people for emotional support.

Is it that obvious that I still have anger towards my ex-husband? Well, I am inclined to agree that I still have issues with him. For the sake of maintaining a positive atmosphere for the children, I have tried, and still do, to put it all behind me. It can be a daily challenge, depending on Jude's willingness to communicate or even to interact with the boys. It does not make it any easier that Jude has been hesitant to speak of the past, to give me closure. The lack of closure has definitely been a source of frustration.

I am sure that part of my anger is with myself for the guilt I still feel over having married the wrong man to be a father to my children. Let me say, that this does not mean that Jude is a "bad" man. In fact, he is usually seen as a "nice" person. He just seems to have something inside that is missing where fatherhood is concerned.

Aside from the anger stage, which I have floated in and out of for the past four years, I probably experienced the first three stages of grief even before Giovanni was released from the hospital. The day Giovanni was released, on February 1st, was the first day I realized I had entered stage four—depression, loneliness and reflection.

After leaving the hospital with Giovanni, I could feel the depression setting in. Being confined in the hospital gave me a shelter to hide from the real world. I was able to put many feelings on hold, as I lived day to day focused on Giovanni. I pushed feelings about the separation aside, in the hopes that this crisis would draw us together. By February 1st, it was apparent to me and to friends and family that Jude had "checked out."

The first stop for Giovanni and me was Jude's new condominium, where I was going to pick up Kenneth, meet the midwife for a well-baby check, and go to my mother's house. When I arrived at the condominium, Esther was there. The place was neat and clean and very much like a "home". Jude was at work.

Lily, the midwife, met me there and we discussed Giovanni's hospital stay. She was pleased that he gained some weight. I tried to explain to her what Giovanni's diagnosis may or may not be. I also expressed some frustration with Jude and our separation. I probably should not have talked so loud, because Esther heard me and I felt bad when I realized that I had hurt her feelings.

I sure was not thinking clearly. I am a mom, and I get defensive and protective of my children, too, even if they may be wrong. I had only expressed confusion over Jude's habit of leaving on his motorcycle while Kenneth and I were home alone during my pregnancy. Esther pointed out to me that Jude needed "alone" time away from me and he went on motorcycle rides to do that.

I continued on to Fairfield where I saw my other in-laws for a few minutes. Needless to say, the atmosphere was tense and not that supportive, so I moved on as quickly as possible. I hugged everyone goodbye and expressed my desire to still work things out.

When I got to my mom's house in Shingle Springs, the loneliness hit. Even though I had my mom, grandmother, and sons around me, I felt alone. I had lost my husband and both my father and brother were in Iraq and Afghanistan respectively. At that point, there was no male role model around for the children. I really felt it would be a struggle, especially for Kenneth, in dealing with the separation without a "father figure" around.

During this fourth stage, one begins to experience a long period of sad reflection where positive encouragement does not help. In addition, a person realizes the full magnitude of the loss, which is depressing. Then a person may deliberately isolate himself or herself in order to deal with feelings of emptiness and despair. I experienced all of these feelings with full force during this stage. Like the feelings of anger, I found over the years that I continued to reflect on the trauma, even as feelings of depression and loneliness would subside.

Though I was probably suffering from some from of depression since November (when Jude told me he did not love me), the feelings became magnified during the transition from the hospital to my mom's house. I would be in a suspended state of transition for eight more weeks until we could move into our new home in Woodland.

I realized that first night how much I really relied upon Giovanni's nurses and those annoying monitors. Because Giovanni was taking Phenobarbital, it affected his breathing and sleeping patterns. Through the night there were periods where he would breathe very heavily and then other periods where I could hardly tell he was breathing. I felt the need to stay awake all night to be his "monitor" in case he should stop breathing. The episodes of apnea were still fresh in my mind.

I had Giovanni sleeping next to me, not only so that I could monitor him and nurse him through the night, but also so he could hear my heartbeat. I hoped that the rhythm would somehow help to sooth him and keep his body functioning normally.

My mother and grandmother were helpful in caring for Giovanni. My mind was operating on "automatic pilot" and I did not have the ability at that point to think critically about anything. My mother tried to guide me and provided answers when I could not think of any.

As depressed as I was, I still held some hope of maintaining contact with my in-laws. Although Esther was too ill to travel far, I had received assurances from Diana that she would be there for the boys and me. After all, she delivered both of her nephews. Indeed, she always had been very hands-on and involved with Kenneth. Therefore, at that point, I had no reason to doubt that she would be there to help Giovanni also.

I am sure that my in-laws were not pleased that I was so far away. Shingle Springs was 85 miles from Fairfield and 120 miles from Petaluma. However, I knew when we moved to Woodland, we would only be 35 miles from Fairfield and 70 miles from Petaluma. In my mind, and with my years of driving experience, I truly felt that these distances were not prohibitive where visitation was concerned. I figured that Jude would be able to see the children at least on his weekends. I worked in Fairfield and never considered it a long ride from Woodland.

For the time I was to be in Shingle Springs, I knew I would really have to go out of my way to drive myself to Fairfield with the boys for them to visit with their other family. I wanted to prove to everyone that my intent in leaving Petaluma was never to deprive Jude of seeing his sons. It was merely out of necessity since I knew I would need family support to help with childcare if I was to continue working only part-time. The guilt feelings I had about moving away from Jude and the frequent reminders from his family that I was the one who made that final decision, only fed my depression.

I fluctuated between feelings of depression and those of anger. I felt that the blame for the separation was landing squarely upon my shoulders. Jude was able to slide away from much of the responsibility merely by failing to take a stand and make any concrete decisions about the separation or divorce. He was able to say from the beginning that I was the one that "left him" and "took the kids away" so he could not see them. As time would tell, Jude blaming me for "taking the kids" would continue to be an excuse for years, when he could not or would not bond with the boys.

Wow. There I go again, lashing out in anger. Truly, I did have a lot of responsibility in being decisive, strong-willed, and moving away when I thought it was best. And in light of the fact that Jude grew to rely on his mother more and more to care for Kenneth as a toddler (she would care for Kenneth just so that Jude could sleep), I felt certain that he would not be any more hands-on with the second child. And this second child, in Jude's words, was a "mistake." A meaningful father/child relationship seemed next to impossible.

In retrospect, knowing even more now than I knew then and having done research on children of divorce, I am convinced that I made the right decision.

Of course, the knowledge that I did right by my boys did not help much in pulling me out of the depression I was in during the first few months after Giovanni was released from the hospital.

Once I was settled at my mom's house, I had time to reflect upon the past few months. I realized my financial situation contributed to my mental state of anger and depression. When Jude and I separated in November, he had agreed to pay a very reasonable $1000 per month in child support for both children. He also promised that he would curb, what I believed to be, his "extravagant" spending habits until we could close out our joint accounts.

By the time I had moved to my mom's, I owed her quite a deal of money. Not only did she loan me the $10,000 that I needed for my new home, but also she took care of the moving expenses while I was in the hospital.

Imagine my dismay when I closed out our one credit card account, which had several thousand dollars racked up. It was 90% from Jude. Apparently, he found the need to go on a $1200 shopping spree with his sisters. He did this within a couple of weeks after promising that he would not spend money. He also found the need to pay $200 to fix a chair that had a small chip in the wood. I should mention that this chip was near the floor and was not visible to anyone except for Jude who knew it existed.

And above all of that, Jude failed to pay for child support for almost two months after I moved to my mom's house. I suppose I should have been happy that in light of everything, we still dissolved the marriage without going into debt—aside from what I personally owed my parents.

I only mention Jude's financial habits because it shows what value he places on material things. Surprisingly, this was not much of a sticking point within the marriage, until Kenneth came along and I switched to a part-time status. I was earning more money than Jude before that time and we were literally "rolling in dough", having only the two of us with two professional incomes.

It is too bad that Jude's spending habits prohibited us from having any savings when we actually divorced.

After having opened my eyes and reflecting on Jude's real priorities, I felt anger and resentment toward him. I was sad and depressed that I now owed my parents money because my husband felt it more important to take care of himself before his family.

Sorting through the many conflicting emotions that ran through me on a daily basis was a constant struggle for me during those first few months.

I was well into my journey of healing by going through the first four stages of grief during the first several months of Giovanni's life. I suffered through the first stage, which was shock and denial. I continued through the second stage, which included pain and guilt. I struggled through the third stage, which included anger and bargaining. During the time I was living with my parents, I found myself in the fourth stage of grief, which included depression, loneliness and reflection. It would take me a few more years to progress through the last three stages.

Chapter 9

Through the last eight chapters, I have focused quite a bit on my family upheaval and my perceptions of my ex-husband and in-laws. One may wonder, "what about Giovanni?" This book, after all, is supposed to be about him.

I certainly do not want readers to think that my intent is to use this as a forum to be critical of my ex-husband and his family, because that is not the case. I was a part of that family and loved them as such for over a decade. But, I do desire to make my position known so that readers do understand why I made certain decisions over the years.

It is an undeniable fact that to understand how Giovanni was, and is, one needs to understand him within the context of his life. Many marriages buckle under the strain of having a developmentally disabled child in the family. I need to make it clear that my marriage was already suffering even before Giovanni's birth. There is no doubt that Giovanni's condition exacerbated the problems that already existed. In addition, it helped to provide clarity of just who I could trust to help support my family and me, and support Giovanni's growth.

I have made mistakes over the past few years in how I dealt with my ex-husband and his family. One of the main mistakes I made was sharing too much information with them—"airing my dirty laundry" so to speak—and fully expecting their moral support. They were my "family" after all. I learned, however, that no matter how close you are to people, they would usually side with the "blood" relative.

I should not have been so surprised or so disappointed in this fact. It was my fault for providing negative information about their son/brother and I am sure that they saw me as a not so supportive wife, regardless of how Jude acted toward me.

One of the problems I had in communicating with my in-laws was our differing definitions of such concepts as "wife", "husband", and "father" and differing views of what was "fact" and what was "perception".

During the first few months of the separation, my in-laws tried to intervene and give advice in order to help us save the marriage. In one of our talks, my in-laws advised me that I needed to be a good Christian wife and not question my husband. It was the husband's place to make the decisions for the entire family. I was to be obedient and follow him. If he made a wrong decision or decided that he was going to live life for himself, I was supposed to keep quite and pray about it.

I was a little disturbed by the fact that Jude had already walked away from the church. He declined to be baptized on at least two occasions during our marriage. He wanted Kenneth "dedicated" in his parents' church, but he would not avail himself of the opportunity to express his belief in God and to be baptized himself.

I know that Jude's family was in turmoil over their belief that Jude was "not saved." I know that the Bible states that "the unbelieving husband has been sanctified through his wife." (1 Corinthians 7:14) Jude was the one who introduced me to his parent's church, and then walked away from it. I continued for years to live in denial of the fact that he walked away by choice, not because he had to "sleep in for work." I realized that as much as I tried to cajole him, I could not make him go back. I could just ensure that our children were raised with my Christian beliefs.

While I believed that the husband should take the leadership role in a Christian home, I also believe that he should consider his family's needs before his own. That is the role of an honorable husband and father. In Jude's case, it appeared to me that his family supported the idea that the "father" did not have to take a big responsibility in child-rearing, as long as he brought home the money. Perhaps I am incorrect in this assumption. Maybe Jude's family was just as disappointed in him as I was, but they just were not communicating it to me.

My belief that a PARENT should put the emotional and physical needs of the children before his or her own needs was a belief not shared by Jude. I do appreciate that he does have his bank send me the child support check the first week of every month. I also know that his job affords him many opportunities to work overtime. All of those extra funds he gets to keep.

While I believe that Jude's family probably agreed with the idea that a parent should be self-sacrificing for the children, I am not sure how much they actually tried to promote that idea to Jude. I am a little different in that I came from a family who loved each other enough that they could confront issues head-on and communicate with each other, even if was not always pleasant.

Our differing views of what was "fact" and what was "perception" have caused problems between Jude and me during the separation and divorce. I like to use the example of "the chair is green." That statement is a fact. Someone can then say, "I hate green chairs," which is an opinion. Someone else can say, "That chair is too small," which is also someone's opinion or perception. Still, someone else can say "so what?" and that is his or her opinion. None of the opinions or perceptions changes the basic fact that "the chair is green."

There are people in the world who are likely to say, "No, that chair is red." Or, "Chair? What chair? I do not see a chair here." This is an example of denial. In my view, Jude and his family preferred to live in a state of denial rather than to confront the uncomfortable realty. If the chair is green, it is green. Period. You may not like the color green, but you cannot change the fact that it is. And you cannot pretend that the fact does not exist when it does.

Over the years, as I have discussed situations with Jude and his family, using facts, I am usually brushed away with "that's just your opinion." In writing this book, I tried very hard to state the "facts", and make note of what statements are my opinions or perceptions. Believe me, when it comes to the family issues in this book, I do have plenty of opinions and perceptions.

One cannot change the facts, but anyone can consider these facts and draw conclusions from them. The difficult part is being able to accept even unpleasant conclusions.

In a recent discussion with my brother about facts and opinions, he pointed out to me that "facts" could be manipulated or taken out of context to serve the purpose of whatever argument is being made. I possibly have taken some facts and placed them into a context that may lead the reader to feel a certain emotion about something or someone.

For the purposes of presenting facts in this book, I shall use the Webster's Dictionary definition as such. A fact is "something that has actual existence, or a piece of information presented as having objective reality." An opinion, on the other hand is "a view, judgment or appraisal formed in the mind about a particular matter." It "implies conclusions thought out yet open to dispute."

Having a severely developmentally delayed child required me to live in the world of facts, not of opinions or perceptions or conjecture. I would eventually have contact with doctors that I would not respect because they would try to "fill in the blanks" when they did not have facts. Opinions drawn from experience or other case studies may be helpful in part when trying to understand what made Giovanni unique. When a professional would take a path based only partially on facts but mostly on opinions is when I usually questioned the wisdom of continuing to use that person as a resource.

All of this focus on my in-laws is to show that there was a difference in communication styles. With my boys and me so far away in Shingle Springs, the differences in communication became more evident. My impression from what Diana told me was that she was going to "be there for me and the boys." I really thought that she might come up once or twice during the first month in order to help with the children or perhaps to play with them. If Diana drove, Esther would probably come. I assumed that Jude would at least try to drive out on his day off or at least meet me at some halfway point.

Since neither of these scenarios happened that first month, it was up to me to try to pull myself together and care for my children with help from my mother and grandmother. I was still lost in a depression. Giovanni had his first pediatric appointment that first week out of the hospital. It was in Davis, which was approximately an hour for Jude and for me. I thought that certainly he would want to be there.

I am not sure if he was working or not. However, he did not come to the appointment and he failed to return my phone calls about the appointment. His lack of interest fueled my depression.

Since depression is fueled by lack of sleep, I had no hope of rising above the depression the first several weeks after the leaving the hospital. I was already suffering from a lack of sleep because of the long hospital stay. Once I arrived at my mom's house, my hopes of "catching up" were dashed when I found myself up throughout the night to monitor Giovanni's breathing.

Certainly, it took my mind and body awhile to adjust to life outside the hospital. In addition to caring for Giovanni, I was also struggling to provide for all of Kenneth's emotional needs. Being separated from his father, and not receiving many phone calls from him, took its toll on his emotional state.

One of the highlights of our day was providing Giovanni with his daily medication. We had to mix his liquid Phenobarbital with the breast milk and have him drink from the bottle. My mother handled this task since I was nursing and I did not want to cause any nipple confusion for Giovanni.

Actually, I did not want Giovanni to refuse the breast as he refused the bottle. To say he hated the Phenobarbital was an understatement. Even mixed with the breast milk, which he loved, the

Phenobarbital was so strong (and it had a strong odor, too) that he was always trying to spit it out. My mom and Giovanni eventually reached some sort of "agreement" where he would take the bottle for her, but no one else.

Giovanni's distaste for his medication foreshadowed his consistent negative reaction to every anti-convulsant given to him.

By March, we had settled into a routine. It was the first week of March when we had our first visitors since leaving the hospital. Giovanni was scheduled for an appointment with Pride and Joy, which was the early intervention program that serviced the county my mother lived in.

I invited all of Jude's family to be there, and to my delight and amazement some of them did drive out to my mother's house. Though Jude was late, he did arrive and visited with Kenneth. Diana helped feed Kenneth and showed interest in Giovanni. Esther was there, too. The staff from Pride and Joy were pleased that Giovanni had so many supportive family members surrounding him.

The physical therapist that examined Giovanni did not note anything out of the ordinary. Giovanni was only six weeks old, and there was no evidence yet of any physical disability. In fact, there was no indication at this point of any obvious disabilities. I hoped that this would mean there would be no serious disabilities.

Since some of Jude's family made the trip all the way to Shingle Springs to attend Giovanni's first Individual Family Support Plan (IFSP), I was hopeful that they really were interested in Giovanni's progress. Unfortunately, this visit was the only visit made by Jude's family during the first two months. The few times that Jude would call this month was usually to talk to me about the separation, divorce, or child support.

Even when Kenneth became very sick with the flu, Jude did not call to check on him. Consequently, Kenneth usually declined to speak with his father when he did call. This flu was the worst illness Kenneth had contracted up until this point (because the chicken pox he had when I was pregnant was a very mild case) and it was the first time I dealt with a child with a fever.

For several days, I was up constantly through the night with Kenneth. What was very interesting was that Giovanni was sleeping in the bassinet next to Kenneth's bed, and whenever Kenneth would wake up feeling poorly because of a fever, Giovanni would wake up, too. When Kenneth would vomit, Giovanni would become restless and cry. And anytime Kenneth would cry out in discomfort, Giovanni would cry out too. Giovanni's temperament was normally on an even keel, possibly influenced by heavy duty medication. However, this illness of Kenneth's was the first time I noticed Giovanni cry out in "sympathy." This was the first indication to me that Giovanni was extra sensitive to the moods and emotions within his environment.

Late in March, Giovanni was scheduled for a follow up EEG in San Francisco. This test was to determine if Giovanni had any subclinical seizures or evidence of epilepsy. I hoped, if the EEG showed no seizures, then we would be able to wean Giovanni off of the awful Phenobarbital.

I took my two-month-old son and drove the 150 miles to San Francisco. I left three messages for Jude in the two days prior, hoping he would be able to meet us there. After all, he worked only about 30 miles away. If his agency was typical, they would allow him "sick time" to attend his son's medical appointment.

Not surprisingly, Jude did not come to the appointment.

The EEG was a stressful process for both Giovanni and me, and possibly the technician who had to carefully place the dozens of electrodes on Giovanni's head. The process took awhile because my two month old was so squirmy. I needed to be in the room with him to console him and hold his hand.

I never knew what the initials EEG meant, but I found out. EEG means "electroencephalography" and it records the brain's electrical activity. It is a procedure in which electrodes are applied to a patient's scalp then connected by wires to an electronics receiver which, in turn, is connected to an EEG machine. The EEG records brain waves as a series of squiggly lines called "traces." Each trace corresponds to a different region of the brain. Epilepsy waves, which are spikes, sharp waves, and spike-and-wave discharges, are specific patterns that indicate a tendency towards seizures.

Thankfully, Giovanni fell asleep for a short time – until the evening janitor loudly knocked on the door, announced himself, and walked in.

After the complete silence in the room for over thirty minutes prior, the sudden interruption woke Giovanni with a startle. That was the end of that test.

I was told that the results would be forwarded to the neurologist and I would be contacted by him with the test results.

It was early evening as Giovanni and I left San Francisco to drive the 150 miles back to Shingle Springs. I was so incredibly frustrated, upset and angry that Jude could not, or would not, make Giovanni's medical test a priority.

When we talked, later that night, Jude tried to defend himself for not visiting Kenneth when he was sick. He claimed that he could not see Kenneth when he was sick, because he "didn't want to get sick," and because he had to work. I told him that I was up constantly, through the night, while Kenneth was sick and I never got sick. Additionally, I was the one with the compromised immune system because I was physically and emotionally exhausted.

Furthermore, Jude "threatened" a divorce, because I was "pushing" him to it. This confused me since he was the one that clearly stated months before his intent to obtain a divorce. I found this was a constant theme in our relationship – Jude abdicating responsibility by placing it on me.

It took me far too long to realize that I had no control over Jude's relationship with either of his children and I really just needed to keep my big mouth shut.

The following day Jude called me to request a divorce. He was upset because he thought that he was paying "too much for child support." I am not sure if he was absent-minded due to stress, but he did not seem to understand that he had yet to pay me any child support!

Jude delivered his first child support check when we met at his parent's home on Easter. He paid me for half of the month of March. I tried to put aside my depression and interact with my in-laws. Jude visited with the boys for about two hours. Near the end of the visit, Kenneth had a temper tantrum. No doubt, he was feeling stress in the room. Jude and his family ignored the tantrum while I took Kenneth outside. Even though the boys had their other "parent" there, I felt like a single parent in trying to meet both Kenneth's emotional needs and Giovanni's physical needs.

The following week, the boys and I moved into our new home in Woodland. Gina and Traci had done us the wonderful favor of painting the entire interior of the house. They did all the hard work free. This was the first of many times my family would willingly come to my aid, asking for no payment in return.

The day we moved in, the movers took all the boxes that were in storage for over two months and dropped off all the boxes in my garage. The entire garage was filled with boxes. My parents and grandmother took care of the boys inside the house while I unpacked boxes and put items away.

I was shocked to open some boxes and find some of Jude's belongings, including gifts given to him by his grandmother. It appeared that everything that was in our hall closet in Petaluma ended up in my garage. Not only was I amazed that Gina, Traci, and my grandmother were able to pack up all my belongings into boxes within four hours, but they ended up packing some of Jude's items also.

I was even more curious as to how Jude and three or four members of his family needed the better part of two weeks to pack and move even a fraction of the items that I had. Thanks to my parents and grandmother, I was able to focus on unpacking and I had everything unpacked and put away within four days.

The hard physical labor of unpacking by myself (with a little help from 3-year-old Kenneth) was easy compared to the emotional adjustment I had to make to being on my own. The transition from the hospital to my mom's home was difficult enough. At least there, I had other people to help care for the boys. Now, for the first time, it was going to be just me.

As strong-willed and independent as I was, the idea of caring for a three year old and a disabled infant all on my own seemed daunting. I questioned my judgment constantly the first few weeks that I was on my own. With Giovanni still taking Phenobarbital in a bottle, I struggled daily to get him to drink it. My mom had the "magic touch". Giovanni reacted differently to her than to anyone else who gave him the bottle.

Although the boys had their own bedroom, I slept with Giovanni in my bed and Kenneth slept on a mattress on the floor in my room. Not only did Kenneth desire to be nearer to me because of his insecurities over his parents' separation, but I also wanted both boys in an area where I could keep an eye on them.

One of the rooms was designated a "home school room," where I could focus on school for Kenneth. I had been home schooling him since he turned one year old, and by the time we had moved in to Woodland, he was ready for some kindergarten curriculum. Focusing on Kenneth's education gave me some comfort in knowing that I had some control over something in my life.

The stress was broken up a little when I had to take Giovanni on a road trip to Sebastopol to see Lily, for my three month follow-up visit. I misunderstood where the appointment was going to be. After making the two hour drive, I had to turn around and go back to Napa. Giovanni was a patient traveler. The appointment was at the home of one of the assistant midwives. Lily examined me and found that I had healed well. She also had the opportunity to visit with Giovanni for the first time in three months. Aside from being drugged out on Phenobarbital, he otherwise appeared healthy and happy.

This was the last time I saw Lily. Sadly, she did not have the opportunity to see how the sick baby she delivered had grown and changed. I called her and sent her an e-mail after Giovanni's fourth birthday to advise her of the changes in his condition.

Other than the chance to leave town to see Lily, we spent April trying to adapt to a new life without a husband or father. Kenneth and I were excited about our first trip to Disneyland during the first week of May. We were going to drive to Disneyland with Gina and Traci. But first, I had to take Giovanni in for his first neurology appointment since his EEG in March. The results of that appointment would cast a dark cloud over our vacation.

Chapter 10

For as much as I was looking forward to a vacation to Disneyland, I was dreading the visit to the neurologist. I always became anxious and nervous at the thought of facing more sad news. I knew I could not change anything about Giovanni's condition. I only could be has prepared as possible for any circumstance, so that I could face it head-on and help Giovanni overcome it.

My mom and Kenneth accompanied me to Giovanni's appointment with Dr. Greenwich, so that I would have moral support. Actually, my mom was there for the moral support. Kenneth was there because I did not have any childcare.

Jude was not present because he had a work commitment.

After a brief appointment and administering the routine tests, Dr. Greenwich provided his opinion of Giovanni's situation. First, he said that Giovanni was "cortically blind" as his eyes did not respond at all to any visual stimulus. He said that the eyes looked fine; the problem was within the brain. Some of the brain injury occurred in the visual cortex, causing a breakdown in communication between what the eyes see and what the brain perceives. At this visit, the doctor did not believe Giovanni was seeing anything.

The doctor also told us that Giovanni had high tone within his muscles, which indicated onset symptoms of cerebral palsy. At four months old, there was no way to determine what the outcome would be. The doctor said he had seen people who appeared to be a "train wreck" while very young, but were able to recover and regain their movement. On the other hand, he also said he saw people who appeared to have only mild symptoms initially, but then ended up in a wheelchair.

By the examples he gave and by what he said, he appeared to believe that Giovanni would be in the latter group.

Furthermore, Giovanni's head circumference had hardly changed in four months. The doctor said his head was still the size of a newborn and gave him the label of "microcephaly." My mom and I believed that perhaps being on the heavy medication Phenobarbital would affect his head size. After all, it affected just about everything else about his personality, his attitude, and mood. Dr. Greenwich said that he did not believe the medication had anything to do with Giovanni's head size. He said that Phenobarbital would not have any effect on brain growth. The size of his head was due to failure of the brain to grow, according to Dr. Greenwich.

Microcephaly refers to a head size that is abnormally small due to failure of the brain to grow. The size of the head is more than two standard deviations below the normal mean for age, gender, race and gestation. The condition may be present at birth or may be evident in the first few years of life when the head fails to grow while the face develops at a normal rate, producing a child with a small head, relatively large face and receding forehead.

In looking at Giovanni, I could see that his forehead was flat, although not receding. His face did not appear to be large in relation to his head.

Sadly, the condition is often equated with developmental delay and mental retardation, though not all children are retarded. Speech skills and motor skills may be delayed. Within a year, I knew the latter to be true for Giovanni.

On a positive note, the EEG that Giovanni had undergone in March showed no signs of epilepsy. Dr Khan had done the reading and noted "voltages were symmetric and appropriate for age." His impression was that the EEG was normal during wakefulness and sleep. There were no epileptic abnormalities recorded. Dr Khan believed that Giovanni's seizure history was strong enough so as not to exclude a clinical diagnosis of epilepsy. However, it appeared that, at least at this point in time, there was no sign of epilepsy or any seizure disorder.

Consequently, Dr. Greenwich determined that we could slowly wean Giovanni off the Phenobarbital over the following four to six weeks. Because I knew of the strong seizure history, I specifically asked Dr. Greenwich's opinion about a possible seizure disorder. Although he did explain to me what specific seizure activity I could look for in someone with cerebral palsy, he admitted that it was "highly unlikely" that Giovanni would have any seizures.

The doctor, who proclaimed almost every scenario as negative, believed that Giovanni's potential for a seizure disorder was very small. Of all the conditions Giovanni had, epilepsy was not one of them.

As the doctor spoke to my mother and me in length about his concerns for Giovanni, I was upset and had a difficult time holding back tears. Kenneth was in the room, playing with a toy, and appeared to notice the stress. His behavior suddenly changed to being anxious to leave. I probably should not have brought him in with me, but I did not have anyone else to watch him.

At the time, I did not think the doctor would say anything that would affect me so strongly. Then again, I may have just been in denial about Giovanni's true condition. Maybe I was just hoping that since he survived and was otherwise healthy (he had not yet had a cold or even the flu that Kenneth had) that perhaps he had improved.

As I walked out to the car with my mom, we were both crying. My mind was racing with the worst-case scenario—having a blind child in a wheelchair who may or may not be able to speak and who may or may not be cognitively disabled.

After over three months of continuous emotional upheaval, I really thought that, in looking forward to a fun vacation, that maybe I would finally find my way out of depression. Maybe Disneyland, "the happiest place on Earth," might finally lead me into the fifth stage of grief and recovery—an upward turn, or adjustment to life. I really wanted to be lifted out of the depression that was draining my spirit.

With the neurologist's grim outlook, I found myself mired even deeper in depression.

After the appointment, I called Jude to tell him about Giovanni's condition. He did say that his work commitment was cancelled and he drove out to Woodland to spend several hours with Kenneth. He took Kenneth out of the house, presumably to get ice cream. They were gone most of the day, stopping at a coffee shop and took their time getting home. I understood that he did not want to spend time with me, but I was saddened that he showed so little interest in Giovanni. I do not remember if we even had the chance to review the doctor visit.

The following week, I took the boys to Disneyland with Gina and Traci. We drove the 400 miles, which made for a long day for the boys. Because Giovanni was weaning off the Phenobarbital, he was extra distressed. I also realized that since he was "blind", he also was probably angry or upset because he could hear sounds but could not see anything.

While we were at Disneyland, I took Giovanni on several of the children's rides. He liked the merry-go-round and he liked the legendary It's a Small World ride. I believe now that he liked It's a Small World because of the continual singing. Though it may be annoying for adults to be "trapped" in such a repetitive ride, Giovanni loved it because of the harmony and rhythm of the music. Even in infancy, Giovanni showed a strong preference for musical rhythm. Though most babies enjoy music, Giovanni seemed to have a special appreciation for it.

One thing that happened that was out of the ordinary was when three-year-old Kenneth faked a seizure. He was sitting in the stroller and he rolled his eyes back, and then would not immediately respond to me. I am sure he sensed my anxiety, because he stopped the charade and told me that he was "only joking." I cannot even imagine how Kenneth figured out what seizures were since Giovanni suffered through the seizures while he was on the hospital and Kenneth was not around much during his active seizure phase. It was disturbing to think that at 3 ½ years old, he could understand enough of what was happening to fake a seizure.

It turns out, that this was not the first time that Kenneth would mimic his brother. I am sure that even though Kenneth never expressed any jealousy over the attention given to Giovanni because of his special needs, I am sure it affected him on some level. Perhaps he faked a seizure at Disneyland because he saw how intense, and sometimes frantic, I was when witnessing any issues with Giovanni. He definitely got my attention.

I realized that I would have to learn to react more calmly when it came to Giovanni's medical issues. That was easier said than done and it took a few years and some counseling to get to that point.

As hard as I tried, I felt too stressed to enjoy myself. I was so concerned about Giovanni that I almost panicked when we missed the last train out of the park and were forced to watch the fireworks show. I tried to cover Giovanni's ears from the constant "booms" of the fireworks. I knew that flashing lights could cause seizures in some people. Since Giovanni was blind, as far as I knew, I thought that maybe the loud distracting noise might cause the same thing. Giovanni was especially susceptible to breakthrough seizures since he was weaning off a powerful anti-convulsant medication. If he were to have a recurrence of seizures, this would be the time.

He had no seizures that night, or any other night, though he was suffering through the effects of being withdrawn from his medication. He struggled to sleep while we were at the hotel. On the way home, he suffered from crying fits. His distress transferred to all of us and probably was magnified and sent back to him.

Even when we returned to the familiar surroundings of home, Giovanni struggled with being jittery and crying for no apparent reason. Kenneth probably was affected, as this was the time Kenneth started having nightmares. My mom had told me that it was normal for children his age to have occasional nightmares. Personally, I felt that in Kenneth's case, his nightmares were exacerbated because of all the stress of being separated from his father and having been a witness to Giovanni's situation.

Since I perceived that Kenneth was missing his father, I tried to call Jude on his behalf. After two days and three messages later, I finally received a return call from Jude. He stated that it was his policy not to deal with relationship or family issues on workdays. He did not sound concerned that Kenneth was having nightmares. I was not aware that parenting had to fit within a schedule of a work weekend.

Anyway, two days later Giovanni had a pediatric appointment. Jude did not come for the appointment, but he showed up later in the afternoon to visit with Kenneth. He was to take him overnight, but cancelled those plans because of work issues. When he came to our home, he only stayed for 30 minutes before he decided to leave because I never said "thank you" to him for driving so far to visit. Again, I was not aware that being a parent required one parent to "thank" the other for visiting his or her own child.

At this time, he also expressed his concern that I had told Kenneth about the divorce because Kenneth was not "old enough" to be concerned with such things. Relative to his relationship to his sons, Jude claimed that his "life" was in the Bay Area and that he would not be moving and would only be able to see the boys once a week.

If only he really did see them that much.

In fact, if history was any indication, I probably could not expect much from him regardless of what he said. During the time we were at my parents' house, he had claimed that he would visit the boys at my parent's house on his days off. Yet, in two months, he only visited twice, and for only a few short hours each time.

During this week in dealing with Jude, I think that I dealt well with the situation, only because I was feeling so much anger and resentment. My feelings over anger overshadowed the depression I felt.

Also adding to my stressors was the fact that I returned to work that week from an extra long maternity leave. Esther was still willing to provide childcare for the boys when I was in town for work. Fortunately, I was still working part-time.

I knew that returning to work would be difficult because I remembered the first day I returned after Kenneth was born. This time it was worse because I felt so much more guilt at leaving a neurologically impaired child in someone else's care. Even as an infant, Giovanni seemed to have preferences to his environment. He had adjusted to living at my parent's house and then moving to his own home. I was not sure how he would react to being at Grandma's house, especially when I was not around.

Not surprisingly, Giovanni had more difficulty adjusting than Kenneth ever did. Unfortunately, my mother-in-law was not in the best health and it was probably difficult to care for an anxious infant and his 3 ½ year old brother. To make matters worse, he was still not completely weaned off the Phenobarbital, and Esther had to give him the medication in a bottle of breast milk.

She was having so much difficulty and was so stressed about it, that she called me at work my first night. She was upset and stated that she did not know how my mom ever got Giovanni to take the bottle. She said it must have been "traumatic," because Giovanni was going through "trauma" now. I did say that I also had difficulty in giving him the bottle with medication, but that my mom had some sort of "system" worked out with Giovanni, in which he would take it for her, and it was definitely not "traumatic."

Apparently, Esther did call my mom that night to get some pointers about talking softly and playing soft music while giving the bottle. Giovanni was easily soothed by music. Both Esther and Diana had some concerns about Giovanni's ability to suck from the bottle, although my mom had been successful in bottle feeding him. In addressing their concerns, I made an appointment with a speech-language pathologist for an oral-motor feeding evaluation set for the following month.

During that first month at work, I had decided that I would get Giovanni "dedicated" at my in-laws church. Although I was raised Catholic, I began attending my in-laws' non-denominational Christian Bible church when I began dating Jude. The pastor married Jude and me and had "dedicated" Kenneth when he was nine months old.

A "dedication" is a ceremony in which the parents dedicate their child to Christ. It is not a "baptism" because there is no water submersion involved. In this church, they believed that an infant is too young to be baptized, because he or she cannot consciously accept Jesus as their Lord and Savior. Therefore, baptism takes place when the child is old enough to understand who Jesus is and is able to make his or her own choice to follow Him.

My Catholic family is open-minded and had no problem in attending Kenneth's dedication. After all, there is nothing in the Bible that prohibits it, and dedicating a child to Christ is a good thing. I wanted to do the same for Giovanni. I did have my concerns about how awkward it might be to have both families at the church to celebrate the dedication of a child who would not actually be attending that church.

Kenneth was at an age where he would ask questions about God and Jesus and he had seen pictures of his own dedication. He knew what it was, and he was excited for his brother to be dedicated also. Truthfully, I really wanted to do something to appease my in-laws, so I figured that if I was going to have my child dedicated, I should do it in their church.

I did feel a little uncomfortable calling the pastor, since he was a family friend of my in-laws I was not sure how he felt about me. I knew he was upset about the divorce. But it never entered my mind that he may deny Giovanni the opportunity to be dedicated in Christ, just because his parents made mistakes in their marriage.

After all, according to the Bible, we are all sinners. As the Bible says, "Let he who has not sinned cast the first stone."

Unfortunately, I think I was wrong. I left two messages for the pastor, which he did not return. After two weeks with no return call, I called to talk to his assistant. She acknowledged that the pastor had the message but that he was so busy and she did not know what he was going to do about the dedication. I was a little bit shocked. I may be wrong, but it seemed to me that he was avoiding my phone calls. Even after I talked to his assistant, he still did not call me back. He never did return my calls.

I was sad by this because in my mind, he was not just turning me away, but he was turning an innocent child away. I had a good cry about that, since I tend to take things so personally when it affects my children. How nice it would have been had he at least the courage and respect to just call me and tell me "no." He just left me in limbo. Even when I asked my in-laws about it, they just re-iterated that he was just "so busy" and he would eventually call me back.

Still having no return phone call from the pastor, I decided I would get Giovanni baptized in my parents' church. I knew that their church had an extremely large congregation of over 7,000 members. This was in contrast to a few hundred members at the Bible church. Therefore, when my mom left a message for the church pastor, inquiring about a baptism, I did not expect a return call for several days.

The priest's assistant returned our call within two hours.

Even though I told him I was going through a divorce, which is definitely frowned upon by the Catholic Church, the priest was willing to perform the baptism. Since I was getting Giovanni baptized in my family's church, I decided to get Kenneth baptized as well. This was because I wanted my boys to be dedicated to Christ in the same manner.

I knew there would be times when Giovanni would be treated differently because of his disabilities. In some cases, it would be necessary because of his special needs. I feared that there would be times when he would be treated differently, because of discrimination, or because of other peoples' ignorance. I decided I would treat my boys the same, as much as possible. I scheduled a dual baptism for later in the summer.

The differences between Giovanni's and Kenneth's development became more apparent with Giovanni's first evaluation by a physical therapist when he was about 4 ½ months old. The therapist noted that Giovanni did not visually track an object, but he turned his head when Kenneth entered the room. Obviously, his other senses made up for his lack of vision, as he was well aware of his environment. Giovanni's gross motor skills were rated at a 3-month-old level. He was able to lift his head to 45 degrees, but was not able to consistently roll from his back to his stomach.

Although Giovanni had a normal range of motion, his muscles were tight and it took some rotation to obtain full range of motion. In addition, he had an overall increase in muscle tone. His arms, especially his right arm, were stiffer than his legs. He kept his hands loosely fisted and both thumbs indwelling. These both were indicators of cerebral palsy. He also had visible redness on his right biceps, which also indicated the general high tone throughout his body.

After all the observation, the therapist estimated his overall delay at 1-2 months. I tried not to worry about that too much, as I hoped that by the time Giovanni was 12 months old, having skills at a 10-month-old level would not be a big issue. I did not realize that regardless of the delay in infancy, it could potentially translate into large delays later in life. A one or two month delay in infancy really could have repercussions, since the brain does some of its greatest growth in the first six months of life.

Because of Giovanni's physical delays, the therapist recommended weekly therapy. Unfortunately, there were so many children needing therapy and so few therapists, that there was a waiting list. Giovanni was placed on the waiting list and I was told to expect a wait of several months.

I was pleasantly surprised a couple of weeks later, when I was informed that Giovanni was going to be placed with the therapist the following week. Honestly, at the time, I was so overwhelmed with everything in my life that I felt my judgment was clouded. I did not realize just how important early intervention would be. Addressing physical issues at the earliest possible time gives the child the best chance to overcome them.

A few days prior to his first physical therapy appointment, I attended a six-month review with his service coordinator at the regional therapy center. I learned that these meetings would take place twice a year to gauge Giovanni's progress and determine his needs for social services. During this meeting, I gave my input for an Individual Family Support Plan (IFSP). This is a written document that is prepared by the service coordinator with input from parents, family members, and therapists. It states in writing what the regional center is willing and able to provide for Giovanni and states goals for his development.

During this IFSP meeting, one of the primary concerns listed on the plan was his delay in fine motor skills. This would also relate to his delay in gross motor skills. Therefore, physical therapy was officially added to his plan. All other areas of development were so heavily dependent on vision that the coordinator wanted to wait to hear what the ophthalmologist diagnosed. Giovanni had an appointment with an ophthalmologist two weeks later.

During the first two of years of his life, Giovanni had very frequent appointments with so many specialists and therapists that I needed a scorecard to keep track. Every doctor or therapist had his or her own experience and opinions, but it appeared that there was still much uncertainty about Giovanni's future development.

Chapter 11

Giovanni's first summer was busy, filled with appointments with doctors, specialists, and therapists.

The week after the IFSP meeting, Giovanni began physical therapy with Sara. She noted that his head was strong and he held it up well. This was positive news for me since I was concerned that the cerebral palsy would affect his ability to control his head. However, he continued to have indwelling thumbs, which showed that he continued to have high tone. Sara instructed me how to massage his thumb, to gently remove it from between the index and third finger.

This instruction on what to do to help Giovanni was really the greatest asset of the physical therapist. Since she only met with Giovanni one hour each week, I knew that she was not going to be performing miracles and getting Giovanni mobile on her own. It would be up to me and family members to follow her instructions on a daily basis, so that Giovanni's brain would be able to form connections in the motor cortex. These connections would strengthen with repetition, forming a "memory" of it in the brain, and would help Giovanni to develop his motor skills.

It would be difficult enough even if it was just repetition that influenced development of motor skills. Because the sense of vision is a primary influence on gross motor development, Giovanni was at a disadvantage. When we visited his ophthalmologist, Dr. Reese, he said that there was nothing wrong with Giovanni's eyes. Giovanni's vision problems originated in the occipital lobe of the brain where vision is perceived.

I was happy his eyes were not affected. The irony was if it were only the eyes that were the problem, it would probably be correctable. The problem was within the brain, which is not correctable. Dr. Greenwich labeled Giovanni "cortically blind", although Dr. Reese claimed that he was not "blind." What Giovanni had, according to Dr. Reese, was "visual inattention." He said that Giovanni's brain was not "paying attention" to the visual images that came in through the eyes.

I was confused, because the doctor said that sometimes Giovanni would respond to visual stimulus and sometimes he would not. I asked, is Giovanni "able to see? Does he have vision?" The doctor's answer was indirect and philosophical. He likened it to the saying "if a tree falls in the forest and nobody is there, does it make a sound?" He rhetorically asked "if Giovanni's eyes take in the images but his brain does not process them, is he able to see?" Well, he did not have an answer to that question.

I left the eye doctor with not much more information than what I went in with except for a very interesting analogy and a different label than the "cortical blindness" that the neurologist gave him.

Esther called that night to inquire about Giovanni's appointment. I waited for Jude's call, but it never came. I could only assume that his mother briefed him with the information.

A few days later Giovanni had the appointment with the speech-language pathologist who would determine if he really had difficulty with sucking on a bottle. Peggy the pathologist noted that he had an adequate suck while nursing. Although she did not witness him try the bottle, she told me that the motor skills that were required for nursing were much more complex than that for bottle-feeding. Therefore, if he could nurse so well, he definitely did not have a problem with the skills involved with taking a bottle. It was a matter of choice. For whatever reason, Giovanni did not want the bottle, not that he was not able to take it.

From her experience, she believed that he would take the bottle when the environmental conditions were preferable to him. For example, he responded to soft voices and soft music and was able to sense any tension or uncertainty in the caregiver. Any tension he sensed in the caregiver, or within the room, would affect Giovanni. He felt it and internalized it.

As part of the appointment, the pathologist also evaluated his speech and eating skills. Giovanni made a variety of vowel sounds and had distinguishable cries and periods of babbling. He did have a tongue thrust problem that became evident as he ate from a spoon. This habit would have a negative effect on his speech, so Peggy suggested utensil placement at the corners of the mouth. This would help him develop good eating skills and a brain "memory" that would help him overcome his bad eating habits. As his eating skills developed, so too would his speech skills.

I was pleased with the outcome of this appointment as it confirmed my belief that Giovanni had no feeding problems. The poor habits he did have were correctable. Most importantly, at this point in time, it appeared that he was developing speech patterns that were typical of a 4-6 month old child.

I realized at this point, that I had reached stage five in dealing with my grief over Giovanni. I was starting to climb out of the depression, just a little bit, and was experiencing an "upward turn" in which I was beginning to accept reality. I felt that I could influence reality in a positive way. This was due in large part to the therapists' treating me as the primary influence in Giovanni's development. They gave me the knowledge to provide him with exercise and therapy in the absence of the professionals. My emotional and mental strength was returning, and I was beginning to feel more in control of my life and surroundings.

I really wanted to share the good news with Jude, but I could not reach him. He came to the house a few days later to pick up Kenneth. He wanted to take Kenneth back to visit with his mother because "she missed him and was not able to see him very much anymore." He also said he wanted to "give me a break." That was a head scratcher since he was taking my semi-independent three-year-old and leaving me with a baby that needed constant care.

He did not ask any questions about Giovanni, I volunteered the information. This became my "bad habit" because all I did was continue to enable Jude instead of letting him take the lead and either be a father—or not—to his son. According to Esther, he did not talk to her about Giovanni's appointments either, so what information I gave him was all he received.

Not only did I feel sadness in Jude's lack of interest in Giovanni, but it also grieved me that comments he did make were usually negative. One day, when he called, I expressed concern about what I perceived to be his negative attitude about Giovanni's condition. He claimed that he was being "realistic." My belief was that a person could be realistic, but also hopeful and actively working toward a better future. It seemed his belief was that realistic meant acceptance of what exists, but not taking control or initiative to make things any better. I believe that God gave us a mind so that we can help to solve our own problems.

As Jude continued to live in his "realty", I continued to live in mine. My reality consisted of being a single parent, trying to make the best of my circumstances in raising two boys to be strong, independent men. I was still determined that no matter what the "experts" said, I was going to help Giovanni become independent.

I visualized Giovanni's life as if he was climbing a mountain. I could place him on a small hill, give him the tools, and tell him to climb it. He may, or may not, reach the top. I would rather tell him to climb a mountain and give him the tools and support needed for the climb. Although he may not reach the top of the mountain, he at least has a chance of making it. If he does not try, he will be destined to remain on the hill.

I intentionally use the visual concept of climbing a mountain because Giovanni's journey can be extremely challenging for him. To be successful and reach the top, he needs lots of physical training, mental preparation, support of those around him, and a strong and indomitable spirit.

In July, when Giovanni was six months old, we began to focus on getting him into a "low puppy" crawling position. The therapist also tried to get Giovanni to get up and sit with assistance. In addition, I began using a black and white mobile to stimulate his vision. He had a mobile that provided sounds of the ocean and one that provided sounds of classical composers like Beethoven. He showed an early preference to the classics.

I am not sure how much Giovanni really saw, but he loved the music and would try to hum along with it.

Besides humming along with music, I noticed Giovanni had a unique ability to "purr" like a kitten. This really is the only way I could describe it. Somehow, Giovanni would growl so deeply that I could feel it vibrating within his body, but there would be no sounds from his mouth. He tended to "purr" most frequently when he was happy or content—like a kitten. I also noticed he would do it to sooth himself. This ability to vibrate his body was the first indication of his sensory processing disorder. At six or seven months old, I did not realize what sensory processing disorder was, so I did not use that to label him yet.

During that summer, when I was focused on providing Giovanni with physical therapy, I also tried to integrate the entire family in doing physical training exercises with him. Esther was very good at following whatever suggestions I gave her. Even with her own medical issues, she did whatever she could to help Giovanni. For the first few months after I returned to work, Esther was the primary babysitter for both children. She occasionally had help from Jude's sisters when they were around. Esther's doctor had expressed concern about her lifting the boys, so I knew it would not be much longer before I would have to find another caregiver.

Perhaps Jude would step up to the plate when his mother became too ill to care for the boys. Well, there was always hope.

At Giovanni's neurology appointment in July, Dr. Greenwich was pleased that Giovanni's head circumference grew two centimeters. This growth rate was about twice the normal pace of growth. Quite coincidentally, this growth occurred after Giovanni was weaned off the Phenobarbital.

That led me again to ask Dr. Greenwich if he thought that the Phenobarbital would affect brain growth and he said, "No." Yet, he had no explanation as to why Giovanni's brain exploded in growth only after he was off the medication.

Regardless of the doctor's opinion, I had hope that now Giovanni's brain had time to "catch up" and maybe his delays would improve. Like the doctor, I was concerned that Giovanni missed brain growth time during the first six months—time he could never get back.

I always made Giovanni's appointments on Jude's days off. Yet Jude also missed this appointment.

In August, when I did meet Jude to exchange the boys, he never made contact with Giovanni and never asked about the recent appointment. Kenneth went overboard with affection for his brother—right in front of his father. He noticed when his father did not respond to Giovanni in kind. Perhaps it was only coincidence that Kenneth had nightmares that night.

At the following week's exchange, I handed Giovanni right to Jude. He kissed him on the forehead and handed him back. He seemingly forgot that I had told him that Giovanni had vision problems and to bond with Giovanni Jude needed to hold him, talk to him, and give him physical affection. In hindsight, this was probably a silly thing for me to do. Why would Jude respond any differently to Giovanni with me as the mediator when he did not respond to Kenneth's mediation?

A few days later, I thought we might have a break through when Jude called and cried that he felt like he "lost everything." Yet, he claimed that he did not miss me. I told him he knew where the kids were if he ever wanted to see or visit them. Since he did not miss me, I assumed what he felt he "lost" were his children. His actions did not exhibit to me that he was a father missing his children. I would have expected a father to want visitation with both children on every day off from work.

The next morning he called me to say he had a hard night and had not slept and his supervisor had removed him from patrol for three hours. If this was an attempt to gain sympathy, I am afraid it was not working. I was a single parent with two children, receiving intermittent child support and also doing shift work. I managed to function fine at work, at least where the relationship with Jude was concerned. My concern and reaction to Giovanni's condition was a different matter.

With Jude not being a big part of the boys' lives, he had no issue with them being baptized. He said he had to work and could not be there. I also invited his family. They declined because they did not agree with the baptism. Thankfully, Kenneth did not question why his "other family" was not there. My family and best friend attended the baptism and that is what was important. Kenneth understood the meaning of the baptism and was excited to be involved.

For his part, Giovanni was patient and quiet. However, for a kid who would later have constipation issues, he had no problems that day. He decided that he had "to go" as soon as he was naked. I had to step aside after the entrance procession to clean him. Gina and Traci stood up as godparents for Kenneth while my brother and grandmother were godparents for Giovanni. It was a special and meaningful day for our family.

It was wonderful to see the closeness between Kenneth and Giovanni, which reaffirmed my belief that these brothers had to be raised together.

As hard as it was to accept Jude's lack of personal involvement with his children, it was also exceptionally difficult at times to deal with his unwillingness to help in child care situations. Sadly, the negative effects spread from me to my own family, who would make sacrifices repeatedly to help the boys and me.

September 11, 2005 is a day that will remain in my memory, and not just because it was the anniversary of the terrorist attacks on the World Trade Center. It was also my parents' anniversary. On this day, I had to work and was also struggling for childcare. Since Esther was no longer able to care for the boys on her own, I had to arrange for someone else to care for them. My parents usually filled in, but they made a special request in advance that I not use them on their anniversary.

My sister had to work and Jude's family members, although conveniently located in Fairfield, were "not available." I arranged weeks in advance for Jude to drive out to babysit his children. As the time came closer, I became more nervous. Would Jude follow through with his commitment this time?

Fear became reality when Jude called at 1:00 p.m. that day to say it "wasn't going to work out." He claimed he was "too tired." Well, I understood being too tired as it was very tiring to work shift work (and my hours changed weekly) and then to care for two children as the only parent. Consequently, "too tired" was not an excuse in my mind for a parent not to care for his children.

I had to be at work at 5:00 p.m., so I had no time to work a shift trade. I could not conscientiously call in "sick" because I was not sick. I reminded him he had promised to take both boys and that it was my parents' anniversary. They had made specific arrangements for this day. This was the first day in eight months that I had asked, rather, begged him to help with childcare. In my mind, I did not think that it was any big sacrifice to provide one day of childcare for his children in an eight-month period.

As was his habit, he did not assertively back out of the commitment, he just "talked around it" for a few minutes. He said he "just got home" and had not slept. I told him I realized that, in his condition, he could not take a special needs child. I asked him for help in finding a solution, but he did not offer any ideas. He said he would take Kenneth the next day, but I told him the boys would be at my parents' house. This meant I would be commuting 85 miles to work the next day. I would have to bring Kenneth with me.

He said he would meet in Fairfield to get Kenneth. However, when I said we would be there at 1:00 p.m., he said that was "too early." I noticed he never committed to say, "I can't do it." I suppose backing out of a visit with his son would have made him look bad. He talked in circles until I pushed him to make a decision. He said he had a friend coming to town and he chose not to visit Kenneth.

It hurt my parents, who came to my rescue again and cancelled their anniversary plans to care for the boys.

Obviously, there was no time for me to be disheartened now as the anger took over. Unfortunately, being the only adult in the household required me to keep my feelings bottled up. I did not want my children to pick up on my aggravation. The best I could do was to not speak negatively about their father. In fact, I went overboard in searching for positives that I could accentuate. As for the bottled up emotions, I am sure the children must have sensed it at some level. Giovanni particularly had the ability to sense emotions and then react to them.

I tried to transform my negative energy into a positive energy to help Giovanni.

As Giovanni continued his physical therapy, Sara kept working on his ability to sit up. He started using an exercise ball to help develop his torso strength. Giovanni responded very positively to bouncing on the ball. He really enjoyed lots of physical activity. Because of his lack of vision, Giovanni craved lots of movement to provide sensory input.

We experimented with using different textures in the toys that Giovanni played with. His lack of vision also tied in with his need to explore his environment using his tactile sense. Giovanni enjoyed experimenting with different textures. From early on, Giovanni showed his preferences with the toys that he liked. If a toy did not interest him, he did not even attempt to pick it up or to hold it. Or, if he did make the effort to feel it, he would drop it.

The toys he liked the most were the ones that made sounds, thereby stimulating his auditory sense. He caught on quickly to the concept of "cause and effect" through use of one of the musical toys. While on his back, Giovanni could use his legs and kick at a pad with different numbers to activate corresponding music and other sounds. He would kick and play with that toy for hours, listening and humming along to the music. Over time, my mom and I would come to realize that Giovanni was humming along with the particular rhythm of the music.

As with any child, there were times when Giovanni became over stimulated. I believe this occurred more easily for him because of his lack of vision. His brain was trying to process a large amount of incoming stimuli from the other senses. His brain had to make some sense of all the input without having the assistance of vision. There were times when Giovanni became uncomfortable and start crying. We found that the best way to calm him was to pick him up and provide deep pressure input like hugs or snuggles. This was another indication that he had special needs related to sensory processing.

As Giovanni experienced more frequent outbursts related to sensory processing issues, I saw that he had his own coping mechanisms. Not only did he like it when another person gave him deep pressure input when he was in distress, but he would also do it himself through his "purr" or deep "growl". This provided input throughout his body that he needed to calm himself. I was happy when he was able to calm himself rather than rely on another person to do it for him. He was showing signs of independence through self-regulation.

He also began showing signs that perhaps he was not totally blind. He would become mesmerized by bright light coming in the windows. It would sometimes distract him from his therapy. At other times, it would be soothing to him. Apparently, what little vision Giovanni may have had, provided some input that was pleasing to him. Until a vision specialist evaluated Giovanni, I would not know how much vision he truly had since Dr. Greenwich believed he was "blind."

As Giovanni grew and changed, he exhibited more signs that he was having difficulty in integrating his senses to adapt to his environment. I did some research on the topic. I found that there was indeed a "disorder" that described Giovanni's sensory problems. Raising a Sensory Smart Child, by Lindsey Biel and Nancy Peske, was the book that gave me so much information about what Giovanni was experiencing and what I could do to help him.

I realized that Giovanni had something called Sensory Integration Dysfunction. It was also called Sensory Processing Disorder. Giovanni was having difficulty adjusting to his environment because his body was receiving sensory input that was not consistent. Therefore, the sensory input was not reliable and Giovanni was having difficulty in responding to his environment. His nervous system was having difficulty in responding to the inconsistent input. I could only imagine, but not truly understand, how frustrating this was for Giovanni.

Because of this problem, Giovanni could become distracted or annoyed with his environment and exhibit certain behaviors to let the caregiver know he was having problems. Giovanni was sometimes oversensitive or undersensitive to certain sensory input. He could become highly distractible. He would sometimes become hyperactive in his attempts to seek out sensory input. When he received too much input, he would sometimes withdraw. Because of difficulties in understanding his environment, he would become agitated during the transition from one environment or activity to another. It was helpful for me, or the caregiver to talk him through the transition. I did not fully understand yet how important this was for him since I could only operate on intuition. I didn't yet have knowledge on how to raise a blind, or visually impaired, child.

It was helpful to understand that his responses to sensory input were not voluntary. He was not intentionally agitated or becoming upset. It was a neurological response. The sensory input

Giovanni received was neurologically processed differently from how we would expect, and so he would have a different behavioral response.

One of the best things I could do for Giovanni in helping him adapt to his sensory integration issues was to watch for sensory overload and provide a program of balanced sensory input throughout the day. Providing the proper input for him would do for his brain what all the other therapy would do for him. The right input would help the brain and nervous system to grown and develop lasting changes.

In their book, Biel and Peske suggested providing a "sensory diet" throughout the day so that Giovanni's brain would become trained in handling various sensory inputs. Giovanni was undergoing physical therapy, and would soon be introduced to other types of therapy. I likened the "sensory diet" to "sensory therapy." Like the aspects of physical therapy which I would integrate throughout the normal day, I would also add sensory input throughout the day to help train Giovanni's brain.

As excited as I was about providing new experiences for Giovanni, I had to be aware of overloading the senses. Giovanni would give me physical indicators that he was over stimulated. Indicators of overstimulation could include: a higher than normal level of activity or sensitivity, increased confusion or distractibility, nausea or vomiting, pale or flushed skin, rapid breathing, change in muscle tone, sudden sleepiness, or even signs of seizures.

In high school, I had learned about the five senses: sight (vision), hearing (auditory), touch (tactile), taste, and smell (olfactory). Now I would learn how they all interacted and influenced one another. I would also learn that there were not only five senses, but actually seven. The other two senses were the proprioceptive and the vestibular senses. It was important for me to understand how these two senses influenced Giovanni so that I could provide the proper input throughout the day. I wanted the input to be helpful, not hurtful or uncomfortable for Giovanni.

The vestibular sense contributes to our sense of balance and sense of spatial orientation. This is the sensory system that provides the dominant information about movement. It is also the primary coordinating system, amongst the other systems, which brings the information together to interpret the environment. Lacking vision, Giovanni relied on this sense to help him orient to his environment.

The proprioceptive sense interprets the relative position of neighboring parts of the body. It is the only sense that provides feedback on the internal status of the body. It is this sense that determines whether the body is moving with the required effort and provides information as to where various parts of the body are in relation to each other. For Giovanni, this sense needed to be trained and tuned. Awareness of his own body parts and their relative location to each other would help Giovanni develop more coordinated movements.

For those of us with complete use of all our senses, we probably do not notice how the senses all coordinate and interact with each other as it is done on a subconscious level. Giovanni, though, was missing his vision, one of his primary coordinating senses. The input provided by all the other senses, especially the vestibular and proprioceptive senses, took on new meaning and importance. In addition, for Giovanni, there needed to be a conscious effort on his part—and my part—to train the other senses to become stronger.

In providing "sensory therapy" for Giovanni, I had to incorporate activities into his day that specifically addressed all the sensory systems. When Giovanni was an infant, no one anticipated that he would have some very specific needs relative to sensory input in his environment. Most parents do not consciously think about what activities can help awaken specific senses. As a consequence, I did not immediately address these issues. For his first year of life, I continued to focus specifically on his physical therapy and motor skills. As he grew and changed and his sensory integration issues became more obvious, I began to learn how to address his need for a more integrated approach on training his senses.

By the time Giovanni's first summer had transitioned into autumn, I had transitioned into stage six in addressing my grief over Giovanni. This stage involves a reconstruction of life and an acceptance of the situation. As my mind began functioning a little more clearly, I became more adept at restructuring my life and working through issues on a day to day basis. This was not to say that I was not still distracted. My own brain was often on overload with the responsibility of helping Giovanni succeed, home schooling Kenneth, and working shift work 24 hours a week. I was at least able to progress forward with my life.

As Giovanni reached the age of nine months old and Kenneth was approaching four years old, I had firmly established myself as a single parent, knowing that with God's help, I could count only on myself and my family with moral support of friends, to provide Giovanni with the love, care and therapy he needed.

Chapter 12

Kenneth's 4th birthday in October afforded me an opportunity to build some bridges between families—or at least observe how far things had strayed off course.

As diligently as I tried to maintain amicable relationships between my in-laws and myself, and between Jude and my family, I definitely felt tension whenever it became necessary to have everyone together. Being the custodial parent, I felt it was my obligation to organize my son's party. It was the first time since the separation that both families got together for any type of celebration.

As nice and cordial as everyone was to each other, there was no denying the underlying tension when everyone was in the same room. Kenneth was definitely "man of the hour." Esther used to call him the little "prince", and sometimes that's how he acted. Even though this day was his day, I expected that Jude's family may have wanted to visit with Giovanni, since they rarely saw him or called about him.

There was very limited interaction between Giovanni and members of Jude's family. Diana and Esther played with Giovanni a little bit and asked some questions about him. Olivia did not speak much. Jude's father sat on the couch and just watched everything. Jude really did not interact much either.

My mom walked up to Jude and handed Giovanni to him. Like me, she got upset with Jude's lack of interest and was as likely as I was to try to "encourage" him to get involved. He held Giovanni for a couple of minutes, but then handed him off to me, so that he could use the bathroom. He never asked for him back. After all the guests left, Jude fell asleep on the couch.

It was during this month that Jude finally said he was ready to proceed with divorce paperwork. His desire was to share custody and to remain amicable. While we were meeting face to face, he said he wanted to help with clothes for the boys and would help with commute costs, since I was paying so much in gas. My parents were providing the childcare and I would drive sixty miles to their house to drop off the boys. Then I would drive eighty-five miles to work. My parents were providing care at no cost to me or to Jude, but I incurred the travel costs. We would revisit this issue several times in the following few years.

He did follow through on his promise to help with commute costs related to childcare this time. He did give me $50.

As disappointing as it was to think about Jude's unreliability, it was even more disappointing to have to take Giovanni in to see Dr. Greenwich. My father came with me for this visit to lend moral support because I knew I would need it. Giovanni's head circumference had grown, however, not to the extent that made Dr. Greenwich happy. He was seriously concerned with Giovanni's brain growth thus far and pronounced that he could potentially have cognitive deficits as a result.

As I was trying to process this sobering information, my analytical father asked specific questions about Giovanni's prognosis. I could sense that the neurologist was uncomfortable with the questions. He talked in generalities around the questions and never provided any substantial information. When my father finally asked in a forthright manner what Giovanni's cognitive abilities would be, Dr. Greenwich appeared exasperated when he said "at this rate, I suspect Giovanni's mental capabilities will be at about a 10 year old level."

I was shocked and I believe my father was also. For myself, I could say that I could not believe that any doctor could examine a nine month old for ten minutes and predict what his mental capacity or cognitive ability would be as an adult. This news, I believe, saddened my father, although my prominent emotion was not one of being despondent (believe it or not) but anger. This was when I concluded that if a doctor proclaimed to able to predict the future, I probably would not trust him.

As I stated before when Giovanni was in the hospital, I did not and do not, respect doctors who are so quickly willing to jump to a conclusion about something that cannot be predicted. The human brain is just too complex for anyone to claim that he knows definitively how any particular brain is going to react to any particular injury.

My analytical mind even started questioning what method the doctor was using in describing what "10 year old mentality" truly meant. Did it mean that Giovanni would function as a 10 year old when he was 18 years old? 25 years old? 30 years old? In addition, did that mean that Giovanni's cognitive development would just "freeze" at some point? Doesn't the brain grow and change throughout life? What measure was the doctor using at determining "10 year old" function? There are some 10 year olds that I have met that could function in high school or even college.

So, I thought, if Giovanni could function at "10 years old" when he was eighteen, perhaps he would function at 18 years old when he was thirty. Therefore, in my perception, he would eventually surpass his father.

I did not ask the neurologist any of these questions since I felt that he had put up a wall between us as a result of our persistent questioning.

While Dr. Greenwich claimed to know what Giovanni's cognitive abilities would be, he could still not confirm a physical diagnosis of cerebral palsy. Dr. Greenwich also believed that Giovanni was still "blind" as he was not responding to any visual stimulus. Yet, he did not believe that Giovanni had, or would ever have a seizure disorder. Although he was pleased that Giovanni was getting the physical therapy that he needed, the doctor did not say one word about how I could make a positive impact on Giovanni's condition.

As we left the office, my father and I were both upset and angry at the doctor's opinion. I realized that there were many people that would take the doctor's opinion as "fact" and would accept the situation as hopeless. I am sure many parents would become discouraged if they felt a lack of control over their child's development.

This was the last time Giovanni saw Dr. Greenwich.

I did not have much time to recover from that stressor, when I had to deal with Jude. He called to arrange an exchange with Kenneth, but never asked about Giovanni's appointment. When we met later, I asked if his family might want me to visit them with Giovanni since I was in town. He stated that he did not "know their plans." He then gave me new clothes for Giovanni that were from his mother. He never showed any interest in Giovanni—he never talked to him or about him.

Jude and I had agreed that we would be the communicators to our respective families in matters pertaining to the boys. I was not sure how I was ever going to arrange visits between Giovanni and Jude's family if Jude was not even communicating with them.

I felt that it should not be that difficult, since we sometimes did our exchanges within two blocks of their family home. Jude's parents and both of his sisters lived in one house. I could not picture a scenario that was more conducive to visitation than this one. It could not be more easy or convenient.

A few days later, Jude had another opportunity to visit with Giovanni and ask about his latest appointment. I was in Fairfield for a dentist appointment and hoped Jude would be able to babysit Giovanni, since he was already in town with Kenneth. Alas, I was unable to track him down. My friend Lisa was more than happy and willing to babysit for a little bit. Giovanni quickly became attached to her.

Even with his lack of vision, Giovanni knew immediately that Lisa was comfortable with him. She held him, hugged him, and showed him affection—all very valuable tactile input for Giovanni. Although Lisa visited Giovanni in the hospital, this was the first time she spent an extended amount of time with him. Even with the infrequency with which they spent time together, Giovanni had bonded positively with her. This reaffirmed my belief that it was not the quantity of time, but the quality of time, that influenced bonding.

After my appointment, I could not contact Jude. I wanted to at least give his family the opportunity to visit Giovanni while I was in town. I called Esther but she was busy. Diana, however, offered to visit and go to lunch with Giovanni and me.

I picked up Diana from the house. We had a good talk that day and I felt, at least at that time, that perhaps we had smoothed over some rough feelings and could start fresh. I told her how thankful I was that she was there to deliver Giovanni. I also told her that I was grateful that she was there when Giovanni was having his seizures. I told her that I had felt there was something wrong with him, but was too upset and distracted to trust my instincts.

When I returned Diana to the house, Kenneth was there with Esther. Jude was in town, but he had gone shopping. Therefore, I was not able to talk to him.

A couple of days later, I was pleasantly surprised when Esther, Diana, and Olivia came out to Woodland to visit the boys. Apparently, I was not the only one puzzled by Jude's lack of communication, as Esther told me that he had not called her either. She and the girls played with the boys and they even brought clothing for Giovanni. Although he received many hand-me-downs from Kenneth, it was nice when he got new clothes of his own. His dad gave him new clothes as holiday gifts.

Jude came the next day for Halloween. Kenneth was excited, since he was able to go to trick or treat with both his parents, while my mom babysat Giovanni. I found it odd during this visit that, although Jude seemed tired, he claimed that he regularly got ten hours of sleep each night. I am not even sure why he would admit this. If Kenneth had not have been there, I may have commented that I had no idea what that felt like as I was only sleeping two or three hours at a time. This was not just because of Giovanni either, but also because Kenneth would have occasional nightmares.

As hard as it was for me to do, I kept my mouth shut. In addition, remembering how he liked to be thanked for visiting his kids, I went overboard in thanking Jude for driving all the way to Woodland. I thanked him at least four times. Maybe that made him feel better, because he actually held Giovanni for several minutes and conversed with my mother. Though he talked with my mom, he did not talk to me about anything of substance.

I really wanted to update him on Giovanni's progress. By this time, Giovanni was willing to be assisted in the quadruped position (on all fours). We noticed that his right arm was strong while his left arm was considerably weaker. He enjoyed when rocking back and forth on all fours. He was also able to sit propped up for one minute before he would allow himself to roll out of it in a controlled fall He also showed a great likeness for bouncing and rocking on an exercise ball.

In mid-November, I brought the boys to Jude's parents' house in Fairfield at 5:30 p.m. for them to visit. When Jude arrived at 7:00 p.m. and after he had greeted Kenneth, I handed Giovanni to him. Jude handed him right back and said he had to "get something to eat." Then he proceeded to talk to his family about how he was working out and lifting weights. I sat there, feeling very awkward as the "wife" who really was not—and listening to how he was moving on with his life without the boys.

Even though Jude's actions, and inactions, caused me heartache and anger, I remained strong for Giovanni. During his next physical therapy session, Sara had him trying to sit for more than twenty seconds by himself. That is when we noticed what she called possible seizure "jerks" from a sleep state to wakefulness. This was not the first time I noticed these "jerky" movements, as I had seen him wake up agitated before. I just thought it was Giovanni's normal behavior during transition.

Sara, however, was concerned it might be seizure activity. She wanted me to note the time and duration of these episodes, and what he was doing during that time. Unfortunately, I became overly fixated on keeping records. With my attention focused entirely on Giovanni, I quickly became mentally exhausted. Within a few days, it was obvious that Giovanni was having dozens of these little episodes very day.

However, Giovanni never "froze" and never had an obvious grand mal-type seizure. Then again, at this point, I did not really know what to look for in a seizure because, aside from the seizures right after his birth, I had never witnessed a partial seizure. I concluded that the "jerky" movements usually accompanied some type of transition or any type of brain work. The primary transition was from sleep state to wakefulness. Efforts he made to coordinate eating skills (a very complex task for him) also caused these jerks. In addition, during his physical therapy evaluation in December, we noticed these jerky movements just prior to responding to visual stimuli such as lights.

The evaluation Sara conducted in December was supposed to be for his yearly evaluation. She noted unique behavior when presented with new sounds. He would stop all body movement and listen intently. He greatly enjoyed vibration and would growl in the back of his throat to provide that input in the absence of sufficient external input. Additionally, he began experimenting with voice inflection. This child was constantly in motion and making noises.

As for his motor skills, he was solid at six months old with 50% of skills at the 7-month-old level. His range of motion was normal, but tight in his upper extremities. Along with an increase in overall muscle tone, Giovanni lacked extensive mobility as he could roll, but had no forward progression. Finally, she noted that he had no protective reflexes to front, side, or rear. He still had a long way to go to become mobile.

As the holidays approached, I felt it would be nice for me to invite Jude's mom and sisters to spend a week with me and the boys at the Lake Tahoe time share that Jude and I owned. This would be the last time I would be able to use it, as I was giving it to Jude in the divorce.

The condominium was spacious and comfortable. It had two separate bedrooms, which provided everyone with privacy. It also had a kitchen, which Diana and Olivia would use daily so they could eat the particular foods that they liked. I was specifically looking forward to the opportunity to spend one-on-one time with Kenneth, as Diana and Olivia said that they would be able to care for Giovanni so that Kenneth and I could spend some time together in the snow.

I thought having family along on vacation would be a benefit for childcare so I could spend some time providing my oldest son with the attention he deserved.

As it turned out, I did not get as much time with Kenneth as I had hoped. The girls had made plans of their own to go out and do some activities during the week, and with Esther in the condition she was in, I did not want to rely on her to care for Giovanni alone. She had become physically weaker and was not able to lift Giovanni. She needed someone there at least do that for her, even if she provided all the other care.

Unfortunately, Esther was the only one who really seemed comfortable with Giovanni. Diana played with him, but Olivia said, "I don't do diapers." Therefore, I had to plan for Kenneth and I to take short excursions for coffee in the morning before Diana and Olivia left for their planned activities.

During this time, Giovanni was eating some solid foods, but was still nursing. Therefore, I could not be away from him for more than three hours at a time. We did a couple of fun activities together. We all rode on a horse-drawn carriage, which was something that was enjoyable to Giovanni because of the movement. We also went out to the ski slope to go sledding. However, it was too cold for Giovanni to be outside, so I took him back to the condominium while Diana and Olivia took Kenneth sledding.

At least Kenneth and I were able to have our daily excursion for coffee, since he enjoyed the ride on the resort shuttle that took us up to the top of the mountain. Kenneth was very observant and noticed the wheelchair lift on the shuttle. He asked questions about how the lift worked and he knew it was for people who used wheelchairs. The shuttle driver was amazed how much Kenneth knew about disability access. Kenneth was only four years old, but he was well aware of people with disabilities, probably because I took time to explain it to him in matter-of-fact way.

Giovanni seemed just happy to be around his family. Though he was 11 months old, he did not have the strength or the balance to sit upright on his own. When I was able to get him to sit up, he had the ability to control his fall when he fell backwards. Using his abdominal muscles, he controlled the rate at which he fell and he would tuck his head to protect it.

He spent time on his vacation listening to music and being exposed to new environments and new sounds. I realized by this time that Giovanni had a unique way of adapting to his environment using sound to assist him. When he entered a new "space" for the first time, he would keep his head down and concentrate on listening to all the new sounds. Then he would hum at different volumes, as if he was actually sensing the sound waves bouncing off the walls. After a minute or two of orienting himself to the new environment, he would raise his head and smile. I jokingly called him my cute "little bat."

Although the vacation was not all that I had hoped for, it really was what I expected based on past history. Additionally, it was a nice for Esther to have some quality time with her grandsons, since it turned out to be the last vacation she would have with them.

The Christmas holiday was not was awkward as I expected since Jude had to work and made no demands on bringing the boys to his family for the holidays. The boys were able to spend time with both sides of the family during December.

I brought the boys to Jude's family house three days before Christmas. I arrived at 2:00 p.m. so that Jude could maximize his time with the kids. This would give me the opportunity to take a break for several hours and to do something for myself. I had planned on going out to a movie, a luxury that I had not been able to enjoy in over a year.

My plans fell through when at 3:15 Jude called to say he "slept in late." Jude's mother was not surprised, as she said that sleeping in late was "the story of his life." When Jude arrived at 5:00, he did not exhibit any excitement to see the boys. He barely acknowledged Giovanni. I had just enough time to go out for dinner and coffee, while the kids opened their presents. Giovanni slept most of the time.

On the other hand, when the boys went to my parents' house for Christmas, they were both wide-awake. Giovanni was alert, responsive, and happy. Obviously, Giovanni was very sensitive to his environment. If he was uncomfortable, he tended to sleep to escape, which was a habit Kenneth had too. When Giovanni was comfortable, he was interactive.

While he was in the comfort of his own home earlier that week, Giovanni had communicated "nee nee" for the first time. "Nee nee" was the term we used to refer to nursing. It was the first time Giovanni had used words to express a specific need. I tried to call his father to share the good news, but he never called back.

Even through the stress, and excitement during the holidays, I still had to organize Giovanni's first birthday party. I made the decision to check with Jude's family first, knowing that my family would make it a high priority to be at Giovanni's party, no matter when it occurred.

Unfortunately something occurred the week after Christmas that would make it uncomfortable to have both families in the same room for a celebration.

Jude's family had the tradition of sending out Christmas cards with a "yearly summary" of family activities. I think we all have received this type of letter at one time or another. Even if we would not send one out ourselves, we are all probably curious enough to read the ones we receive.

Well, for the year 2005, I was curious enough to read the letter. I was feeling stuck somewhere between "family" and "non-family", since Jude and I were physically separated but not legally so. I was wondering what tidbits of information Jude's family was willing to share with the more than 200 people on their holiday card list.

Among news of family vacations, I was shocked to find some very personal information about me as well. My jaw dropped when I read, "Jude's and Lisa's marriage continues to disintegrate," and "Lisa and the boys moved to Woodland" so that "Jude doesn't get to see the boys very much." Well Merry Christmas everyone!

Granted, I was emotional, but the tone I read in this letter led me to feel condemned by Jude's family. The fact that they wrote about me "moving away" right after commenting on the 'disintegration of the marriage" indicated to me that they placed the blame primarily on me.

If I had been able to communicate with Jude's family and we all had been given the opportunity to "clear the air" once and for all, I believe that we could have had a stronger and more amicable relationship. Instead, we would spend years in which I felt like I was on a roller-coaster, getting along one day and then I would inadvertently say something to offend someone the next day. Then I would be "written off" again.

Again, however, I speak from my own perspective, having come from a strong family who chose to communicate our issues as straightforward as possible. Even if it was uncomfortable (sometimes) and our voices were raised (rarely), we always reached a fair conclusion.

Not all families communicate in that manner. In some families, it is more comfortable to bury or ignore any negative feelings rather than address them as they occur. Part of the problem Jude and I had over the years, and continue to have, is our major differences in our communication styles. I continue to be a "bulldog" and he continues to be an "ostrich." I am sure there are benefits and pitfalls to both, but it sure would be best for everyone involved if we could find some common ground.

As far as the letter was concerned, I was hurt and angry that my personal information was being broadcast to hundreds of friends, family, and strangers, including the entire congregation at their church. My parents, grandmother, sister, brother, aunt and cousin all received this letter. My brother's wife burned it and my aunt ripped it up. My entire family expressed their outrage to me.

I, of course, expressed our collective outrage to Jude. I did not think it would be wise to approach his family directly as they had already expressed their preference not to deal with any uncomfortable situations or feelings. In addition, this was indeed an uncomfortable situation. I was hoping that Jude could take what I told him and rephrase it into something that would be acceptable to his family.

He claimed that he had not even read the letter yet and that it was no big deal. How he could say it was no big deal was beyond me if he had not even read it yet. He assured me that his family did not intend to hurt me. Regardless of their intent, they had hurt me, and my family.

This sad incident happened as I was going to the trouble to schedule Giovanni's birthday party around their schedules, to ensure that everyone would be able to attend. I went to great lengths to ensure that no one felt left out. In light of all the emotion surrounding this incident (probably mostly my emotion), I suggested that we have separate family parties for Giovanni. A combined party at this point would be even more stressful, mainly to me, than Kenneth's party had been. Jude readily agreed with me, as he liked to avoid situations with potential for confrontation.

Jude agreed that it was his obligation to be the one to communicate with his family about the letter. Sadly, Kenneth saw the letter within the Christmas card that he opened and he wanted me to read the letter to him. I do not believe in lying to my children, but it is a delicate balance in telling the truth without being negative or hurtful. I managed to read over a few of the happy vacation-related sections without any questions from Kenneth.

I suppose, in looking back on this very emotional episode, I could say that this book is my opportunity to set the record straight. I have approached Jude and both his sisters for input on this book. I really would have liked a more balanced account of everyone's perceptions, especially since this whole process is a chance for me to relive and reflect on certain parts of my life so that I can learn and grow.

Giovanni really was the catalyst in prompting me to address issues of the past. We all learn from our children and Giovanni in particular motivated me to question all the incidents and emotions in my past that led me to the point where I am today.

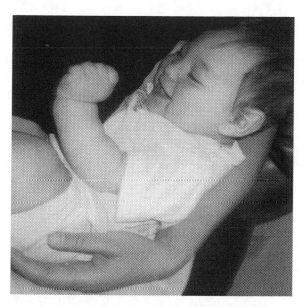

When Giovanni was an infant, he would usually
close his eyes to process the other sensory input
that he relied on to interpret his environment.

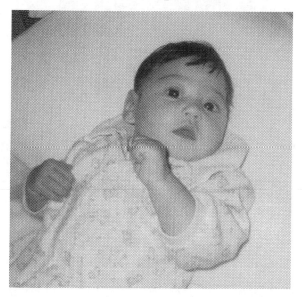

Giovanni did not respond to visual stimulus
as an infant and behaved as if he was blind.

Even as an infant with no vision and no ability to
move or roll around, Giovanni was usually a happy boy.

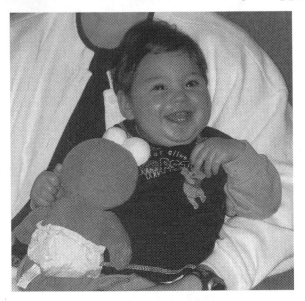

This is Giovanni on his 1st birthday. Though
he was free of medication during this
brief time, he still appeared unhealthy.

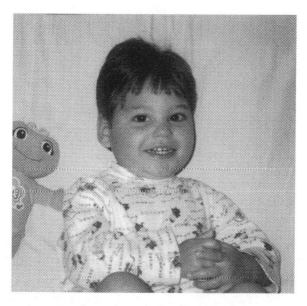

Giovanni loved toys that made music. He
loved to count to ten and sing the alphabet song.

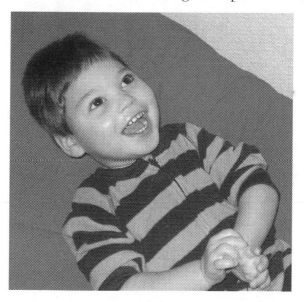

By Giovanni's 2nd birthday, he was able
to bounce and roll around for mobility.

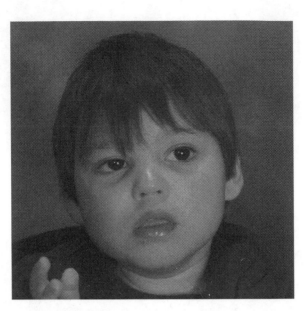

This was Giovanni's first portrait that captured his face with his eyes open.

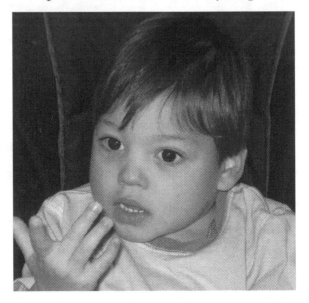

Even from an early age, Giovanni used his hands to test his visual acuity and perception.

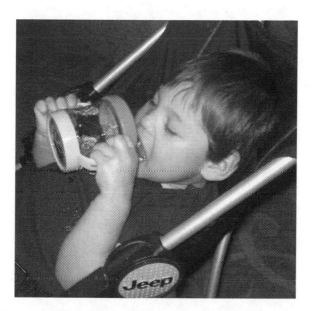

We were so excited when Giovanni finally had the motor skills to drink from a cup. Before this, I would have to sit next to him and help him hold the cup.

This photo was taken during a family vacation when Giovanni was 2 years old. His cousin Christian is holding him. Kenneth is holding their younger cousin, Marissa.

Giovanni enjoys going in the pool with Papa. From his first moments in the birth tub, Giovanni has enjoyed water.

We were all excited when Giovanni had the strength to sit up on his own and keep his balance indefinitely.

Giovanni loves music. He experiments with many different instruments and noisemakers. He usually begins by feeling the object with his mouth.

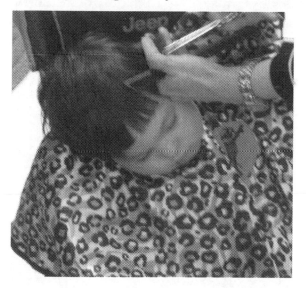

Giovanni put his head down and closed his eyes for his haircut. We talked him through the procedure because it was a new sensory experience for him.

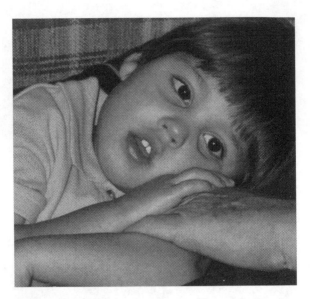

Although Giovanni was comfortable resting on his Papa's arm, he was not feeling well this day. This was one of the days he had a vomiting episode because of his high dose of medication.

Giovanni is exploring his new Braille books that he received for Christmas.

Giovanni with his brother Kenneth on his 4ᵗʰ
birthday about 10 minutes after Giovanni faked
a seizure to get off the phone with his father.

Giovanni is so much more happy and alert when he
is not on medication. In this photo, he was down to
187 mg from his high of 275 mg. By this time, he
was having functional vision more often than not.

Giovanni is practicing standing and walking in his special training walker. He has since "graduated" to a lighter weight walker that focuses more on actual walking than standing.

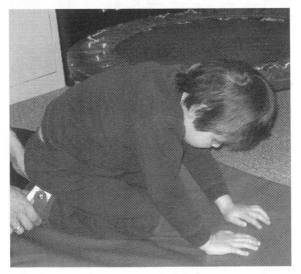

Giovanni is practicing the "low puppy" position in physical therapy. The therapist was trying to build up his arm strength in preparation for crawling.

Kenneth likes to help Giovanni during his physical therapy. This photo shows them taking a break from therapy that took place at Giovanni's pre-school.

This photo was taken during a family vacation when Giovanni was 4 ½ years old. By this point, his legs were strong enough to stand tall with minimal assistance for balance.

Giovanni enjoyed his second trip to Disneyland
much more than the first trip. He was almost free
of medication at this point and was very alert.

At school, Giovanni shows that he does have the
ability to feed himself, although at home he acts like
he doesn't know how. His fine motor skills improved
significantly has he became medication-free.

Chapter 13

With the dawn of a new year, and the approach of Giovanni's first birthday, I occasionally had feelings of hope that this year would be better than the last. While Giovanni made slow strides forward with his physical and cognitive development, his relationships with his father and father's family continued to stagnate.

New Years day was disappointing. Neither Jude nor his family called the boys. Kenneth was disappointed as he waited up until 1:30 a.m. hoping for his father to call. When I suggested he call his dad, he declined and finally fell asleep. Of course, Giovanni did not know any better and did not exhibit any negative behaviors.

Several days later when I met Jude in Fairfield to exchange Kenneth, I also brought Giovanni so he could bond with both boys. If not bond, he could at least see them. We met for coffee, and his friend Simon was there. He showed more interest in Giovanni than Jude did. Jude did not interact with Giovanni. He never got any physical attention or affection from his father.

While Jude had his visitation with Kenneth, I took Giovanni to San Francisco for his annual neurology appointment. Since I was disappointed with Dr. Greenwich, I had asked Kaiser for a new neurologist for Giovanni. I chose to drive to San Francisco to see Dr. Shayne, who was his original neurologist while he was in the NICU. I really liked her and trusted her, as she was the one that tried to remain positive while providing me with the facts.

I found that Dr. Shayne still had a positive, yet realistic, attitude. She examined Giovanni and determined that he was probably not totally blind. She was not sure what type of vision that he had. She also could not diagnose him with cerebral palsy as his tone had actually improved over the past year. Furthermore, he apparently did not exhibit any of the physical attributes of cerebral palsy.

Already Dr. Shayne was providing some information that was contradictory with what Dr. Greenwich had predicted. Dr. Shayne was able to witness Giovanni nursing and noticed his "jerks" and "twitches." Even as they occurred right in front of her she could not say for certain if they were seizures or not. Whatever they were, he was not too distracted by them. Because he continued to nurse without incident, Dr. Shayne was not concerned about a seizure disorder.

Dr. Shayne conceded that Giovanni's head was small. When I was concerned about the label "microcephaly," she stated that all that the term meant was that a person had a small head. She said that she had microcephaly also. It just meant that both hers and Giovanni's head sizes were within the bottom two percent of the population. Dr. Shayne said that microcephaly may or may not have any relevance to his intelligence or cognitive abilities

Dr. Shayne did believe that in Giovanni's particular case, the fact that he had microcephaly had to be addressed as a more serious issue than for someone in the general population. This was because Giovanni was ill at birth and did suffer resulting brain injury. Because of his history, his head size could not be discounted as irrelevant.

Dr. Shayne did not feel the need for an EEG at that time. She never discussed the possibility of any medication. It appeared she wanted to maintain a wait-and-see philosophy, and continue to treat Giovanni as a unique individual with unique neurological issues. Even after having had a year between visits with him, Dr. Shayne still could not provide a diagnosis for Giovanni's condition.

Therefore, there were still no answers. But by now I was okay with that.

Overall, I was pleased with the visit, primarily because of the doctor's realistic, yet not gloomy, outlook. She did not want to make any prognoses or predictions since the brain was still so young and was growing and changing. She did not appear too concerned about the jerks either. It was about this time that I decided to describe Giovanni's muscle movements as "sparks." From that point on, my family and I would use the term "spark" to describe, either when Giovanni would throw up his arms, or if his eyes would twitch.

Even later when the doctor would label Giovanni's "sparks" as myoclonus (a seizure type), the term "spark" would stick.

The next day, I met Jude so that I could pick up Kenneth. I tried to share the positive information I had received at Giovanni's appointment. All he said was, "Well we love him, even though there is nothing we can do for him." It appeared that this attitude was going to be his prominent attitude about Giovanni. How frightening that a child with multiple disabilities would have a father who would just allow him to exist without any attempts at all to find answers or therapy to help him.

That was about the only thing that Jude had to say about Giovanni that day. When I asked about his family's plans for Giovanni's birthday party, he stated that he was not sure what was going on because he had not talked to his family. He did say that they were going out for his own birthday the week after Giovanni's birthday.

Jude's family did decide to have their family party for Giovanni on his actual birthday, January 10th. Diana took the boys to get pictures while I went shopping. When I returned at the designated time, I found that the party was just immediate family, and that Giovanni had slept most of the time. In fact, he still had not opened his gifts.

I really did not have much choice but to stay while Diana brought out the cake and presents. For Giovanni, Kenneth blew out the candles on the cake. Then, Kenneth opened the presents. I had no problem with Kenneth opening presents for his brother, who was unable to, but it seemed that all the attention was focused upon Kenneth as well. Kenneth was four years old and of course he loved the attention. However, no one seemed comfortable enough to engage Giovanni. The only other person Giovanni appeared comfortable with was Esther.

When I left that night, I was sad. I had imagined that having a birthday party for Giovanni would give Jude's family the opportunity to focus on him for a change. And, since I was unintentionally in attendance at the end of this party, I had hoped that the family might ask questions of me in order to better understand Giovanni and his needs. I was hoping they may try to get to know him so that they would feel more comfortable around him in the future.

I do not think that anyone in that family realized that Giovanni slept most of the day probably because he was escaping from an uncomfortable environment.

Giovanni reacted like a completely different child four days later at his party at my home. We had immediate family and a few extended family members in attendance. I had decorated our home. I did not know how much Giovanni understood about this day or even how much he could see, but I tried to treat him like I would have treated Kenneth on a birthday.

Giovanni responded with excitement and enthusiasm. He refused to nap, but was happy all day long. Unlike the party at Jude's family's house, this party lasted eight hours. When my family has the opportunity to be together, it lasts for hours. Kenneth helped Giovanni open his presents, but all the attention was on Giovanni as he was "the man of the hour" on this day. Not only did Kenneth not exhibit any jealousy, but he was wide-awake and happy, too.

Giovanni responded positively to all the attention he received. He especially enjoyed the sensory input. When my sister held him and rocked him in the rocking chair, he laughed and giggled. He obviously enjoyed the vestibular input. It seemed to energize him.

Since Giovanni was now one year old, it was time for his yearly appointment with the First Steps Infant Program. My mother also came to the meeting. Others in attendance were the infant teacher, the First Steps nurse, and the First Steps coordinator. We discussed Giovanni's progress over the past year, and what we thought would be his needs and objectives for the next year.

One item of discussion was his possible seizure activity. I informed the group that Dr. Shayne was not sure if these "sparks" were related to seizures or to some other neurological anomaly. What we did know was that these "sparks" seemed to precede a change in his vision. Since his vision seemed improved at these times, my family and I started to believe in the possibility that these "sparks" were brain synapses connecting to foster brain growth.

By this time, we all realized that Giovanni was not completely blind, but had a cortical visual impairment. This was a term I had never heard of before and was not sure what it really meant for Giovanni. As a result of this meeting, the coordinator determined that Giovanni needed monthly visits from a vision specialist. I anxiously awaited that first visit.

On the positive side, I was able to tell the nurse that he had no ear infections that first year, and no illnesses. I believe this was a surprise for the nurse since many children with neurological impairments also tend to be physically weaker than other children. This could, in part, be because of a compromised immune system. I guess this goes to show that what people perceive as normal for infants just does not fit every individual child.

We also discussed Giovanni's progress with physical therapy. By one year old, he was able to sit briefly with support. Because of his strong abdominal muscles, when he fell, it was always controlled and he never injured himself. Unfortunately, his arms were still weak and we were struggling in trying to teach him transitions from prone to sitting. He did show improvement in catching himself to the front. He continued with his preference to reach for toys that made noise.

In addition to the weekly physical therapy, the service coordinator authorized a vision specialist once a month, a special education teacher twice a month and consultations with an occupational therapist and speech therapist. The First Steps teacher, Maddie, came the following week and brought toys to test Giovanni's preferences. Giovanni was particular in his choice of toys. He was mesmerized by lighted toys, but really was motivated to reach for the toys that made sounds or vibrations. Those were the toys that he would initiate himself.

When Sara found out that Giovanni had preferences for toys, she provided information about the Woodland Toy Library. Even though Giovanni was fortunate enough to have hand-me-down toys from Kenneth, and many of his own, there was an opportunity to borrow other toys with which Giovanni could experiment. Sara said that many communities have this resource, which is especially helpful for low-income families. Though I never found the time to take advantage of this resource, I did speak to several parents who were grateful for it.

When Janet, the vision specialist, came the following week, I was so excited to finally have the chance to ask an expert about Giovanni's condition. First, Janet made it clear that Giovanni was not blind. She confirmed that he had cortical visual impairment. When I explained that Dr. Greenwich's description for it was "cortical blindness," she asked how old he was. When I said he was in his late 50s, she indicated that he must not have read up on the subject in several years because "cortical blindness" was no longer a correct term. It led people to believe that there was no vision at all. I told her I was not surprised that he was inaccurate, based on some of his other opinions.

I really liked Janet as she was very energetic and positive about what parents and caregivers can do for a visually impaired child. She observed how we interacted with Giovanni and immediately gave her input on how we could do things better for him. She was trying to give me input from Giovanni's perspective because it is one that I could not grasp. I suppose some people may have seen her as too "direct" and may have taken offense to her telling them what to do or how to do it. However, she was always very friendly about it. I really wanted to know what to do to help Giovanni. After all, my ego was not a consideration. She was providing a lot of input about Giovanni's point of view.

Janet was in her 60s, but was full of energy and full of knowledge. I wanted to glean as much information from her as possible. She was the most experienced and knowledgeable vision specialist in the Northern California region. I felt fortunate to have her to help Giovanni. I was especially grateful that she was able to come so quickly for a home visit and evaluation since I was told by the First Steps coordinator that there may be a waiting list to see her. When Janet came by my home, she had a camera and took many photographs. I was not sure what it was all about until the following week, when I received her evaluation in the mail.

Even though Janet had a lot of advice to give me while she was at my home, she also documented the visit and sent a written evaluation and summary. She used the photographs to illustrate her conclusions. Janet used the photographs with captions to describe an action from Giovanni's perspective and what I could do to help him. Her advice was straight-forward, basic and understandable. For Janet's first visit, she explained how to teach Giovanni to process the whole object in an organized way when we introduced him to an item for the first time.

She also discussed using Braille with Giovanni. I was more than ready to start Braille with him, even though he was barely one year old. Some people told me that he was too young and I was moving too fast. Janet agreed with me that Giovanni was not too young to be introduced to Braille. Introducing him to the raised dot system, though he obviously would not be able to read it for years, would train his tactile sense.

I began to have memories of that day at Java City and smiled in wonder at how things in life do come full circle.

Another aspect in helping Giovanni interpret his world was to foster body awareness. Janet showed me how to use Giovanni's feet to help bring them up to his "midline", and to help him touch his feet and toes. I could make a game of this by counting to five and doing these exercised in a pattern. Doing activities with a pattern helps the brain form memories, which will be solidified and become second-nature after lots of repetition.

One of the most helpful things Janet did during her first visit was to review cortical visual impairment (CVI) with me. Since she had so much experience with many visually impaired children, she was able to give some idea of what it might be like for Giovanni since he was unable to speak and tell me himself. The most important thing I had to understand about CVI was that it was highly variable, not just from person to person, but from day to day or even hour to hour, even in the same individual. Giovanni was unable to verbally express his current state of vision, making it more important for me to be able to read his body language. Just as every song has its own rhythm, Giovanni has his own unique communication style.

Some people with CVI describe it as similar to trying to see through several layers of cellophane wrap. Others describe their vision as looking through Swiss cheese because they do not have a full picture. Some individuals may have only peripheral vision, some may have only central vision, and some may have a little of both. Some may even have double or triple vision in which their world is like a kaleidoscope, making it more difficult to determine where things are in space. Having double or triple vision gives me a headache just thinking about how my brain could process that.

If and when they do have vision, many of these individuals are attracted to motion, or to bright colors with high contrast backgrounds. Tracking a target is difficult because of either unclear or inconsistent vision. Because of "jerky" or saccadic eye movements, the eyes do not track in a smooth fashion. Therefore, it takes more time for the brain to process the images. In addition, the delay in processing causes poor hand-eye coordination. Children need to be constantly reinforced with words to label their environment and cues to help anticipate their environment.

Janet gave me some advice about things I could consider when helping Giovanni decipher his world. First, I needed to be aware of avoiding crowding of images since Giovanni's mind cannot separate images that are too close because they blend into one. He needs items to have a clear and defined separation. I can help Giovanni by using hand over hand movement for guided processing. This will help Giovanni to internalize the movement and patterns related to certain activities. In addition, I should provide consistent locations of objects and organized placement of materials to facilitate a quick and logical scanning method. Randomness may cause Giovanni frustration.

Since having a visual image was not always be possible for Giovanni, it was necessary for me to realize the importance of providing him a mental image. Everything I introduced to Giovanni needed to be hand over hand and described to him with time to allow for processing a complete mental picture. This would require a completely new way of thinking for everyone in Giovanni's life. It would also require open lines of communication among everyone so we could share information about Giovanni's actions and reactions. Communication between caretakers would be important in providing consistency for Giovanni.

Because of that lack of communication that existed between Jude and me, and within his family, there were many opportunities lost for them to get to know Giovanni better. As a result, Jude's family became even more detached from Giovanni.

When I finally met Jude for an exchange, I tried to tell him about the meeting with Janet. He expressed surprise when I told him I was introducing Giovanni to Braille. Whether he thought Giovanni was too young or just incapable I will never know. I tried to explain the complexities of CVI to Jude, but he did not want to discuss it for more than a couple of minutes. As he departed, I felt that the concept of CVI was too much for him to comprehend. Anyway, it was not a concept that could be grasped in a quick conversation. He was still too uncomfortable to be in the same room with me for more than a few minutes, so I was not able to really have a discussion with him.

I considered January 31st as the date Jude and I physically separated. As the first anniversary of our separation approached I became more anxious to actually get divorced. By this time, my feelings for Jude had dissipated, due in large part to his lack of interest in the boys and his ignorance of Giovanni.

Jude, though, was dragging his feet to make a final decision. No matter how much I expressed my stress over being in this intermediate state. Jude failed to act because he thought he was doing me some financial favor. In actuality, he was the one reaping the financial benefit, as I would realize much later when I discovered how much child support he was legally obligated to provide.

In my mind, I was prepared to file for the divorce myself if he did not make a decision before January 31st. I was wary since I had no control or influence in Jude's financial affairs. I knew his spending habits from prior experience, and although he never became so overwhelmed as to be unable to meet his obligations, I did not want the same liability with him in that regard.

As it turned out, by mid-month, he called me to tell me he was filing for divorce and that the divorce would cost me $350. He thought it was fair to split the cost.

I was shocked. I, again, told him that as a matter of principal, I would not pay for the divorce since I was not the one who initially wanted it. Besides, I reminded him I spent my life savings on OUR wedding. The amount for the divorce was a pittance by comparison. I could not believe his audacity to expect me to pay for it. He quickly backed down. Perhaps he did understand my feelings.

For the next several weeks, not much changed regarding Jude's involvement with the boys. Giovanni was making slow, but continuous, progress in physical therapy. I tried to focus on the positive, which was that there was progress and no regression. As March approached, I gave Jude the opportunity to attend a follow up IFSP.

As was my habit, I made the appointment on Jude's day off so he could be there, and could not blame me if he was not there. He did not attend.

Esther attended as a representative for their family. I was amazed that as ill as she was, she still cared enough to make the trip to show her support. If anyone had an excuse to run, hide, and avoid the children, it was her. Although alternative medicine had helped lower her cancer tumor count, her body was still becoming weaker from the fight.

During the meeting, the coordinator commented how much Giovanni had changed. His tone had improved and he was very aware of his environment. I attributed his awareness to being free of heavy medication. Maddie and Sara provided their input on Giovanni's strengths and weaknesses.

Among Giovanni's strengths were that he was able to anticipate routines. He was interactive, he liked music and sounds, he was motivated by Kenneth, he was usually easy going and content, and he liked water and new experiences.

Some concerns we all shared about him included his language development, mobility, and fine motor skills. My goal was that he would grow to become an independent adult, even if it meant climbing a mountain to reach that independence.

I was thankful that Esther was there, because I felt she was the most positive person on that side of the family. I hoped she would return home and provide her family with a positive explanation on Giovanni's situation and progress. Even if they did not want to confront the uncomfortable reality of his disabilities, they may at least keep a positive outlook about him.

I really did not know how much Esther relayed to Jude because he only called irregularly for the next three weeks and then only to talk to Kenneth. When I did call to plead for help regarding a childcare emergency, he avoided my calls for several days. By then, the emergency was over and my family had come to my rescue again. When I confronted him the following week about his failure to return messages when I had childcare issues, he offered to help with the kids, if no one else could do it.

Unfortunately, that did no good now, after the fact. Additionally, if this was some attempt at commitment to help with future childcare issues, I found this would not be the case either. Jude's actions showed me that he did not want to deal with unpleasant conversation.

I am not sure why it took so much effort to get this family to visit with Giovanni. The little guy was as lovable and snuggly as they come.

During the following week's exchange, Giovanni became hungry because Jude was late again. When I called Jude's family, no one seemed to have much of a desire to see Giovanni. They did not say "no" outright, but they never extended an invitation either. I had to assume that they were not comfortable with me either.

Again, I sat alone in a parking lot to nurse Giovanni while I waited for Jude, who was again late, to return Kenneth. Thankfully, I had taken the initiative to change the exchange place from a busy Starbucks to the police department parking lot. I felt a little safer there. I felt more comfortable knowing there was a restroom available for Kenneth

When Jude arrived, he deflected my concerns about having to nurse in the van while his family home was only two blocks away. I asked again about childcare issues in an attempt to pin him down on a commitment. He waffled and failed to commit. Every comment was that we would, "...cross that bridge when we came to it." Never mind the fact that we had come to that bridge several times already. I always crossed that bridge alone.

And if there were any tolls to be paid (child care and commuting costs) I also paid them.

Again, perhaps to placate me, he claimed he would take Giovanni for a visit "someday."

Jude always forgot that I worked 24 hours a week, and had to take care of our children's daily needs. Perhaps I should add here that my schedule changed weekly. Sometimes I worked two 12-hour days. Sometimes I worked three 8-hour days. I worked every shift, around the clock. Because I switched weekly, there was never any consistency. My parents were my sole childcare at this time, so I commuted 170 miles round trip to work every day that I had to work.

Consequently, Jude's complaints about his lack of sleep because he had to occasionally work more than 40 hours a week brought no sympathy from me. Besides, he was able to retain the overtime salary for himself when he worked more hours.

It always seemed to be an uphill battle in trying to get Jude to understand my extreme work schedule and that I was trying to raise two children alone. On top of that, as I had to remind him, one of those children was severely developmentally delayed and needed lots of additional attention. That uphill battle I had with Jude was more exasperating than any climbing I did with Giovanni.

With the approach of spring, and the hope of renewal in our lives, it was heartbreaking when everyone's life took a sad turn when Esther passed away in April. Jude called and asked me to bring Kenneth to the hospital. I brought Giovanni also.

I was concerned about how Giovanni might react in a hospital atmosphere since he had experienced so much stress and trauma the last time he was in an emergency room.

Much to my surprise, Giovanni became extremely calm when we entered the hospital. As we entered the outer corridor near Esther's room, he started smiling and babbling. Even as the family gathered in shock and grief in the cafeteria, Giovanni was laughing and giggling. His gaze seemed fixed on the ceiling.

I am not sure if Giovanni had vision that day, but I did believe that Giovanni's other senses were heightened. As a spiritual person myself, I believed that day Giovanni was even more spiritual than me, and could have been sensing that Grandma was at peace.

I had assumed that Jude would want the comfort of having his sons around after losing his mother. He explained that he was so shattered that he was in no condition to even take Kenneth home with him to share his grief. Consequently, I took the boys home and attempted to make sense of everything and to explain it to Kenneth.

As it turned out, that evening we experienced what I could only describe as a paranormal experience that brought comfort and closure to Kenneth and to me.

Several days prior to Esther's death, I had misplaced the key to my locker at work. This key was one that I always kept in a specific jacket pocket. After searching the jacket, the car, and all my bags, Kenneth and I searched the house to find it. I looked in every room, including rooms where the jacket had never been.

As I searched the dresser in my bedroom, I noticed how dusty it was, and I took the opportunity to remove items and then wipe down the entire dresser. Having searched the entire house, I gave up on ever finding the key.

Upon returning home after Esther died, I went into my room to change, and there on my dresser, in plain view, was my locker key!

I may have thought nothing of it, had it not been for the fact that I had specifically dusted that dirty dresser. In addition, the jacket in which I kept the key was always hung in the hall closet and had never been in my room.

This incident had a special meaning since Esther was the one who found my car keys at her house on two previous occasions after I had misplaced them. She had given me an audible key chain for Christmas that year so that I could locate my keys by whistling. It was an inside joke between the two of us that she would find my keys whenever I lost them.

I was absolutely convinced that the reappearance of my keys had something to do with Esther.

When I told Kenneth the story, he immediately believed it because he knew that Grandma always found my keys, and he had helped me search the house for the locker key.

Kenneth and I both felt a sense of peace in knowing that Grandma was okay. She was letting us know she was in a better place.

With Esther gone, I fully anticipated the family to fracture, as she was the strength and the glue that held them together. Only time would tell just how much the family would change.

This would probably not be the year for improvement in family relationships for Giovanni.

Chapter 14

After the emotion over Esther's death had calmed a little, I tried to get the boys back into a daily routine. Having a routine helped me to focus on other things besides the sad events. Our routine consisted of tending to Kenneth's home school and Giovanni's therapy.

Knowing I was seeking out all information related to brain function, Maddie suggested that I attend a seminar presented by neuroscientist Bruce Perry, M.D. I was amazed and energized by the information he provided. I obtained some insight about how a child's brain actually worked and a new hope that I could have some influence over how Giovanni's brain developed.

Dr. Perry presented concepts of child development in relation to neurodevelopment. In his article "The Power of Early Childhood", Dr. Perry emphasized the "malleability of the human brain, based on its ability to modify itself through repetition and use." He described the process of how billions of connections are made everyday within the neurons of the brain. I was excited when I saw that he supported the strengthening of the brain through repetitive activity.

Since the brain changes through repetition, I hoped that I could help re-wire Giovanni's brain to function in the way he needed it to. The article also explained much of what therapists told me about repeating tasks until they became habit for Giovanni. From a biological perspective, Giovanni's brain function was beginning to make sense to me. Dr. Perry helped me to understand that the "acquisition of memory", which primarily occurs during the first years of life, is a change in the neural connections. Again, repetition facilitates the neural changes.

One of Dr. Perry's points that really resonated with me was his description of how vision worked. He described this sense as a chain of interconnected neurons that communicate by neurotransmitters. Any interruption in this "chain" would essentially affect the sense of vision. This really helped to explain Giovanni's problem in a neurobiological way. He had a brain injury that was causing interference between neurons.

Dr. Perry maintains that "each brain adapts uniquely to the unique set of stimuli and experiences of each child's world." This gave me the hope that I could influence Giovanni's brain development regardless of how doctors expected him to develop based on others' experiences.

I also determined that this was the time that I would learn Braille. I remembered the desire I had to learn Braille some years before and how it never came to fruition then. Well, now was the time to learn it. I found that I could go on-line and register at the Hadley School for the Blind. Among the many classes they offered to blind students, they also offered Braille to parents and caregivers.

I highly recommend that every parent with a visually impaired child at least take an introductory course in Braille. I took the introduction to Braille as well as how to read and write uncontracted Braille and contracted Braille. I learned how to use a slate and stylus and a Braillewriter. I do not expect everyone to get as involved in this as I did. Since I had a degree in education, my tendency was to learn a topic, sometimes to the extreme, so that I could teach people that topic. I still had a mind set of a home school teacher and I expected that I would need to at least supplement Giovanni's instruction with some teaching at home. I could not expect a vision specialist to teach him everything he needed to know. The specialist had so little time to devote to him.

When my brain finally began to function somewhat normally, I realized some of the slight changes in Giovanni's behavior that became concerning to me. Giovanni was beginning to have episodes in which he would gasp and stop what he was doing for several seconds. He would appear as if he was startled.

Though I noticed these episodes about once a week in the spring, I realized that he may have actually been having them on occasion since January. Prior to January, Giovanni's episodes consisted only of myoclonic "sparks" which could have been non-epileptic myoclonus. He was not exhibiting actual seizures. Ironically, it was only two weeks after his yearly vaccinations that I first noticed the episodes. One of his vaccinations was for varicella (chicken pox vaccination).

I was not concerned about the first few episodes, primarily because I did not actually see them. I only heard them. At the time, I did not even know what I was hearing, until I heard and witnessed what was happening. The sound was unmistakable – a gasp, sometimes followed by a "squeak" in which it sounded like the windpipe was constricted. If I was out of the room, I would run back and check on Giovanni. By then the episode was over and he was acting normal again.

It was about the April or May period that I noticed the episodes occurring with more frequency because I was witnessing them more often. Again, I really did not know what I was dealing with and Giovanni would always act normal again within several seconds. As far as I could tell, he never stopped breathing and he did not exhibit any obvious signs of seizures. I was not even sure if the episodes were voluntary or not. They manifested as a "startle reflex" and would occur at times when a "startle" would be appropriate.

In hindsight, I realized that what Giovanni was beginning to experience were seizures. My fears grew through the spring and early summer as they came with more frequency.

As I became more concerned about Giovanni, I found I was not getting any support from Jude. I was still obligated to send Kenneth off for visitation, whenever Jude's schedule permitted. Frankly, I was relieved for the break. I was trying to control my stress over my concern about Giovanni and trying not to have Kenneth see it.

Much to my surprise, Diana offered to do me the favor of providing childcare for the boys while I worked. Unfortunately, she was an hour late and I had to bring Kenneth and Giovanni into work with me. When she arrived, she said "I'm sorry," which stuck in my head since that was the first time in so long, if ever, that I heard her actually say, "sorry". Usually I was the one doing the apologizing, many times righteously so, but many other times just to placate the family, because if I did not say it, no one else would. Therefore, the communication would continue to suffer.

When Diana arrived to pick up the boys, Kenneth was clingy and did not want to leave me. Diana was distracted and did not show any interest in Giovanni. In addition, as for me, I was anxious my entire shift that day, wondering how wise it was for me to leave the boys with Diana as she was obviously struggling with grief over losing her mother. I was grateful for her attempt to help with childcare, even if it was for a few hours, because it took some of the responsibility away from my family.

In late May, I brought the boys to the care home where Jude's grandmother was living. It was her birthday, and Jude's family was there for a party. I brought both boys, but Olivia was the only one who talked to and held Giovanni. Diana showed no interest and hardly acknowledged him. It appeared that even though everyone in the family was experiencing sadness and grief, it was highly distractible for Diana. In my perception, it was beginning to affect her cognitive function.

It was evident that Esther's death was profoundly affecting Jude's family. As much as I loved her, and as sad as I was about her passing, I had to move forward with life and raise my children.

One of the things that kept me occupied during this time was getting Giovanni to weekly appointments at the Children's Therapy Center. He met weekly with Suri the occupational therapist and Peggy the speech therapist. Peggy was the therapist that had provided Giovanni's initial evaluation when he was four months old, so she was already comfortable with him.

Suri provided weekly activities for Giovanni that gave him the sensory input that he needed. The center had a sensory gym containing all the equipment necessary for stimulation of all seven senses. Giovanni's lack of vision required that he have extra stimulus for the vestibular and proprioceptive senses.

Suri utilized several different types of swings for vestibular stimulation. Each swing provided unique input. Since Giovanni was young, and developmentally delayed, Suri needed to hold him during swinging. She used a platform swing in which she sat Giovanni between her legs and balanced him as she swung the platform from right to left and forward and backward. She also used a bench swing, which just provided input forward and backward. Giovanni was usually pleased with the platform swing. We noticed that too much stimulation would activate the myoclonus.

Peggy would provide oral motor stimulus in conjunction with other sensory input. It seemed that Giovanni's senses would "warm up" by swinging on the platform swing for several minutes. Then he would be more cooperative in doing his occupational therapy. It was as if his brain had to be primed to be able to properly integrate his senses.

After witnessing his behavior during his physical therapy sessions, I realized how important it was for Giovanni to get vestibular input in order to help organize his brain. Since the vestibular sense was the primary organizer of all the other senses, it made sense that Giovanni's brain needed a great deal of this input to help calm his brain and organize his other senses.

Regardless of what therapy Giovanni was going to do, I made sure that he had several minutes of swinging or rocking to help get him focused. His concentration was so much better if I did this. Over time, his need for so much vestibular stimulation declined. I suppose with brain growth and a decrease in Phenobarbital helped Giovanni outgrow some of the intensity of sensory input.

After I saw what a positive effect the swinging had on Giovanni, I decided I needed to have something like that at home. This was when I decided that I would make my own sensory gym in the garage at home.

My parents purchased an indoor swing set that had an infant swing and slide. Even though Giovanni liked the swing, it did not swing very high or very fast, so he did not get that excited about it. He really enjoyed sliding down the slide. Knowing that Giovanni wanted even more vestibular input than an indoor swing could provide, I purchased a special swing from a physical therapy catalog and set it up in my garage. My dad, who had the knowledge to assemble the equipment, set up special beams in the garage that would hold the carabineers for the swing.

I purchased an infant swing and a platform swing as well as gym mats to place underneath. Thus began Giovanni's home sensory gym. My parents and grandmother contributed a great deal to this home gym. In addition, I established a special fund for Giovanni in which gift money could be saved up to buy specific therapy items. Although I explained my intentions to Jude, he never expressed any interest to help.

Jude was more inconsistent than usual with phone calls to Kenneth. He called one night and Kenneth was upset and refused to talk on the phone with him. This gave me a moment to speak to Jude.

As if he anticipated my questions, Jude offered up, "Oh, yea, I want to take Gio, when he's mobile and done with therapy." I said, "Therapy may never be done." In light of the possibility that he may never take Giovanni, or at least not for a long while, I asked if he could at least ask his sisters if they would be willing to help with childcare. My family was taking on all the responsibility. He stated that he did not want to ask his sisters to help, because they were busy working and had busy lives.

I suppose Jude believed that my family had nothing going on in their lives. This was not the case, as both my parents had other obligations. However, they always chose to make their grandchildren their first priority. I was, and always will be, forever grateful for that. They raised their children and had every right to expect to live their own lives, but they were helping their divorced grown daughter care for her children.

I did not expect Jude's sisters to take on a major role in childcare, but I thought that they would at least want to visit their nephews once a month. It would work out for me if the visits coincided with my work schedule. After all, I worked two blocks away from their house. I was even more disappointed because it was Diana who claimed that she would always be there to help with the boys no matter what happened between Jude and me. Thus far, this had not been the case.

As Father's Day approached, Jude called because his sisters wanted to have Kenneth over to do something for Father's Day. I asked, "Well, what about Giovanni?" He said they did not mention Giovanni to him. How could it be that anyone would expect to take a child to celebrate Father's day, or any holiday for that matter, and leave his brother behind?

I had to reiterate my position that I wanted Jude's father, Grandpa, to have a relationship with both boys, and not just on special occasions. In addition, I explained that my family and I were upset that Kenneth and Giovanni were treated differently. He never denied it, but had nothing to say about it. I told him that it frightened me that a four-year-old felt the need to ask if he and his brother had the same daddy. Jude totally ignored this comment and just said, "Well, I'll check to see when the girls can return Kenneth." I said, "Did you not hear what was just said? Don't' you even care?" He said, "About what?" and I said, "About Giovanni." He replied, "Yea, of course, but it's hard under the circumstances."

What circumstances are too hard that a parent cannot care about how his son is treated?

After venting to my parents that night, I left Jude a message the next day, inviting him to our family Father's Day barbeque. I did not expect that he would come, but my family and I felt this was something we could do for the boys. This way both boys could spend that day with their dad, since Jude's family still had not finalized any plans yet.

The following week, I decided to take matters into my own hands where communication between families was concerned. This should come as no surprise as I was still trying to find some common ground between Jude's family and me. Since Jude was not succeeding in fostering a relationship between his children and his family, I felt that I was obliged to at least try for the children. Part of me felt that maybe I was overstepping my bounds. If I did not make a move forward in repairing our relationship, past experience indicated that no one else would.

I stopped by the house in Fairfield to see Diana and Olivia. I explained how I felt and that it was my desire that we communicate because it was evident to me that Jude was not exchanging messages between us very well. For at least the third time in less than a year and a half, we began to break down the barriers to our communication. Both Diana and Olivia told me that they had been ready to do so for a while, but had been waiting for me to "make the first move."

I suppose if I never took the initiative to approach them, they would have just let the situation remain unchanged. I believed that God would have wanted us all to make peace with each other. Perhaps Jude's sisters did not place the priority on it that I did. On the other hand, perhaps it is just that some people have personalities that are proactive while others are reactive.

It was a good thing that I made peace with the Diana and Olivia, since the following week Jude finally confronted me about my "nagging" voice mails. Finally, I got a passionate and assertive reaction out of him! I had been waiting for this reaction for a long time, as it showed that he finally cared about something.

I explained that the tone of my messages reflected my frustration because he ignores the boys and me and refuses to return my calls. He claimed, yet again, that he wanted to see Giovanni, but the separation in the beginning made it so difficult. Without directly saying so, I believed he was blaming me for having taken the boys so far away.

In my defense, I explained to him again my reasons for having moved to Woodland. I needed to find a home I could afford that was near my family. They were providing my childcare. By this time, it should have been evident to him that my family had made a larger commitment than his family in caring for and visiting the boys. He made another claim that he would "help" with childcare costs. I still was not sure what his perception of "help" was, because I had not seen it yet, expect for the $50 he gave me the prior summer.

I did not need the stress of dealing with Jude because I was becoming increasingly alarmed at Giovanni's condition. Near the end of June, he finally exhibited what most people would recognize as a seizure. This time, Giovanni did much more than "gasp." He threw up his arms above his head, his eyes glazed over, his face grimaced, and his head slowly averted to the left. While breathing heavily, he stayed frozen in this position for about ten or fifteen seconds.

As he came out of the seizure, his arms came down slowly, and he appeared disoriented.

I could feel my legs weaken as I fell down into the cellar of depression again. Forget the phrase "one step forward, two steps back", because I think for all the steps forward I had made, I just fell back about a mile.

I called his pediatrician, Dr. Lewis, who suggested an EEG. However, it would take at least a week to schedule it. We were leaving on an Alaskan cruise the following week. Dr. Lewis believed that the EEG could wait until after we returned.

I called Jude to leave a message about the seizure. He did return the call several hours later, which was a quick response for him. As I explained what happened with Giovanni, he kept acknowledging me with "okay." Then he abruptly changed the subject to Kenneth. I figured that when we met the next day for the exchange, Jude would see Giovanni and ask for more clarification then.

The next day, Jude made no mention of Giovanni's seizure. It was as if it had never happened. Of course, if Jude had acknowledged the seizure, he would have had to deal with uncomfortable feelings. It also would force him to engage me in a conversation, which was something he probably wanted to avoid. I believed that Jude preferred to stay firmly in the stage of denial. He did make an attempt to connect with Giovanni by holding him in the standing position.

Giovanni, who was barely able to hold his weight and had motor planning delays as well, made obvious attempts to get away from his dad. He took two steps away from him. Usually, Giovanni wanted to walk TOWARD someone. That day I did not think too much about Giovanni's reaction to his dad. I would find that over the next couple of years Giovanni's behavior would become a pattern. This would lead me to believe that his behavior was intentional and not mere coincidence.

Kenneth spoke with excitement to his dad about our upcoming cruise to Alaska. This was a family trip that we had planned for almost two years. Besides the boys and me, my parents, grandmother, aunt, cousin, and his wife, were all going. The cruise was a gift from my grandmother. Before we left, I spoke to Dr. Lewis and he provided me with the prescription medicine Diastat and instructions on how to use it in case of an emergency.

The emergency I never hoped to have was a condition called status epilepticus. This condition was potentially life threatening. It occurred when a seizure did not end after several minutes, or if one seizure followed on top of another without ceasing. The medication was designed to stop the seizures. However, the medication was so powerful that a doctor's examination would be required afterward to assess the affects of the medication.

I remembered the long-ago conversation the transport doctor had with my mom and me the night Giovanni was transported from

Santa Rosa to San Francisco. He had said that once the brain was "wired" for the seizures, it was hard to calm it down. I hoped that I would never have to use the Diastat.

We left out of San Francisco on a windy day. My parents were not able to accompany us on the trip. Therefore, instead of having my parents to help care for the boys on this trip, it would just be me and my grandmother, and occasionally, my aunt.

Giovanni had a small seizure inside the terminal. I began to wonder if the strong winds aggravated Giovanni enough to cause a seizure. During the cruise, I also noticed that Giovanni had seizures that may have been brought on by certain foods, or certain environments. I suffered through a lot of stress that week as I tried to analyze the circumstances surrounding every seizure in order to find a possible causal link. I kept a log of every seizure and Giovanni's activity or environmental conditions just prior.

Obviously, the cruise was not the relaxing vacation that I had planned, as Giovanni's seizures increased to several each day. Thankfully, they never became more severe, just more frequent.

I kept in contact with Dr. Lewis every few days during the cruise. He assured me that the seizures were not causing Giovanni any pain. However, the grimace that was frozen on his face made it painful for me to watch. Kenneth handled everything very well, although he was clingy that week and did not want to participate in any onboard activities. I am sure he was feeling the stress, even if his outward demeanor seemed calm.

Giovanni's seizures seemed to be influenced, at least in part, by his environment, but there was no one particular cause. The dining room caused him some distress as his senses were overloaded with all the noise and odors. As a result, mealtime was particularly stressful, especially since I had to feed Giovanni. He was 18 months old, but essentially had the physical skills of a six month old. He had not yet developed the fine motor skills to chew food.

Although I specifically ordered certain baby foods through the cruise line the week before we sailed, I found that they did not always have the food on hand that I ordered. One night all they had were three jars of green beans. There was no variety at all for Giovanni. At least he received food to eat. I tried to feed myself in between feeding him, while keeping an eye on Kenneth to make sure he behaved.

Needless to say, I did not have time to savor the food as it really was more for sustenance at that point rather than for pleasure. Since Giovanni would either have a seizure or a tantrum during meals, I would usually have to leave early and take him back to the cabin. I missed out on a lot of the delicious cruise line food. Kenneth liked to ride the elevators, so we did get the opportunity to go to the late night buffet a few times.

When Giovanni was not having seizures or feeling over stimu-lated, he was generally happy. He seemed to enjoy the movement of the ship. During times of rough seas, when I could barely walk a straight line down the halls, Giovanni would laugh. He liked elevators, also.

I tried to enjoy the two times that Kenneth and I left the ship for excursions, while we left Giovanni in the care of my 81-year-old grandmother. She was capable of caring for him for a few hours, but I was stressed because of the seizures. Although Kenneth and I were able to see humpback whales and lumberjacks, my mind was always distracted.

As if I was not stressed enough about Giovanni, then Kenneth became sick also. He started having some difficulty breathing along with a whooping type cough, and I had to take him to the ship's medical clinic. I woke my aunt in the middle of the night to watch Giovanni. I sat near Kenneth's bedside while he was given albuterol to open his airway.

After all the worry about Giovanni needing medical attention aboard ship, it was Kenneth that had the problems. I spent the last third of the cruise holed up in our cabin, reading books and hoping that neither child needed emergency care while at sea. By the time we reached San Francisco, Kenneth was feeling better, and I was anxious to find out answers about Giovanni's seizures.

Giovanni went in for an EEG the week we returned from Alaska. My mom went with me to help keep Giovanni calm. Since he had sensory integration issues, he was very particular about anything being on or around his head. I could not expect him to keep a hat on his head, let alone numerous electrodes that needed to stay in place for sixty minutes.

The plan was to keep him awake half the night before the EEG and not allow him to sleep until we got to the hospital. I hoped that he would sleep through the EEG. He made it into the waiting room and we could not force it any longer. He fell asleep.

Much to my frustration, the technician decided to take her coffee break right after she showed us in the room and told us to get comfortable. I knew she took a break because she returned fifteen minutes later with coffee in hand. Then it took her twenty more minutes to place the electrodes properly. By the time the EEG test actually began, Giovanni had been asleep for over 45 minutes, and I had never known him to take more than a 20-30 minute nap.

Sure enough, Giovanni startled awake about 20 minutes into the test. He started thrashing around, and I had to hold his hands to prevent him from tearing out the electrodes. I figured by now that there was probably some sub-clinical seizure activity going on in the brain keeping him anxious. It was common for Giovanni to consistently wake from naps with a startle. When he awoke, he never seemed rested and ready to wake up. It was not the natural process of waking up that most people experience (without an alarm).

The technician indicated there was enough brain wave activity to be read. Though they set up for an hour EEG, they only need about 20 minutes worth of brain activity to read it. The negative side was that someone could have a seizure disorder, but it may not be seen on the EEG if there were no seizures during that small time frame.

As it turned out, twenty minutes provided enough information to determine Giovanni's condition. The neurologist who read the EEG gave his impression that "this was an abnormal EEG tracing, recorded in sleep state only, with multifocal epileptiform activity." In other words, Giovanni was having sub-clinical seizures.

The most ironic twist of all was that the on-duty neurologist who read the EEG was none other than Dr. Greenwich – the very doctor who had stated with great confidence that Giovanni would most likely NOT have a seizure disorder.

We visited Dr. Shayne's replacement, Dr. Khan, to get Giovanni started on medication. We were fortunate that Giovanni's new neurologist happened to specialize in epilepsy. He confirmed that Giovanni did have a seizure disorder, or epilepsy. We discussed several medications. First, he suggested Phenobarbital, to which I immediately objected. Not only would Giovanni be a "space cadet", but his brain growth would probably slow down.

Next, Dr. Khan suggested Lamictal, but that was a more long-term medication that he said required frequent blood tests to ensure that the blood levels were tolerable to Giovanni. He said that this medication usually was suggested for older kids. Giovanni was still so young, and so small, that I did not want to have to bring him in for blood draws.

The best medication Dr. Khan could suggest was Clonazepam, otherwise known as Klonopin, which was in the same class of medications as Phenobarbital, but supposedly would not affect brain growth. I decided Giovanni should try this medication first.

As nervous as I was about medication, I thought it wise to be familiar with the possible side effects of anti-seizure medications. My first concern was the cognitive side effects, which is a negative effect since medication reduces excitability of the brain cells. It can also dampen normal ability and impair cognitive function such as attention, concentration, memory, mood, and drive.

I also wanted to have awareness of what factors might provoke seizures. These factors included missed medication, sleep deprivation, emotional stress, environmental factors, illness, fever, and gastrointestinal illness or diarrhea, which reduced absorption of the medications. I would find several of these circumstances affecting Giovanni, so I was not surprised when he began having seizures during these particular times.

Thankfully, Giovanni's seizures were greatly reduced almost immediately after starting the medication. By now, I was so anxious and fearful of having witnessed so many seizures that I felt it would take awhile for my own brain to calm down and relax.

I did not realize what high toll Giovanni's seizures took on my psyche until I took a 911 call at work that involved a child having a seizure. For the first time I could remember in twenty years of dispatching, I froze, and then I handed over the call to my partner as I started to cry. I had never experienced a situation like this in which I was unable to function.

I had to take a long break from work that day to regain my composure. My boss, and friend, Dawn told me that she had been noticing my work performance suffering in recent weeks. This all seemed to have originated with Giovanni's condition changing a few months prior. She suggested that I talk to someone with our work place assistance program.

She believed I was suffering from some type of post-traumatic stress disorder. Even though I thought I had grieved over Giovanni's condition and reconciled all the facts in my mind, there must have been some reason I kept falling into the dark pit of sadness and depression.

Even during some of my darkest and saddest days, I always found there were sources of inspiration. Obviously, I prayed a lot and I relied a lot on my love for the boys and support of my family to help regain my focus. I also had a network of friends and even co-workers who were willing to listen to me and offer advice to help me.

It was a co-worker and his family that provided me with perspective and inspiration many times throughout the years. Joe Allio is a patrol sergeant that I have known for years. He and his wife have six children. Two of their five children, Catie and Annie, have a very rare genetic disease called Battens Disease.

Battens disease, or Neuronal Ceroid Lipofuscinoses, is an inherited disorder of the nervous system that usually manifests itself in childhood. Symptoms usually begin in early childhood and may include visual problems or seizures that may begin subtly. In some cases, early signs may take the form of personality or behavior changes, slow learning or clumsiness and stumbling. Over time, affected children suffer mental impairment, worsening seizures and progressive loss of sight and motor skills. Children become totally disabled and eventually die. There is no prevention or cure for this disease.

Despite their daily struggles in caring for two terminally ill children, the Allios continue to have a strong faith. Joe always has a smile on his face, belying the heartache he must have been feeling for his daughters.

Instead of feeling sorry for himself or his family, Joe is proactive. He became a spokesperson for Batten's Disease. He is involved in organizing golf tournaments and other events to raise public awareness. One of the major events of the year is the The Relay, a 199-mile race from Calistoga to Santa Cruz. Teams of 12 members run the relay in the course of a weekend. When I ran The Relay in 1998, we had one team with 11 members. The latest Relay had five teams, each containing 12 members, primarily from public service and their families. They now run under the name "Catie and Annie's Cops."

Even through the most daunting circumstances, the Allios are true examples of living a life of faith and handling hardship with grace and dignity.

Although the Allios were, and remain, a primary source of inspiration for me, I am grateful to Dawn for pointing me in the direction of a therapist. The therapist explained that I had suffered some great trauma that my brain had failed to process properly. Whenever something would occur, like Giovanni having seizures, or even someone else having seizures, my brain would revert to the stress and uncertainty of being in that hospital when Giovanni was so sick. It would be as if I was living those memories all over again in the present. It was draining me emotionally.

The therapist provided a therapy called eye movement desensitization and reprocessing, or EMDR, which was designed to reprogram the brain to place memories of traumatic events into long-term memory. He would have me remember the traumatic events and then have my eyes follow his finger, while thinking about an individual event. My brain would move that memory from short-term to long-term memory.

Within a few sessions, I was able to remember all the events surrounding Giovanni's hospitalization and observe them as an outsider. I no longer felt the emotion of being in the moment. I was able to function with a clearer head. I felt empowered to be able to handle the sad memories without falling apart.

In the end, it turned out that seizure calls would be my specialty, because I felt I had the experience to identify with the callers and provide some insight and guidance.

My parents were right by my side in dealing with Giovanni's seizures and I know that my mom was particularly bothered by witnessing them. With the start of medication, Giovanni responded quickly and ceased having the seizures.

Jude was not in contact with us much during this time as we were still in the process of the divorce. I had authored a marital settlement agreement, which I had reviewed by an attorney and then agreed to by Jude. I hoped that we could be divorced by the end of the year. The one element that I did agree to that would cause me concern and doubt over the years was joint custody.

As much as I really did want Jude to be a father to the boys, I knew I had no control over it and I could see that the situation was deteriorating and probably would continue to do so. Against advice from family, friends, and even my attorney, I agreed to the joint custody because I felt I owed it to my boys to at least give their father every chance to be one.

Evidently, Jude did not feel the need to be a father during this stressful time of dealing with Giovanni's seizures, tests, and medications. Additionally, as Kenneth was approaching five years old, I am sure that his father's lack of involvement was having an impact on him.

After the EEG, Jude reiterated again that he wanted to take Giovanni, when "he's all done with therapy." And I told him again that he "may never be done with therapy." In addition, when I called him about Giovanni's neurology appointment, he dismissed what I was trying to say to him and started talking about divorce paper-work.

As high of a priority as the divorce was to my state of mind, it was nowhere near the priority that I placed on caring for the children.

Over the next month, Giovanni suffered some breakthrough seizures while I increased his Klonopin (Clonzepam). Fortunately, the frequency of his seizures was much less than before.

One of the problems Giovanni had with his medication was that it was in liquid form, which doctors referred to as a suspension medication. The pharmacy needed to mix the correct amount of the Klonopin with the liquid. The strength of the medication always depended on how it was mixed Unfortunately, Giovanni was highly sensitive to the medication, and if it was not mixed quite right, he would have breakthrough seizures.

The inconsistency in the potency of the medication was disturbing. On more than one occasion, either my mother or I would have to return to the prescription and have it prepared again. Some pharmacists were more competent than others were. I ended up dropping my local pharmacy and travelling 40 miles to a different pharmacy because the pharmacist was more competent. By the time I figured all this out, I had grown frustrated with the entire process. I asked Dr. Khan to recommend another medication with more consistency that would not be so reliant on an individual person's competence.

As it turned out, Klonopin also came in the form of a wafer, which dissolved in the mouth. I was not sure if Giovanni would accept a wafer straight into his mouth, as he was sensitive to taste. The wafer would immediately dissolve as soon as it touched the mouth, so if Giovanni was uncooperative and tried to turn it away, it would start dissolving in my fingers. Once it dissolved, it was gone. It would become such a sticky mess on my fingers that I would have to wash off, as Giovanni sat with his mouth clamped shut.

When Giovanni did get his wafers, the dose was consistent and he had fewer breakthrough seizures.

I saw that Kenneth was starting to exhibit some behaviors that indicated he was having a difficult time in dealing with Giovanni's seizures. In eighteen months, the poor kid had lost his dad, his grandma, and was by my side in helping his disabled brother.

I felt that I should at least call Jude to tell him about Kenneth's emotional difficulties. I had done the best I could in explaining Giovanni's condition to Kenneth. Since I had been in therapy, I was a lot calmer and able to deal with the seizures. Jude failed to return calls for several days. When he finally did call, Kenneth absolutely refused to speak to his father.

One of the issues that Kenneth was having with his father was his frustration with the inconsistency of phone calls. When Kenneth did have phone conversations with Jude, they were usually short. Usually at the end of the conversation, Jude would say to Kenneth, "Give Giovanni a kiss for me." When Kenneth would hang up the phone, he would give Giovanni a kiss, then look at me and say, "Why can't Daddy do this himself?"

When I got on the phone with Jude, I asked if Jude received any of my messages about Giovanni, since it had been weeks since we had really talked. He admitted that he had received the messages and it sounded like Giovanni was "doing fine." I told him, of course, he is doing fine now, but his seizures were last week.

When Kenneth became ill several days later, Jude was nowhere to be found again. When he finally did call, I calmly explained my frustration with him, and that I was "tired with two sick kids" and getting no support from him. All he could say was he understood, but he cannot answer messages during the work week because his mind had to "be on the job."

In all these months, there was still no progress on his part to be a parent, not even on his days off. If he worked overtime, he was unavailable on his days off, too.

Adding to my stress was the fact that Giovanni was a "frequent flyer" to the doctor's office. There were times I took Giovanni to the doctor's office and there was nothing wrong. He could not speak, so I had to have the doctor examine him every time he had even a small issue, like an earache. This was to make sure there was nothing seriously wrong with him.

During our family reunion in September, Giovanni became sick with a wheezing cough. We were concerned he was having difficulty breathing. My dad and I drove him to the nearest weekend emergency room, which was forty minutes away. Sure enough, when they took his oxygen diagnostics, his numbers were low.

Giovanni was 22 months old, and was still nursing at least once or twice a day. I felt that when he was not feeling well, he might want to nurse in order to feel more secure. This weekend was the first time Giovanni turned me away during nursing. He weaned himself that day by going "cold turkey". He never nursed again.

We had to spend most of the day in the hospital, waiting for chest x-rays for possible pneumonia. He did not have pneumonia, but he did have asthma. That was the first day Giovanni would need to use an inhaler.

Giovanni had asthma. Just what I wanted to hear – Giovanni had another medical condition that I needed to monitor.

As Kenneth's birthday approached in October, the situation had not really improved. Kenneth was still refusing to get on the phone on the occasions that his father did call. He would even turn and walk away when I would play messages on the answering machine for him.

Due to the stress and uncertainty surrounding Giovanni, and the fact that I was working and commuting at all different hours from my 24-hour work week, I decided to put Kenneth in kindergarten. He needed to be around other children. There was some concern initially at the school because he started so young. He was only four years old at the beginning of the school year.

In large part as a result of the home schooling I provided to Kenneth, he was advanced beyond the public school kindergarten. He became a "teacher's helper". He seemed more comfortable around his teacher than the other children. He did get along well with everyone.

Because he was advanced academically, I found that I still had to provide some home schooling to supplement what he was doing at school. His teacher said that he had reading and math abilities that were close to second grade level. I was proud, yet nervous. I really needed to focus on keeping this kid challenged so he would not become bored.

Just before his birthday in October, I was able to arrange a visit with his father. We met at Starbucks, where Jude admitted that he felt uncomfortable with Giovanni. He also admitted he was not doing well by Kenneth in failing to call him.

Jude claimed he would do better and I watched him write a memo to himself to call Kenneth "every other day." Since when does a parent need a written reminder to call his own child?

One surprise that came from this meeting was that Jude agreed to be at Giovanni's next neurology appointment, which was scheduled, as usual, on his day off. Additionally, it was in San Francisco, which was a much closer drive for him than for my parents or me.

Jude did indeed show up even though he was fifteen minutes late and arrived on his motorcycle. I am not sure why the fact that he came on his motorcycle bothered me so much. Perhaps I was upset because I related a motorcycle ride to something done in leisure time, which I had little of, because I was a single parent with no childcare help from the other parent.

It was probably more related to the fact that Jude purchased the motorcycle after we found out I was pregnant with Giovanni. It had been reminiscent of the big money he spent on braces for vanity purposes after we found out I was pregnant with Kenneth. Just at the times when I felt we should be watching our budget, Jude would decide to spend thousands of dollars on himself, without any apparent concern for his family. I wonder now if he did these things out of resentment towards me, because I was the one primarily pushing to have a family

Besides, I had helped find financing for the motorcycle, and he was still reaping the benefits of being on my insurance policy because he could not find a company to provide motorcycle insurance at such a low rate. I felt frustrated that he continued to benefit monetarily because he had been married to me.

Although the appointment was routine and uneventful, Jude had the opportunity to ask any number of questions about Giovanni or to even show an interest. He was silent the entire time.

Dr. Khan's pediatric assistant was a helpful and friendly woman named Deborah. She had been a Godsend to our family from the time Giovanni was first assigned to Dr. Shayne. Deborah was our point of contact for the office. Every time we had a question or concern about Giovanni, she would be so helpful in providing advice. No matter how many times my mom or I would call during the week, or even during any one day in some cases, she was always very patient.

Deborah was on a first name basis with my mom and me. She also knew the story of Giovanni's birth and Jude's involvement, or lack thereof. My mom and I had met Deborah during our first visit with Dr. Shayne earlier in the year. During that visit, Deborah had given us her personal business card and had officially introduced herself. She knew that Jude was coming to this appointment. At the end of the visit, Deborah came in and gave a friendly "hello." She then gave my mom and me her business card. She barely even looked at Jude and did not offer her card.

I found the incident quite humorous and I felt vindicated. Whether she had intended to or not, my belief was that she had snubbed him. However, in looking at Jude, he did not appear to be affected by it at all, so maybe he did not even recognize it.

I gave Jude credit and thanked him for coming to Giovanni's appointment. I still had hope that he would experience a change in priorities and make Giovanni a priority in his life.

This turned out to be the first and only time that Jude would take part in any of Giovanni's numerous appointments—emergency or otherwise—in the first years of Giovanni's life.

Chapter 15

Epilepsy or seizure disorder? Which sounded more palatable? Both essentially mean the same thing. I personally did not like the word "disorder", so I decided I would use the term epilepsy to describe Giovanni's condition.

Now Giovanni had yet another label I could attribute to him, in addition to microcephaly, severe developmental delay, cortical visual impairment, motor planning delay, and sensory processing disorder, which I found could also be labeled as sensory integration dysfunction. Besides the developmental labels, he was also diagnosed with asthma and epilepsy.

Here again I had a choice of what label to use. I am not sure if "dysfunction" was any better a term to use than "disorder." Both terms implied there was something wrong. They both had negative connotations.

During one of Giovanni's IFSP meetings, one of the social workers gave me a list of "acceptable" terms for different conditions. I had no problem in calling Giovanni epileptic. However, I found the correct terminology was "a person with epilepsy." I imagine this was the politically correct term. I was confused because when I used the term "epileptic", it was meant to be descriptive of Giovanni's condition, not a negative term to define Giovanni as a person.

It was frustrating that I had to actually think about which term was "correct" to describe Giovanni. There were literally several pages listed on the form I was given. I was not even consistent myself in the terms that I used. How could I expect anyone else to determine the least offensive terms on his or her own. Thankfully, the social worker said that I was the mom of the special needs child, so I was the one who was able to choose what terms were appropriate for Giovanni.

Over the years, I have used many different terms to describe Giovanni in general terms. I can describe him as "handicapped," "disabled," "exceptional," "challenged," "developmentally delayed," or "a person with differing abilities." I am personally not offended by any term used to describe Giovanni, as long as it is not used in a derogatory manner.

I set about trying to absorb all the information I could about epilepsy. First, I needed to know what doctors actually considered a seizure. A good definition of epilepsy that I could understand is, "a brief, excessive discharge of brain electrical activity that changes how a person feels, senses, thinks or behaves." During a seizure, there is a breakdown between the regulatory systems that maintain the normal balance between stimulation and dampening of nerve cells.

Epilepsy is considered the chronic condition of recurrent and unprovoked seizures. Seizures may result from a hereditary tendency or a brain injury as Giovanni suffered. From what I understood, many doctors would label someone with epilepsy if they had more than two unexplained seizures. Giovanni most definitely met this standard.

Next, I needed to know the different classifications of seizures. Like many people, I pictured a seizure as a very dramatic grand-mal type seizure where there is lots of shaking and jerking and possibly loss of consciousness. I found that there are many other types of seizures that may not be obvious to an outside observer. Indeed, some types of seizures are not obvious unless people know what to look for.

There are two general classifications of seizures: primary generalized seizures, which originate in both sides of the brain and involve the entire brain; and, partial seizures, which originate in one region of the brain

There are six types of seizures which may occur within the classification of generalized seizures. First are absence seizures that consist of brief episodes of staring with impairment of awareness and responsiveness. They usually last from 10-20 seconds and are not associated with a warning or post episode symptoms. At Giovanni's age, I could not determine if this seizure type pertained to him at all.

The second type, myoclonic seizures, is brief, shock-like jerks of a muscle or group of muscles. This condition causes abnormal movements on both sides of the body at the same time. Involved body parts are the neck, shoulders, upper arms, and legs. They often occur within one hour after waking, but are most easily controlled by medications. This condition is usually a lifelong condition. This list of symptoms described what I had been seeing in Giovanni. Therefore, before the neurologist even had the chance to analyze Giovanni's seizure patterns, I had determined rather quickly that his seizure type was primarily myoclonus.

Many people have sleep jerks that are actually a benign nocturnal myoclonus.

The third type of generalized seizure is the atonic seizure. This manifests as a sudden loss of muscle strength, which cause sudden falls, thereby earning the nickname "drop seizures." I did not notice this type of seizure in Giovanni.

The fourth type of generalized seizure is the clonic seizure. This condition is the rarest and involves the rhythmic jerking movement of arms and legs. There is no confusion or tiredness after the episode. Giovanni's jerks did not fall under this category.

The fifth type of generalized seizure is the tonic seizure. An episode usually lasts less than 20 seconds and is associated with sudden stiffening movements of the body, arms, and legs and involves both sides of the body. They are most common during sleep or in transition into or out of sleep. Giovanni exhibited this seizure type on occasion. Sometimes, the tonic seizures would occur in conjunction with the myoclonic seizures. I also believed that I may have witnessed a few episodes of this type of seizure during sleep.

The last of the generalized seizure types is the most recognizable, the tonic-clonic seizures (also called grand-mal). These are the dramatic convulsive seizures in which the person stiffens, loses consciousness, falls, cries out, and begins jerking. This type of seizure causes extreme tiredness and confusion. I was so thankful that Giovanni had not exhibited this seizure type.

Dr. Khan told me that seizure patterns could change over months or years. I hoped that those changes would not include having to witness the frightening tonic-clonic seizures. My hope for Giovanni was that he would "outgrow" his seizures over time. Dr. Khan was not so hopeful. Based on the severity of Giovanni's brain injury, Dr. Khan believed it was "highly unlikely" that he would be a candidate of ever outgrowing his epilepsy.

The second seizure classification is called a partial seizure, which can be broken down into simple or complex partial seizures Simple partial seizures include: motor symptoms, somatosensory or other sensory symptoms, autonomic symptoms or psychic symptoms. Complex partial seizures can begin as simple partial seizures or they can begin with impairment of consciousness. During some of Giovanni's early episodes, his pediatrician classified some of his seizures as partial seizures.

In all of the seizure types I have described, there are three phases: the aura phase, the ictal phase and the post ictal phase. After Giovanni exhibited several seizures, I learned to anticipate when they might occur because the aura he presented just prior to entering the active seizure, or ictal, phase.

Many people with epilepsy can describe the aura they experience before a seizure. They are able to anticipate seizures with a warning of several seconds. I believe Giovanni probably intuitively knew the aura surrounding his seizures, but he could not speak to describe them to me.

What I noticed before a seizure was that Giovanni would become quiet and would begin to stare. Sometimes his eyes would twitch. Then he would have a myoclonic jerk of his arms and pull them inward toward his body. His head would slowly turn to the right and he would breathe deeply. He would freeze for 10-20 seconds during the active seizure, or ictal, phase.

The post-ictal phase occurred as Giovanni came out of the seizure. Usually he was disoriented and tired.

I tried to keep track of all of Giovanni's seizures for the purpose of sharing the information with Dr. Khan. He wanted to be able to correctly classify the seizures since medication was prescribed based on the specific seizure type. I was not very good at verbalizing every action since I was always afraid I would miss something.

During Giovanni's October neurology appointment Dr. Khan revisited the possibility of prescribing Lamotrigine, or Lamictal. Although it would require periodic blood tests, I decided at this point that blood testing was preferable to the breakthrough seizures he was experiencing with the Klonopin. By this time, I had come to accept the fact that Giovanni's epilepsy was a lifelong condition. Lamictal was a medication doctors prescribed for long-term epilepsy patients.

What would be most difficult for me now would be the transitioning of Giovanni from one medication to another. He needed to be slowly introduced to Lamictal while taking the Klonopin. This process would take three months, and if successful, I would be able to wean him off the Klonopin. The tapering of Klonopin would take another four or five months. I resigned myself to the fact that this whole process of switching medications would take the better part of a year.

With the Lamictal prescription was a form that discussed the side effects. I was anxious to know all the various side effects with every medication Giovanni used. Even though serious side effects were considered rare, I was concerned because of all the various disabilities that Giovanni had. My mind was not eased much just knowing that the serious conditions were rare, because I felt Giovanni was high risk.

One of the many risks of the medication was a potentially life-threatening rash. I had no idea what this rash was supposed to look like. Giovanni tended to get frequent rashes. During this time it was stressful because I did not know what to look for in a life-threatening rash. Later, I learned that the rashes Giovanni did have were related to food allergies. He would also develop rashes by rubbing his face around on the bed and the carpet to get tactile input.

Deborah was helpful when I called the neurologist's office. She tried to allay my fears every time I reported a normal rash, thinking that it was the "death rash." I found out by searching on the internet that the life-threatening rashes were obvious, almost disfiguring rashes.

Over time, I stopped worrying about the rashes. Giovanni did suffer other side effects such as headaches and constipation. I could figure this out for myself based on Giovanni's behavior.

Even as Giovanni was changing his course of medication, he still was involved in weekly physical therapy. Since the medication affected his mood, there were some days that he just did not want to put forth any effort with the therapist. As he approached his 2nd birthday, he was able to sit on his own for an extended period and could stand with assistance. He knew the sound of Sara's voice and would usually become angry and agitated when he heard her voice because he anticipated he would have to work.

Meanwhile, he was having his monthly meetings with Janet, his vision specialist. We were trying to get him interested in Braille. Janet showed me how to help him scan the Braille book. Kenneth liked to help in this area.

She also showed me the importance of helping Giovanni feel centered in his environment. I did this by pressing down at his waist and pressing rhythmically on his shoulders while he was sitting. It was important to provide sequenced exercises to allow his mind to process a movement in relation to a consistent pattern, so that his anticipation would lead to his participation. I helped him scan whole toys. When he rolled around, I would name objects that he came into contact with.

Another way Janet instructed me to provide stimulation was to scoot Giovanni around the house in a sling made from a large blanket. I placed Giovanni face down with his tummy on the blanket and his arms and legs sticking out. Then I would simulate the movement of crawling by swinging him forward, and allowing Giovanni to feel the floor as he was propelled forward.

Janet also noticed that Giovanni was exhibiting signs of receiving visual input. Janet believed that he could probably see some motion, light and color. But since he could not speak clearly, we did not know for sure just how much he saw and for how long. When he did seem to have his vision "on" he would get the biggest smile like he just received a treat.

Giovanni began exhibiting behavior that I understood to be him "testing" his vision. He would bring his hand in front of his face to look at his fingers. Janet said that this provided a form of stimulation, and it also served to turn his vision "on" and help his brain to focus.

Janet was full of resources. Since she knew I was learning Braille, she gave me a Braillewriter so that I could make my own labels to place on objects for Giovanni. Kenneth also learned some of the Braille code and was able to type on the Braillewriter. Every time Janet came to visit, she provided a Braille book. These books had both Braille and other types of tactile pictures.

Another resource Janet provided was a book that she authored. The book provided parents and caregivers advice on how to promote the sense of touch in children with visual impairments. This book gave an excellent perspective of how blind children perceived their environment and how critical tactile learning is to them. As a mother, it was my responsibility to provide Giovanni with the exposure he needed to build up mental images of his environment.

I could tell by reading Janet's book that I had a very difficult and complex task ahead of me in teaching Giovanni abstract concepts. Even the most basic of concepts took on new meaning for me. I had to think through how I would introduce the concept to Giovanni so that he would gain a clear understanding without having fragments of ideas.

From my education and experience I knew learning takes place in three ways: concrete learning, manipulative learning, and abstract learning. The concrete learning refers to using tangible objects that are effortlessly processed through vision. The manipulative learning tools refer to items like toys that are used for interaction. Abstract learning is done through the use of words producing associations with real things and imitation of purposeful activities. The bottom line is that learning is different when vision is different. Being an active participant of what is going on would help Giovanni to learn.

I knew that it was going to take a lot of commitment and patience to involve Giovanni in every aspect of life. There have been times that I have felt guilty that I could have done more to integrate Giovanni into different activities. However, I found that there were just times that I was too worn out and it was so easy to allow Giovanni to sit and relax and play happily, while I relaxed also. I knew that it was unrealistic to expect that I would have the energy to be able to address his every sensory need 100 percent of the time.

I came to realize that even if he was not actively involved in a physical activity, Giovanni was learning just by being in the same room with me and taking in all the auditory input. At least, I figured that I had the idea in the back of my mind to keep Giovanni involved and to walk him through activities throughout the day. It was the same mindset that I had when home schooling Kenneth, which was to take regular activities throughout the day and turn them into learning experiences.

Well, I was excited anyway to be armed with new knowledge that gave me insight into Giovanni's world and I was ready to share it. Of course, my family was there every step of the way in learning about Giovanni's disabilities and how to help him, teach him, and communicate with him. In fact, my mom and I would talk at least twice a day about the children.

Now it was Jude's turn to learn a few things. I sent him Janet's book, and I talked to him in positive terms on how this book would help him to understand Giovanni better. Maybe if he could understand Giovanni better, he would feel more comfortable in interacting with him. I never gave up hope that Jude would become a father to Giovanni.

I was disappointed, though not surprised, that when I asked for the book back several months later, Jude had not read it.

I did not give up so easily though. Having helped Jude study in college, I knew he was not a big reader. Janet's book was over 70 pages, large print, after all. So I made it a lot easier. I typed up a synopsis of Giovanni's issues that I could share with Jude as well as anyone else that was curious about Giovanni.

This is what I wrote:

Hi, my name is Giovanni!

I am not able to speak clearly – yet – but I can understand nearly everything you say.

I have a cortical visual impairment, but I use all my other senses to organize my world.

I am non-ambulatory at this time, but I love to move around and bounce around.

I have motor planning delay, which means it takes a little extra time for messages from my brain to travel to other parts of my body. Please be patient as I process your requests.

I have sensory integration dysfunction. This means I process sensory input differently than you do.

My tactile sense is hyposensitive. I use my mouth frequently to gain sensory input.

I have epilepsy, which is controlled by medication. However, you may notice me "spark" or my eyes "twitch", which can be related to fatigue or overstimulation.

I like people talking to me, various types of music, lots of movement, swinging, vibration, deep pressure input like hugs, the alphabet song, counting to "3" before changing my position, being outdoors, toys that have texture or make noise.

I dislike very loud places with too much background noise, getting too close to my face unless I know you, soft plushy toys, and cold foods.

If you have questions, please ask my mom. She loves to talk about me.

I figured that this summed up Giovanni pretty well in just half a page. I gave the information to most of my friends as well as to Jude and his family. I honestly cannot say if he even read it or not, because based on some of the rudimentary questions he continue to ask about Giovanni, it would seem he did not read the information that was on the paper I gave him.

Aside from Jude, my co-workers really made some sacrifices to help me out. During our staff meeting before the holidays, there were two different schedules proposed to cover staffing shortages. When a vote was taken, one schedule was unanimously approved with one sole dissenting vote.

That dissenting vote was mine.

The schedule that the majority of the dispatchers wanted required me to work three eight-hour shifts. The worst part was that one of the shifts ended at 10:00 p.m. and I was required to be back in to work at 6:00 a.m. the next morning. I explained that this would create a hardship for me, since Giovanni was going through a stage in which he would become upset when I left. This was a time when Giovanni was having some intense sensory issues and I needed to spend extra time preparing him for the transition of my leaving. I knew that the "turnaround" between shifts would not allow sleep, let alone for that time Giovanni needed.

When I explained to the group what my situation was, they agreed to take a re-vote. The vote was unanimous for the schedule that worked best for me. I cried on my way home from the staff meeting that night because I was so touched by the support I had received.

Even as my friends and co-workers were showing empathy and support as the holidays approached, I opened my mailbox to find a nice Christmas card, along with a letter. This letter turned out to be "The Letter – The Sequel".

My jaw dropped again as I read "a year in the life" of Jude's family. They covered everything from Esther's death (in April), to the tropical family vacation (in May), to celebrate Diana's 30th birthday. There was the obligatory section about Kenneth and Giovanni. There was information printed about Giovanni that pertained to his disabilities. Most of the information, specifically related to Giovanni's vision, was inaccurate. It was not information that I provided to their family and it was not information that Jude was able to provide, since he did not really understand Giovanni's condition at all.

It was odd enough that I was on the list, but again, my entire family was on the list also. I was angry and upset as I had been led by Jude to believe that he would talk to his family and have them remove my family and me from their Christmas mailing list. This year, my father did not stand by and say nothing. He was very protective of Giovanni, as we all were, and was upset that false information was being spread about him to total strangers.

He sent Jude's family a very unemotional and non-confrontational letter explaining to them that it was illegal to release sensitive medical information to strangers without permission of the parents. I of course never gave permission, and Jude claimed he did not give them permission. He claimed, again, that they never intended to hurt anyone's feelings. Further, he also admitted he had not even read the letter. Therefore, I did not feel he really could comment one way or the other until he had done so.

Whether or not Jude ever did talk to his family I will never know, but my father's letter was enough to remove us all from their mailing list.

What made the whole situation mindboggling to me was that the divorce was finalized in early December and I would not have expected ever to be included on a list of "family" correspondence. If they had treated me as family in every other way, it would have been different. However, they did not treat me as a close family member.

All the hurt feelings going around put a damper on my hope that Giovanni's 2nd birthday could be celebrated all together with a positive atmosphere. Consequently, we were back to our plan of having Giovanni's birthday celebrated separately. Giovanni spent his actual birthday with me and my family and went to his dad's family for a party two days later.

One of the disadvantages for children having birthdays during the holidays is that their own personal special day is sometimes lost in the holiday celebration. For Giovanni, his birthday was almost two weeks after major holidays. He shared a birthday month with his Grandpa, his father and at least one close family friend. Consequently, his birthday was celebrated at the same time with the same party as two or three other birthdays.

Perhaps I am being a little petty and melodramatic. I just wanted my little boy to have his own day. I still had memories of the prior year when Giovanni was not the center of attention of his own party. Kenneth had received most of the attention. I was afraid of the same thing this year.

As it turned out, I did not have to worry too much about what Giovanni experienced at the party, because he spent the first hour and a half, of his four and a half hour visit, sitting in the van with Kenneth and me. Again, we were sitting in the van in a parking lot two blocks away from the family house. However, Jude still insisted that I wait for him so his family did not "have to get involved in any exchanges." When Jude did show up to get the boys Kenneth was upset that his dad was so late and Giovanni was somewhat agitated. I tried to offer Jude instructions on how to give Giovanni his medication, but he stated, "I've done it before." I was not too worried since I would be getting Giovanni back at 9:00 p.m., and if Jude failed to give him his medication, an hour late on medication would not hurt.

Jude returned the boys right on time at 9:00 p.m. It was ironic that he was nearly always punctual when giving boys back to me. Jude looked a little agitated. He was concerned that Giovanni "made a mess" while eating. I had to explain to him that Giovanni had motor planning delays that made it difficult to eat, and that a mess would be expected. He handed Giovanni back to me, showing no affection towards him whatsoever as he left.

While unpacking Giovanni's gifts later, I realized that Jude never even gave Giovanni a birthday gift. On the off chance that it was forgotten at his family's house, I called Jude and Diana, but neither returned my calls.

Since Jude and I were not on very good speaking terms, and the divorce was final, I had no reason to expect that Jude would attend Giovanni's neurology appointment at the end of the month. Nevertheless, I called him and texted him with my usual invite to the appointment that I had scheduled on his day off.

Of all the neurological issues we could have discussed about Giovanni, this appointment was focused primarily on seizures and medication. I had purchased a new digital camera after Giovanni's October neurology appointment so that I was always ready to capture the seizures as they occurred. It was not until Halloween that Giovanni had a seizure that I was able to capture in pictures. It took several seconds for the camera to reset between each picture, so I was only able to get a series of eight pictures.

Dr. Khan was pleased when I showed the pictures of Giovanni's seizures to him at his January appointment. Dr. Khan noted that although the last actual seizure was the one I photographed on Halloween, Giovanni was still having intermittent myoclonic jerks with some eye twitching. By now I figured this would be the norm.

I did not want to overmedicate the poor kid, so I decided I could live with the intermittent myoclonus.

As far as the label for the seizures was concerned, Dr. Khan commented that they appeared to be partial complex seizures. Given the findings on the EEG, which indicated generalized seizures, he hypothesized that Giovanni may have several seizure types. At least all the "scary" looking seizure types were controlled by the medication. I was just learning to live with the myoclonus, hoping that it would not cause too much distraction or cognitive delays for him.

I was thrilled when Dr. Khan gave his permission to taper Giovanni off the Klonopin medication. Here we would begin our several-months long process of getting this awful medication out of his system. Meanwhile, he was on 150 milligrams per day of Lamictal with expectations of having to increase the Lamictal as he tapered off the Klonopin.

Dr. Khan confirmed that Giovanni was not responding to any visual stimulus that day. He was pleased that Giovanni was making vocalizations and was trying to mimic him.

I called to leave a message for Jude to let him know what information I learned at the appointment. He did not return the call for a few days. When he finally did call, about Kenneth, I questioned him about his interest in Giovanni. He claimed he still could not take Giovanni on a visit because he did not have any place for him, and there is no place to sleep. Jude's excuse was the environment is not acceptable to a visually impaired child. So, now it was not an issue anymore with being done with physical therapy. Suddenly it was about Giovanni's visual impairment, which was a permanent condition.

Giovanni was not going to be visiting his dad anytime soon, if ever.

Chapter 16

I was disappointed because Giovanni's medical issues interfered with his progress in all of his therapies. His brain certainly could not concentrate on cognitive growth when it was spending so much time just trying to keep Giovanni healthy. Truthfully, Giovanni was actually quite healthy for a child with his multiple disabilities. It just seemed that every couple of weeks Giovanni would have some minor medical issue.

Shortly after his neurology appointment, Giovanni was exhibiting symptoms of wheezing again. My parents were babysitting while I was working, and they did not want to take any chances. They made an appointment with the on call pediatrician. In Giovanni's medical record she noticed his prior prescription for albuterol and flovent for asthma. She prescribed that course of action again.

Providing Giovanni with an inhaler was about as much fun as giving him his medication. He would whip his head around, refusing to be still. He was very sensitive to sensory input on and around his head and he would always try to get away when someone would try to do something to him around his head or face. This included brushing his hair or brushing his teeth. We all did the best we could in providing him with a warning and talking him through whatever procedure we were doing for him.

Giovanni had a mind of his own and usually would not cooperate taking the inhaler. Traci had the most success with him, because she had long legs and was able to position him in just the right place so that he was lying on his back with his head between her ankles so he could not move it around. Perhaps it was the proprioceptive input he was receiving by being snuggled between her ankles, but he seemed to be calm and cooperative in that position. My mother and I did not have long enough legs to have much success with this position.

Whether we were giving Giovanni medication, or just caring for his needs in general, we saw that if Giovanni became agitated, he would have an increase in his myoclonic sparks. I am sure that during this time there was a correlation with him being tapered off the Klonopin. Since Klonopin was a powerful drug, Giovanni suffered some powerful withdrawal symptoms as he was weaned off the drug. These symptoms included insomnia, headaches, constipation, and crying for no apparent reason. Consequently, I kept in frequent contact with Deborah at Dr. Khan's office. Dr. Khan requested lab work for Giovanni's Lamictal levels. They all came back normal.

During that winter and in to spring, I kept a close eye on Giovanni so that I could document any breakthrough seizures. When he was healthy, he did not have any such seizures. On the occasions when he did become ill, or run a slight fever, Giovanni was highly susceptible to seizures. I pretty much expected that Giovanni would have at least one breakthrough seizure if he felt even slightly under the weather. I came to think of these seizures as "precursor" seizures, because these seizures would usually occur right at the beginning of an illness, preceding the onset of the illness. At least it gave me warning that Giovanni would need extra attention.

These seizures tended to be similar to the partial seizures that he used to have when I first realized he had epilepsy. He would have eye twitches and tonicity, or stiffening, in the upper extremities, as he would seize and freeze in position for 10-20 seconds. I did not like to see these seizures, but they were no surprise. Dr. Khan had warned me that Giovanni would have a low seizure threshold when he was ill, and any breakthrough seizures would probably happen at this time. If we noticed that he was having these seizures it indicated he needed to increase his medication.

In Dr. Khan's opinion, the ultimate goal was to have complete control over Giovanni's seizures, even during illness. It was a stressful time as Giovanni was weaning off the Klonopin and increasing his Lamictal. I had to find just the right balance of medication.

One of the difficulties I had with giving Giovanni his Lamictal was his constant effort to spit it out. I tried to hide the tablet in a variety of foods. Each time, Giovanni would taste the Lamictal and drool out his Lamictal with his food. Sometimes, he would actually eat the food while keeping the Lamictal in his cheek. Then, he would spit it out later. Giovanni was capable of eating the food around the Lamictal and then spitting out the tablet, much like eating a cherry and spitting out the pit. It was a blessing in disguise. Giovanni did not have any difficulties with his fine motor abilities within the muscles of the mouth.

Dr. Khan was supportive of parents taking control of their child's health. I was always trying to educate myself in order to make the best decisions for Giovanni. In my opinion, any medication that Giovanni was taking was a "necessary evil." I preferred him to be at the lowest possible dosage and the fewest medications as possible. Dr. Khan explained that many parents just chose a medication that took away the seizures, even if it meant making the child lethargic or delayed.

I was saddened to think how many children may have been needlessly overmedicated because it was the easiest thing for the parents to do. Giovanni was already severely developmentally delayed and did not need any further obstacles to his development. I had no problem in taking on the challenge of monitoring his medication and analyzing his reactions, so that I could decide as his mother what the best balance of medication was for his unique body.

I had no doubt that Jude probably would have chosen to have Giovanni on the highest safest dosage of medication, so that he would not have to think about how to tweak the dosage to the lowest effective dosage for him. I firmly believe that my willingness to help Giovanni wean off the most addictive drugs and to find the lowest effective dosage of medication is what helped him move forward with his development.

In April, my family decided to take another cruise for our annual family vacation. This time my entire family was able to go. My grandmother went with us, which was helpful to me because she helped pay for the cabin. I did not have the money to be taking extravagant vacations. I did know how to budget for a nice vacation once in awhile. This cruise to Mexico was fun because my entire family was able to go this time.

The boys had a great time. Giovanni especially seemed to enjoy the movement of the ship. He liked being outside and in the pool. Having my family there made it nice for me, as I had people ready and able to watch Giovanni so I could do some activities for myself. Moreover, I was able to spend one-on-one time with Kenneth. It was great having the family together.

During the cruise, Giovanni was still going through withdrawal symptoms from weaning off the Klonopin. I did notice that he was becoming more alert as his dosage was decreasing. It was during the cruise that he was able to finally grasp a child sippy cup and drink water himself. Before this, someone else would have to help him hold the cup and tilt it the right way so that he could get to the water. This was a major improvement in his fine motor skills. It gave me hope of continued improvement.

The week after returning from the cruise, I became sick and was having difficulty caring for the boys. Jude was on a day off, and I called literally begging for childcare help. He refused to return my calls.

Diana was kind enough to take Kenneth for the evening, so that I could rest and recover with the responsibility of just one child. When Jude finally called that night, he only asked for Kenneth. I stated that Diana took him because I was sick and desperate for some childcare help. My family was not available that night. He literally hung up on me.

The next day, Diana returned Kenneth and I found he was sick, too. This was the first time that I had to handle a sick child at the same time I was sick. Although I was trying hard to keep Giovanni healthy and well, he was totally exposed to whatever Kenneth and I had. Jude called only to speak to Kenneth and to ask one question about Giovanni's medication. He did not express any empathy for me or Kenneth being sick. Kenneth was feeling too ill to get on the phone with his father. Jude still did not comprehend the difference between the Lamictal and the Klonopin and which one Giovanni was being switched to.

April and May were very difficult months for me, the children, and my family. We had different colds and flues, which all of us were exposed to and became sick at one time or another. Giovanni held out the longest. Even though my mom was still sick, my very stoic, and supportive, parents were caring for the boys. I had to work and we could not even reach Jude for help in childcare.

One night my parents had to bring Giovanni in to the emergency room, because he appeared dehydrated and was having break-through seizures. I left work to meet them at the emergency room. As I was leaving work at 6:00 p.m., I left a message for Jude to let him know his son was in the ER. He called back at 10:30 p.m. He did not understand how Giovanni could become dehydrated. I explained he was still having some difficulty in coordinating sipping and swallowing from a cup. Even if we were right on top of him, it was not impossible for him to become dehydrated. I explained that Giovanni was probably fighting off the same flu or cold that we all had. Thankfully, Giovanni never did get sick with the flu.

Jude was not very much concerned about Giovanni. He was more concerned about where Kenneth was located, because he did not want Kenneth in the hospital. I told him that my sister was home and she was staying the night with him. If my sister had not been home, I would have had no choice but to bring Kenneth. I turned the question back on him and asked him what he would expect that I do if I had no childcare and he was unreachable. He refused to answer that question. He claimed he had to handle something at work and hung up. I left him a message at 11:30 p.m., as we were leaving the hospital. This was to let him know we were on our way home, even though Giovanni was still having occasional breakthrough seizures.

Jude left a message at 1:00 a.m. stating that he would call Kenneth "later." In my world, "later" meant a matter of hours when it had to do with a child. Jude's "later" meant five days.

One of the frustrations I had, and would continue to have, with Jude was his unavailability, even when his children were sick or in the hospital. He was a police officer and had hundreds of hours of sick time he could use to help us out. That never happened.

I was thankful that Jude at least provided Giovanni with access to medical insurance. Giovanni had yet another referral in May to see Dr. Smith, an orthopedic specialist. I hoped that maybe there was something he could do to help Giovanni with his walking skills. Or perhaps, the evaluation could at least provide Giovanni with a label that could get him some assistance through state sponsored programs.

Although I firmly believed in my responsibility to care for my child, I was grateful for whatever assistance social services could provide for him. Some very experienced and talented therapists work for state agencies.

The appointment did not provide much information. Giovanni was uncomfortable in the office and with the doctor. The doctor spent the majority of the time revisiting Giovanni's history. I was not sure why I needed to explain everything in detail yet again; since Kaiser had a computer system that provided physicians the access to all of Giovanni's medical records.

I felt fortunate, however, because Dr. Smith had an observer with him who happened to be a doctor who worked for the U.C Davis Medical Center. Giovanni had two highly respected professionals present to examine him.

Aside from confirming that Giovanni did not have cerebral palsy, neither doctor could provide any other input. They talked back and forth with each other, sounding puzzled as they exhausted their list of possible conditions. There was no medical label they could attribute to Giovanni's condition, so he did not meet the criteria to obtain additional state services or therapy for his physical condition.

Dr. Smith's suggestion was to participate in sensory integration activities, and gross motor activities, at home and school. Well, since these were the very things that I had been doing for months with Giovanni, this visit was not entirely revealing. I was upset that I had driven so far and wasted half of a day to have the obvious stated to me. I was also a little upset that two experts could not give Giovanni a medical diagnosis. I knew that they really did try, but they had exhausted the list of medical conditions.

A few weeks later, Giovanni had the opportunity to participate in some sensory integration activities with family members. Jude and his sisters decided to take both boys to Stinson Beach. I was a little concerned because of Giovanni's tendency toward seizures and his sensitivity to temperature. Because his dad was showing some interest in taking him out, I wanted to support that. I figured that three adults could handle my two children. I was accustomed to handling them by myself.

Diana and Olivia knew I was concerned about how Giovanni would handle new environments. They called me in the early afternoon to say he was doing well. Diana said that she was keeping him under an umbrella and he seemed happy and not agitated. By evening time, Diana called to say he was having "issues." He did not take his Lamictal well and was starting to spit up. I waited up anxiously for the boys to get home.

When the boys returned at 9:00 p.m., Giovanni was pale and cold. He appeared windblown and sandy. Most concerning to me was that he was spitting up and was "sparking" quite a bit. At times, his eyes would roll back in his head and he would become stiff.

These were perhaps signs of tonic seizures. He was refusing to eat or drink for me. I was up all night with him, as he was spitting up and he could not hold any food down. The next day he was very lethargic and had to drink water constantly.

My plan to involve Giovanni with Jude's family went awry. A child with Giovanni's disabilities would be more sensitive to weather. I am not sure if Jude and his sisters realized that. It appeared from what they said that they had treated him like any typical child. As much as I appreciate people respecting Giovanni like any other child, the fact is that he has issues that require special attention. I would have thought that Diana might have realized this, as she was a nurse. On the other hand, I would have hoped that if they did not understand all of his issues, that they would ask questions.

As it happened, Giovanni had an appointment with Dr. Khan a few days later. His glands were still swollen, which indicated an illness. Dr Khan concurred that Giovanni probably suffered from heat exhaustion or at the very least, had become ill due to exposure. As I suspected, what Giovanni was experiencing the night he returned was some type of seizures. This was upsetting to me, since he was already up to 200 milligrams per day of Lamictal and was still weaning off the last few tablets of Klonopin. The tiny little guy was drugged up as much as I could safely drug him up. Needless to say, this whole incident did not ease my fears about leaving Giovanni with people who did not understand him.

I felt torn because, although I wanted Jude's family to spend time with Giovanni, I was also fearful when they did because they did not have much knowledge about his disabilities.

When Diana called a couple of days later to take the boys to a "special" park in Berkeley, I was not too thrilled with the idea. I was concerned about Giovanni being exposed to the elements. He had barely recovered from his beach trip. I was hoping that if Diana wanted to visit both boys, that maybe she would adapt the plans to make it more conducive for Giovanni to attend. Even after I expressed concern about Giovanni, she declined to modify the plans for him. She said, "This is the only time" they could go to the park and she really wanted to take Kenneth. I was not going to deny Kenneth the opportunity to visit with his aunt, so I agreed.

Diana also discussed having Kenneth stay with her an extra day, because she was sad about Granny who was ill. She wanted Kenneth around to cheer her up. When Granny died that week, Diana called me to cancel all the plans with Kenneth.

A few days later, I found out that Diana had made plans for Kenneth to attend a graveside service for Granny. She did not invite Giovanni or me. I would not have expected to be invited, since I was no longer part of the family, but I would have thought that Giovanni would be, especially since Kenneth was actually taking part in a special ceremony at the gravesite. Diana explained that nobody was invited to the service. She did not have the time to call people, and that friends and family had to call her for the information. So, I suppose Giovanni and I were not invited because we did not call her to ask for details about the service.

Since I was part of the family for over a decade and I knew Jude's grandmother well, I thought that I may have been given an opportunity to attend her service. After all, I had attended Esther's service. But I did not feel slighted at not being invited. I was more upset that Giovanni was not invited since Kenneth was invited to actually take part in the service. I really just needed to learn to calm down, relax, and not take everything as an affront to Giovanni.

A few weeks after the service, I stopped by Jude's family house to drop off some information on sensory integration dysfunction. It was actually a three-page synopsis of an entire book on the subject. I wanted to make it quick and easy for anyone to read. I gave it directly to Diana and asked her to give it to Jude when she saw him, since the boys and I were not seeing him much. I also suggested that she read it since it would provide some information about Giovanni's condition. Perhaps I was being too assertive in providing this information, but I really did have the best intentions at heart.

I must not have offended Diana, because a week later Diana surprised me when she and Olivia and Jude's father spoke to me about Kenneth's education. They all wanted to help in sending Kenneth to a Christian school. I was flabbergasted, and very thankful. However, I was worried about Jude's unreliability and I did not want to be the one footing the bill if he "bailed out" on us. I told her my concerns, because the expenses for Giovanni's needs were substantial.

Diana made it very clear that they were committed to help for the entire twelve years of education, unless they had major financial trouble. She assured me that if Jude "bailed", that they would take care of his portion of the tuition since Kenneth is part of their family. I expressed my appreciation. I was not able to afford sending Kenneth to a private school on only my income. I was nervous because I knew that once we committed, it would be crushing to Kenneth, who would probably like being at the school, to remove him later. Again, I was assured by Diana that I did not have to worry about it.

Diana felt that this was something their family could do to help Kenneth. She trusted that the "state" would take care of Giovanni. I made it clear that the "state" helped with a total of about 10 hours a month of various therapies, but it was my family and me that were taking care of Giovanni.

Having five people contributing to Kenneth's tuition made it possible for him to attend Christian school. As I anticipated, he loved it and told me he never wanted to return to the public school.

Ironically, it was not Jude that backed out on Kenneth's education, it was Diana. Within a few months, she had met a man and been married and decided that she could no longer afford to help with Kenneth's education. Even though she had promised twelve years, I was thankful for the one year she did provide tuition for Kenneth.

I think I am angry and disappointed that she made a promise to her nephew which was done lightly. Also, I realized if this was the priority she placed on Kenneth, then there really was very little hope that she would ever bond with Giovanni. Having a family of her own would put further constraints on her ability to visit with her nephews.

I struggled throughout the summer to be as pleasant as I could to Jude whenever he would take Kenneth for visitation. I did the best that I could to talk in positive terms to Kenneth about his dad. But it was impossible to hide the fact that he treated Giovanni completely differently than he treated Kenneth. Although not a negative word was said aloud, Kenneth took notice of how Jude treated Giovanni.

Jude's treatment of Giovanni was not lost on Giovanni either. During one exchange he faked being sick while Jude was holding him. He started to fake a cough so that Jude immediately handed him back to me saying he did not want to get sick. I tried to tell Jude that Giovanni was not sick and that he was probably faking it, but he did not believe me. Giovanni laughed about it when we drove out of the parking lot.

When I tried to talk to Olivia once about Jude's behavior, she explained that Jude had hurt feelings and was unable to see the children because he can't talk to me. In addition, he could not bond with Giovanni because he had missed out on infant bonding time caused by moving the children away. Like Jude, she believed that the children are too far away! When I tried to defend myself and tell her that I did what I had to for the children and their care, she said Jude didn't walk out and would never leave us high and dry. However, Jude did walk out by his behavior.

Actually, he did not really walk out as much as he walked down-stairs and out of our lives. In addition, he did not leave us high and dry because he did pay the child support that he was legally required to pay.

Even though I realized that Jude's family was probably not aware of all the information surrounding child custody and childcare, it still did bother me a little bit that they seemed to feel that I took the children away from Jude. In my opinion, it seemed that they felt Giovanni's physical well being took second place to Jude's convenience at being able to bond with him.

In order to reassure myself that what I was doing was indeed the right thing for the boys, I did my own research on father-infant bonding. Well-known pediatrician Dr. William Sears had some good information about infant bonding. His website contained information from Dr. Marshall H. Klaus and Dr. John H. Kennel, which explored the concept of bonding. They speculated that there is a "sensitive period" for humans at birth where mothers and newborns are uniquely programmed to be in contact with each other.

Although bonding during this biologically sensitive period gives the parent-infant relationship a head start, the authors state, "Immediate bonding after birth is not like glue that cements a parent-child relationship forever." The authors believe that catch-up bonding is possible because humans are adaptable. They go on to state, "The conception of bonding as an absolute critical period or now-or-never relationship is not true."

That last statement validated my personal belief that having moved away with the children did not preclude Jude having a relationship with them. I only wished that Jude's family would realize that Jude needed to take some responsibility as a father and make the commitment to spend the time with his children.

Then again, we return to our differing concepts of distance. As long as we lived 70-80 miles away from each other, Jude could always make the claim that it was just too far for him to drive on his days off.

Since Jude had three days off work each week, he did have many opportunities to get involved in Giovanni's therapy. Not only was Giovanni in physical therapy once a week, but by this time he was having combined occupational and speech therapy once a week. I took Giovanni to the Children's Therapy Center where he would have therapy with Suri the occupational therapist and Peggy the speech therapist.

Giovanni was still having withdrawal symptoms because of the Klonopin. This affected his mood and willingness to work during therapy. He always did best when he was in a swing. This vestibular input was extremely important to him.

Although I tried several times to contact Jude to discuss Giovanni's progress, Jude did not call much that summer. During those sporadic phone calls, when Jude talked to Kenneth, Jude never asked for information. He did not ask about Giovanni for an entire month.

In August, I wanted to meet with Jude to discuss Giovanni and the concerns I had about child custody. The marital settlement agreement stated we had joint custody, although I was the primary parent with 95% custody. More specifically, I had 90% custody of Kenneth and 100% custody of Giovanni. Jude had given no indication that he desired any increase in his custody. He did express frustration in the amount of child support he was required to pay.

When I finally got my meeting with Jude, he was interested to discuss his girlfriend with me. He refused to discuss Giovanni or the MSA (marital settlement agreement) because he felt it was not appropriate. A couple of weeks later, Jude called to discuss Kenneth starting first grade at his new school. He avoided all questions about Giovanni. Instead, he focused on what specific foods I needed to pack for Kenneth for his lunch.

After Kenneth started school, there were several days where Jude did not call to ask him about school. Kenneth was upset, but refused to call his dad to tell him how he felt. Leave it to me to get involved and send a text to Jude to advise him about Kenneth's mood. At the same time, I mentioned Giovanni's IEP appointment in late September. I figured that would give Jude plenty of time to ask for the time off. Jude never returned any calls, even on his days off. I often wondered how Jude's lack of interest was affecting Kenneth.

I kept busy throughout the summer getting Giovanni to his therapy and providing therapy at home. Although Suri was addressing Giovanni's sensory integration issues in occupational therapy, I wanted to do more. I was thankful that I could provide sensory therapy at home with the home gym that my dad had helped to install.

Jude arrived for Kenneth's back to school night. Jude did not express any interest in Giovanni. He stared at Giovanni, but did not talk to him or touch him. I could not decide if Jude still did not understand the scope of Giovanni's visual impairment, and that he would need to speak to him or touch him in order to bond with him, or if he just did not care. Here was a perfect opportunity, neither the first nor the last, for Jude to do some catch-up bonding with Giovanni. There was no excuse this time about the distance being too far, unless he considered two feet away to be too far.

The back to school night gave Diana and me the opportunity to break down the barriers of communication – again. She apologized to me for all the mean things she had thought about me and done to me. I forgave her and again thought for Giovanni's sake, that we were on the road to better communication. I came to understand that communication was a matter of individual interpretation. Like Giovanni, communication that did not necessarily involve spoken words.

By the end of the night, Jude's attitude had thawed a little bit and he did hold Giovanni for a few minutes and asked some very basic questions about him. These questions were the same questions he had asked in the past, which indicated that his retention of information regarding Giovanni was not that great. Or else, he just did not care enough to remember details about his son, or just was not listening. I reminded Jude that Giovanni had an IEP in a couple of weeks and it was important that he be there as Giovanni's dad. This would be a great meeting to attend so he could learn more about Giovanni and his issues and his progress.

Since Jude and his family made the effort to drive the 35 miles to see Kenneth at his back to school night, I had hoped that they might want to make that same effort for Giovanni's school IEP. Giovanni's school activities did not warrant the same attention from Jude and his family as Kenneth's activities did.

After talking to Diana and feeling better about the possibility of more positive interactions with their family in the future, and being the eternal optimist, I decided to take a leap forward and send Jude a conciliatory letter. This was not the first time that I made conciliatory overtures to Jude, and it would not be the last. For some reason, I always held out the hope that if I was "extra nice" and was not quite so assertive, that maybe Jude would not be so fearful of me.

I suppose that the mere fact that I took initiative and sent an apology letter was probably an assertive act in itself. If Jude interpreted this as an aggressive action, perhaps that is why Jude never acknowledged the letter.

Although he did not directly respond to the letter, maybe the letter helped to soften Jude up a little bit. The following week he was willing to drive to Woodland to visit the boys. He spent time playing with Kenneth and trying to teach him to ride his bike. He still showed no interest in Giovanni.

A few days before Giovanni's IEP, Jude angered me when he called just before midnight to tell me that he had not called Kenneth because of work that past week. Additionally, he would not be going to the IEP because of work this week, too. His reason, again, was that, "You guys live in Woodland and I live in Rohnert Park. I can't do things for Giovanni." When I asked about any possibility of things improving in the future, he said, "I live too far away." Then he declined to commit to helping Giovanni in other ways, like in purchasing therapy equipment for him.

I had to pull myself out of my anger toward Jude, because Giovanni was not feeling well. It seemed that Giovanni was having more incidents of illness and upset stomach as he was being switched from one medication to another. As his Lamictal levels increased, so did his flu-like symptoms. He was having episodes of vomiting which, like clockwork, occurred every two weeks.

On the one hand, Giovanni needed his medication to control the seizures. On the other hand, it seemed the medication was causing frequent stomach upset. I figured I just had to accept that Giovanni had a sensitive stomach and, like my mom, would occasionally throw up anything that agitated his stomach.

In late September, Giovanni had an episode that was especially concerning to me. Usually when Giovanni had an upset stomach, he would vomit a few times, usually in the morning, and then sleep for four or five hours. By the afternoon, he ordinarily was like himself again. Before these episodes started, Giovanni would typically have a lot of myoclonic activity. During this particular incident, he was pale and he had a partial seizure in the morning. Sara was there for his physical therapy and a representative from the company providing Giovanni with his walker and special wheelchair were present and witnessed the seizure.

I called Deborah with my concerns and we discussed a plan of action in the unlikely event that Giovanni had more serious seizures, or any seizure activity that lasted more than three minutes. The plan was that if Giovanni had a single seizure lasting more than one minute or a cluster of seizures lasting more than three minutes, I would give him a dose of rectal Diastat, otherwise known as Diastat. This medication would stop seizures almost immediately. Having a plan made me feel more secure and in control, even though neither Deborah nor I ever thought I would have to resort to that plan. After all, I had this Diastat in my possession for over a year and I had never had to use it, even on the cruise when Giovanni was having uncontrolled seizures. Even though Giovanni was ill most of the day, he did not appear to have any more seizures.

In the early evening, I noticed Giovanni having a different seizure type than I had ever noticed before. He became stiff in his upper body and made deep guttural sounds while throwing his head back. His eyes were rolling to the back of his head and it appeared to me that this was definitely not a voluntary movement. I think I was slightly in shock at what I was seeing, since it was a new type of seizure for Giovanni. After a few minutes, I realized that these seizures were almost constant.

I was thankful that I had spoken to Deborah earlier that day, because I had to resort to our plan of action. I gave Giovanni the dose of Diastat and then I called 911 for an ambulance.

Kenneth was asleep and I did not want to alarm him, so I asked the dispatcher for a "silent approach" which is when the ambulance shuts down their sirens a few blocks away. This was one of those times where I was extremely thankful for family nearby. I was able to call my sister to come over and she actually arrived at the house before the fire department. I anticipated a visit to the hospital and I needed someone to watch Kenneth.

When the fire department arrived, their EMT, or emergency medical technician, asked all the required questions about Giovanni's condition. I explained everything and told him how I administered the rectal Diastat. I was wondering if I had administered it correctly, and what the side effects might be. He told me he did not know anything about that particular medication and I needed to ask the paramedic.

When the ambulance arrived, the paramedic asked me the same questions as the EMT, which I fully expected since I am a dispatcher and I knew how medical calls are handled. I asked the paramedic about the side effects of the rectal Diastat. She stated she had never heard of that medication and I would have to ask the doctor.

Even though Giovanni was sleeping peacefully, I had him seen by a doctor, since none of the paramedics knew anything about the medication that I had given him. The firefighters were helpful in getting the car seat out of my car so we could bring it on the ambulance. The situation became more stressful when Giovanni woke up as we placed him on the stretcher. He made it clear the he did not want the paramedic anywhere near him with the oxygen mask. He still had sensory issues in which he did not like anything on or around his face.

I sat next to him in the ambulance and held the oxygen mask just above his mouth so that he was able to breathe the oxygen without having the mask on his face. Then the ambulance drove the speed limit the three miles to the hospital. My sister was staying at the house with Kenneth, and my father was enroute from Shingle Springs. When I arrived at the hospital, I remembered that Jude was off work and had the next day off. I called him to report to him that Giovanni was in the hospital and the circumstances. I did not expect him to come. He did not.

This was not just another trip to the ER. Giovanni had been transported by ambulance to the hospital after suffering a series of seizures.

I could not get reception on my cell phone from the ER, so I sent Jude a text and a picture of Giovanni being transported by ambulance and his condition. He texted, "Is he okay?" I replied, "Yes and he should be released tonight." He said, "Okay, I'll call and check on him tomorrow." That was it. "Tomorrow" turned out to be three days.

When Giovanni was released about midnight, my dad and Kenneth picked us up at the hospital. Even though I never said a word about his dad, I am sure that Kenneth was aware that his dad did not come to the hospital to see Giovanni, and did not come out to help care for him either.

I was so full of emotions that night. I felt sadness that Giovanni had to go to the hospital again. I felt anxiety that his seizures were not completely under control, even with all the medication in his body. I felt heartbroken that he had no dad that showed any interest or love for him. I felt guilty that I was the one who chose this man to be the father to my children. And I was angry and frustrated with that man for living his own life, where his children existed to him only when it was at his convenience.

Chapter 17

Although Giovanni's medical emergency was emotionally draining, I was proud of how I handled it. I had remained calm and followed the plan. Even though I was distracted with Giovanni's immediate needs, I still had the ability to think clearly and provide for Kenneth's care. I had maintained my composure without becoming an emotional basket case.

It was upsetting when I found out how much the trip to the emergency room cost. Not only did I pay $40 out of pocket, but also the ambulance ride was $1200. Calculated, it cost approximately $400 per mile. I cannot believe gas cost that much. I should have put in a bill since I actually provided more medical care than the paramedics did. I suppose they charged for the oxygen Giovanni used. I will never understand how medical insurance and billing works.

Keeping my attitude in check over Jude's non-interest in Giovanni's condition was more difficult. Once again it was necessary to mask my resentment with Jude so that the boys would not notice my negative vibrations about their dad. As hard as I tried, I had no doubt that my attitude and demeanor gave away my true feelings.

When Giovanni went through his ordeal I was not scheduled to work. One of my most difficult tasks being a single parent with a disabled child was working shift work. I was fortunate that I only had to work 24 hours a week. However, those 24 hours could be in three 8-hour shifts, or two 12-hour shifts or a combination of 10-hour shifts and a 4-hour shift. My hours changed weekly which compounded my work schedule leaving me constantly tired. At times, I felt overwhelmed, although I was pleased that this was not the case this particular week.

When Jude came out to visit the following week, he once again did not give any attention to Giovanni. He did not ask about the hospital visit, either. Jude played with Kenneth and occasionally looked over at Giovanni. I am sure that Giovanni knew that Jude was his father. Over the course of his short life, I had discussed in length with Giovanni who this man was that kept popping in and out of his life. I am not sure how much Giovanni understood about the meaning of "father" since it was my own father who was the male role model in his life. But I did know that Giovanni's reactions during some of the exchanges indicated to me that he was agitated and upset when Jude would barely acknowledge him and then walk away.

Giovanni's annual neurology appointment came up the following month, so I gave Jude several reminders throughout October so that he could meet us there. The appointment was in San Francisco and he lived and worked only twenty minutes away. I probably should not have bothered to remind him. His history was an indication of how he would probably respond. I figured he would not come to the appointment. It would not matter if I reminded him or not. I figured that one advisory would be enough for him to put it in his planner.

As the appointment for Giovanni was still a few weeks away, I was not so concerned at that point if Jude would come. I was more concerned with how Kenneth would respond to his dad coming out to the house on November 3rd to carve the Halloween pumpkin. At least that was the plan, although Jude showed up without any pumpkin carving supplies. Although Halloween was over, Jude did follow through with his promise to help Kenneth carve the pumpkin with supplies he borrowed from my sister.

Kenneth was just thrilled to see his dad. His dad ignored Giovanni, leaving him with me, while he took Kenneth to dinner.

Later that evening Jude did ask a few questions about Giovanni. It must have been only as a formality, because Jude walked away as I was literally in the middle of a sentence. This was another opportunity Jude missed in getting to know his youngest son.

Since my parents were not able to come to Giovanni's appointment in November, my friend Lisa and her boyfriend Bobby volunteered to drive with me to San Francisco so that I did not have to travel alone. Lisa's nine-year old daughter came along, too. It was nice to have company for the long ride. I am sure that having a male along for the ride made Giovanni happy. Giovanni responds differently to male voices than to female voices. I believed he responded positively to the deep male voice. We knew, though, that he did like female voices when it came to music.

During this visit, Dr. Khan and I discussed Giovanni's progress and his continuing myoclonus. He was still having constant episodes of these "sparks" which were not completely controlled even by the high dose of 225 milligrams of Lamictal. Since these episodes were not disruptive, I preferred to keep him on the lowest possible dosage of one medication rather than "chase down" every spark with higher dosages or more medications. It appeared that 225 milligrams was the lowest effective dosage. My feeling was that Giovanni needed to have an alert brain as often as possible in order to progress in his development.

Dr. Khan noticed that although Giovanni had motor planning delays that affected his walking, he had very strong abdominal muscles. Actually, he preferred to do abdominal crunches in order to sit up rather than use his arms. Consequently, his arm muscles were still weak. His vision had improved a little since his last visit, as he was able to track objects a little bit. He also babbled a lot more than the last visit and tried to mimic simple sounds for Dr. Khan.

Two items that had been introduced to Giovanni since his last visit were orthotics for his feet and a walker. The orthotics helped keep Giovanni's feet in correct alignment so that he could at least attempt to walk. Giovanni's feet were over-pronated and affected his ability to walk straight. At this point, he was only standing in his walker and was not very much interested in walking. His legs were not yet strong enough to support his weight for sustained periods. He also tended to cross his legs when he did try to walk. It took a lot of brain concentration for him to make the steps that he did make. I could tell he was concentrating because he would close his eyes and not make a sound because all his brainpower was focused on walking.

Giovanni still was seeking sensory input in other ways. He still preferred the swing for vestibular input. He also liked to put everything to his mouth in order to obtain tactile input. He especially enjoyed his "z-vibe", which was an oral-motor vibrating tool that had attachments for a toothbrush and a spoon. This provided him some sensory input that he was willing to accept. I also believed that the "z-vibe" helped in desensitizing him enough that he was accepting new textures in his foods, although he was still sensitive to temperatures. He still refused to eat or drink anything cold.

Finally, I talked to Dr. Khan about my belief, as well as the belief of a holistic practitioner, that Giovanni's issues may have been caused by exposure to the varicella virus while I was pregnant. While stating it was less likely, he did confess to a lack of certainty in this regard. He was supportive of my desire to explore alternative medicine.

Dr. Kathryn Picoulin is a holistic healer. Before she began practicing holistic healing, she was a registered nurse. Her formal education includes a Baccalaureate degree in nursing. She also has a Masters degree and Doctorate degree in homeopathy. I met Kathryn through my mom, who had been seeing her for several months. Dr. Picoulin said she was willing to evaluate a child as young as two years, with epilepsy. Before Giovanni's neurology appointment, I took Giovanni to see Dr. Picoulin. She took some DNA samples to do an evaluation both for me and for Giovanni. She also discussed my pregnancy and Giovanni's prior history. After his neurology appointment, we went back to see Dr. Picoulin for our results.

Giovanni was comfortable in Dr. Picoulin's office. I was pleased. This was a child who generally was quiet, withdrawn, or otherwise stressed in hospitals or clinics. He was completely at ease in Dr. Picoulin's office, as if he was feeling positive energy.

Dr. Picoulin believed that Giovanni still had the varicella virus in his body. She also believed that it was his exposure to this virus while I was pregnant that affected his brain. We discussed the dramatic increase in seizure activity and the inclusion of different seizure types within a few weeks after his varicella vaccination. She explained that many alternative healers believed that epilepsy was caused primarily by the varicella virus. Therefore, removing the virus from his body may actually cure the epilepsy. It was worth a try since traditional medicine could not cure the epilepsy. It could only provide the drugs that acted as a band-aid on the problem. Dr. Picoulin said there was a homeopathic remedy for the varicella virus. Removing a virus from Giovanni's body would take close to a year, and she told us we might not notice any major difference in his seizures for quite awhile.

I started him on a course of remedies that would possibly take up to a year or more to rid Giovanni's body of the varicella virus.

Aside from epilepsy that was causing Giovanni major issues and affecting his development, he still had a chronic problem with asthma. Dr. Picoulin said that Giovanni was allergic to wheat, gluten, corn, and strawberries. She said that the asthma was an allergic reaction specifically to wheat and gluten. This empowered me, as I knew that I had total control over his diet and I could immediately make the necessary changes.

I removed wheat and gluten from Giovanni's diet that very day. The asthma disappeared. He has had no breathing difficulties of any kind since then. He has had no sniffles, coughs or any major allergic reactions of any kind since that day, except for the rare occasion when I have accidently given him corn, which causes him sniffles and coughs for about an hour or two after ingestion.

I was so excited about this development in Giovanni's health! For people who do not understand or believe in alternative medicine, I always hold up Giovanni as an example. All you have to do is see his reaction to the allergens and his health since they have been removed from his diet and compare the two. There is no doubt in my mind that food allergies do exist.

Dr. Picoulin also determined that Giovanni's primary stomach problem was caused by a specific strain of bacteria in his stomach. She suggested a homeopathic remedy for that condition and recommended a daily supplement of probiotics to add "good" bacteria to his system that would help fight off the "bad" bacteria. Thankfully, this course of action did the trick. Giovanni's bi-weekly vomiting episodes soon disappeared.

At least they disappeared for a little while, until his Lamictal levels were increased again. Although the "bad bacteria" influenced Giovanni's general health, it was not the only factor in his vomiting episodes. Through trial and error, I found that it was indeed the Lamictal that was the primary factor in the vomiting.

I also had Dr. Picoulin do an evaluation on me while I was there with Giovanni. I was also allergic to wheat and gluten. Additionally, I was allergic to shellfish. That was a bit disappointing since I loved lobster. My lymph glands were unhealthy due to parasites. I also had chronic back and neck problems that were related to tetanus and parasites. Moreover, I was constantly tired, no matter how much I slept. This was because of a virus called Epstein Barr. There were also homeopathic remedies for all of these conditions.

Within a year I had lost 60 pounds, and was feeling energetic even when I only had a few hours of sleep. My whole body felt so much healthier. I was also excited when my neck and lower back pain disappeared. This was so important since I was always carrying Giovanni.

I still take several remedies in order to make my body healthier and detoxify from environmental toxins, viruses, and parasites.

Two weeks after visiting Dr. Picoulin, I was invited to a retirement dinner for an old friend. Since my parents were invited and my sister was not available, I had no one to watch the boys. Jude was unreachable. Jude's sisters offered to care for the boys. I saw this as a validation of their commitment to taking a more active role in their relationship with Kenneth and Giovanni. I admit I still had visions of their beach trip and the condition in which Giovanni was returned to me. However, this was our home. I figured that two grown women could handle two children in a home environment for a few hours. Everything went fine that night.

Although Jude's sisters did fine the night they babysat the boys, I was still concerned that if something happened to me, Jude was not capable of caring for Giovanni. He had admitted so himself. My attorney advised me that a judge would not separate the boys. Therefore, if Jude wanted custody of Kenneth, he would have to take Giovanni also. I was afraid that if something awful happened to me, that Jude would find himself with sudden 100% custody of both boys. Considering how little he really knew about Giovanni, I was concerned for his health and development in his dad's care.

Even though I believed that Jude would not contest custody of Giovanni, he might do so for Kenneth. I was hoping that if I kept accurate and specific records of Jude's interest, or rather lack of interest in the boys, the family court would consider granting custody to other family members besides the biological dad.

Giovanni responded to Traci like a second mother. I had no doubt that he would progress in her care. With his father, he would likely suffer further developmental delays.

My secondary concern was that Jude might actually be willing to take custody of both boys in order to get Kenneth. Then he would probably need to rely on his sisters to help with their care. These were the same sisters that he claimed were "too busy" to help with childcare. I could not imagine they would have time for the children if I was out of the picture. I realize that I am probably being too paranoid. It is probably due to my controlling nature that I feel this way.

I anticipated a possible custody dispute even from the very day of our separation. At least, I anticipated that Jude would want Kenneth. I knew he did not want the responsibility of Giovanni.

In anticipation of the day of reckoning and being a very analytical personality (and a control freak), I kept a journal of conversations, exchanges, disagreements and so on. I began this journal the day Giovanni was released from the hospital in 2005.

Well, as it turned out, I have yet to take Jude to court for custody. However, the hundreds of pages of documentation that I kept came in very handy in writing this book.

If Jude and I were able to communicate better I probably would not be so concerned about the future. After nearly three years, though, we still had difficulties in finding common ground. Actually, it would have probably been easier to find common ground if I was able to speak to Jude, but he continued to avoid phone calls and refused to return messages.

Just before Thanksgiving, Jude did decide to return one of my messages. I had called Jude because I was concerned about the reasons Jude kept providing about his lack of involvement with the children. He told me several times that all he had time for in his life were working, eating and sleeping.

Even as he used these reasons for his lack of involvement, my friend found pictures of him on a social networking site. The pictures showed him at parties and at bars. Normally I would have no problem with a grown man participating in these activities during his free time. The problem I had was that Jude continued to claim that he had no free time. I believe that the only reason that Jude returned my call was because he knew I had found out about his dishonesty.

Jude certainly did not call to check on the boys because he did not mention them during the conversation.

During the conversation we were having, Giovanni was playing on the bed. Giovanni was very sneaky as he would sometimes lay still, sing, and play and then he would suddenly move. This time, he suddenly moved and he rolled right off the bed.

I told Jude I was not able to talk anymore because Giovanni had rolled off the bed and I needed to check on him. Jude showed absolutely no concern about Giovanni and never asked if he was okay. Giovanni was fine, but Jude did not ask, and so I did not tell him. I told Kenneth later that his dad had called and that he could call his dad back. As usual, Kenneth declined to call his father back. I have wondered since this incident if Giovanni possibly rolled off the bed intentionally. It certainly would not have been the first, or the last, time he had done something distracting to inhibit my interaction with Jude. However, mostly he did these things to cut short his own interactions with his dad.

Communication with Jude did not get any better that week. I tried to let Jude know by text message that Kenneth was having issues with calling him or talking to him. Of course, this did not go over well with Jude. Perhaps he assumed I was trying to control his relationship with his son. Actually, I was just concerned about Kenneth's emotional state as he was alternately excited to talk to his dad on some days, and then angry and resentful with him on other days. Jude maintained that he was, "Pretty much out of the picture" because I had moved.

Apparently, Jude was going to keep to the excuse that I had moved and therefore he could not have a relationship with his children. He was upset because he thought that people stereotyped him as a father who is not around for his children. I made it clear that no one "stereotypes" him based on someone else's actions. My family, my friends, and I judge him based on his own actions.

After our heated text controversy, it was no surprise that he did not call for Kenneth. He texted that he would like for me to have Kenneth call him. Kenneth knew his dad's phone number and how to use a phone. He was six years old and I did not believe that he should have to be the "adult" in this relationship. However, I suggested that he might want to call his dad since I had just texted him. I knew he was by the phone. Kenneth did call, but it went to Jude's voice mail.

Following his past practice, Jude disappeared for nearly a week after our uncomfortable text exchange. When he did call, he actually asked to speak to Giovanni. There was a first time for everything. Since Giovanni was a captive audience in his high chair, I placed the phone to his ear. He paused and listened to his dad for about ten seconds. Then he pushed the phone away without making any of his usual attempts to babble on the phone.

I was not surprised that Giovanni pushed the phone away. After all, Kenneth would also try to avoid his dad's phone calls. Giovanni had even more reason than Kenneth to resent his father, so he had no reason to talk to him either.

Since Jude had specifically called to talk to Giovanni, I thought maybe we had reached a turning point. I felt renewed hope when I called a couple of days later asking for assistance with a childcare issue. I had no one to watch the children and it was Jude's day off. I left Jude a detailed voice message and then a text asking, "Please listen to my message reference childcare. I'm begging for help."

Apparently "begging" did not affect Jude any more than "politely asking" or "demanding." He disappeared for another week. He did not reappear until after the childcare issue had passed. Indeed, we had not yet reached that turning point.

When Jude finally did call, at the end of the first week of December, he volunteered to meet me at his family's home in Fairfield so he could visit the boys. He was going to take the boys for several hours to give me some time to myself. At least, that is what he led me to believe.

This was not the first time Jude had offered to take the boys to give me a break. Therefore, I did not have any expectations that this attempt would be any more successful than the last.

Sure enough, when Jude called to say he was on his way, we were already sitting in his family's living room. Kenneth was upset. He said, "Daddy is always late. Why can't he be on time? He never does what he says he's going to do." These were the words of a six-year-old who had his dad all figured out, based entirely on Jude's own actions and not a word from me.

I did not know how to respond to him, especially since I agreed with him. All I could say was "I'm sorry about that." In a repeat from eleven months prior, he told me, "Thanks, but it's daddy's fault."

Not only was Jude late, but he showed up on his motorcycle. That way he could tell me he had to leave early, "before it gets too cold." It turned out that the six hour "break" he had promised me was actually 1 ½ hours. In another repeat from earlier in the year, I had just enough time to get dinner and coffee before having to return to pick up the boys.

The next opportunity Jude had to visit Giovanni was on December 23rd, when I brought the boys over for their family Christmas. This time, I did get 5 ½ hours to myself. Then again, Jude was not entirely responsible for the boys as there were several adults in the house celebrating the holidays. Indeed, when I returned at 7:30p.m. to pick up the boys, they were wide-awake while Jude was asleep on the couch.

During our family Christmas, I found out that Gina and Traci were going to be gone for three weeks in January. My father had a previous commitment. My mother was not able to lift Giovanni by herself due to her osteoporosis, so I started leaving texts for Jude on December 28th in the hopes that he could offer some help with childcare in January.

I also left messages regarding Giovanni's 3rd birthday party, asking if he planned to help either with the planning or the financing. Jude never answered these texts.

I wanted to have a large party for friends, family, and therapists to mark Giovanni's graduation from the First Steps Infant Program to pre-school. I also wanted to take the opportunity to thank everyone for his or her love and support.

Jude made one passing comment on the phone that he would help, at least with the cost, which never happened. Then he disappeared again and he was unreachable until he met to pick up Kenneth for visitation just four days before the party.

As Giovanni approached his 3rd birthday, I was both excited and nervous at the prospect of him attending school outside the home. It would be a transition for both of us. I anticipated the positive changes that would be happening in Giovanni's life.

Chapter 18

A s we transitioned to a new year, Giovanni and I were preparing for him to transition from the First Steps infant program to the special day school. I wanted to make his birthday party special, not just for him, but for everyone in his life that had been there every step of the way to provide support to me and to the boys.

I had decided to have Giovanni's birthday party at a nice restaurant that had a banquet room. Everything was progressing according to my plan as I coordinated with the manager and finalized plans a few days before the event.

However, the weather had other ideas.

During the first week of January there was an intense storm that caused power outages and flooding. Our backyard fence was knocked down. Because of the power outages and phone problems, the manager of the restaurant could not reach me the night before the party in order to cancel it.

I walked in to the restaurant one hour before the party to find out that the power had been out all night and the restaurant had no food. I was told that power had just returned about an hour before I arrived. Their chef was traveling around the area, trying to get food for the day. The manager asked if I could postpone the party.

Though I would have been happy to reschedule, there was no way that I could. Family members were already on their way from many miles away and were due to arrive within the hour. The manager agreed to continue with the party, but it would require a menu change and a lot of patience since the chef had not yet returned and some of the kitchen staff were not yet at work yet due to road closures.

What some people might look at as a catastrophe, I merely shrugged it off and adapted to the situation at hand. I suppose in instances like these, it helps to have a special needs child because I was an expert at adapting to changing circumstances. Frankly, I was not affected by appearances or the need to have perfection. I knew that the people that showed up were there to celebrate Giovanni, regardless of what food was served.

Even though there were road closures, everyone who had agreed to come had arrived. My entire family was there, except for my brother who was out of state on a military assignment from which he could not be released. Quite a few friends showed up. Jude arrived with his sisters. Jude's father was not able to be at the party because of another commitment. Although most of the people I invited were family and friends who were supportive of Giovanni, I invited Jude's sisters and father because of their relationship to Giovanni.

Kenneth had been visiting his dad for a few days prior to the party, so he arrived with him. As they arrived, Jude and his sisters greeted Giovanni, gave him a kiss, and then walked away. They sat at their own table, and did not interact much with anyone. When it was time to eat, they sat away from Giovanni. They watched as my family fed Giovanni since he could not feed himself. Maybe they did not realize that my family would have been more than happy to allow Jude, Diana, or Olivia to hold or to feed Giovanni. All they had to do was ask.

I felt sad because I had thought that Jude and his sisters might have taken this opportunity to visit with Giovanni, or perhaps to talk to me about his progress. Maybe they felt uncomfortable because my family was there. Members of my family had a strong bond with Giovanni and hugged him and cuddled him a lot.

I could imagine how uncomfortable Jude and his sisters may have felt uncomfortable if they were thinking that I may have "poisoned" everybody's mind against Jude. Actually, I do not believe that was the case. My friends and family judged Jude by his own actions. However, I do admit that some of my closest friends and family knew the truth about my feelings because I did confide in some people how disappointed and angry I was at times.

In fact, when my friends Lisa and Bobby showed up, the boys responded more to Bobby than their own father. When it was time to open presents, it was Lisa who helped me and Giovanni open his presents. Jude and his sisters acted more like friends or acquaintances than family members.

At least this year Giovanni got a present from his father. He got some nice clothes and a special toy that taught children sign language. The toy provided a visual on how to form several words using sign language. I admit, when I opened the present in front of everyone I really did not know how to react. Everyone there knew enough about Giovanni to know that he was visually impaired and was learning Braille, not sign language. In fact, my friend Suzanne, who was not able to attend the party, sent a special gift, which was a t-shirt with Braille embroidery.

In his defense, Jude did say that Kenneth picked out that particular toy. Kenneth told me that he picked out that toy because it had some raised letters and animals on the opposite side of the sign language. As it turned out, Giovanni liked to put the raised side in his mouth for tactile input.

During the party, I had a special ceremony for Kenneth as the party boy's big brother. In contrast to Giovanni's birthday with Jude's family in which Kenneth opened gifts and acted like the birthday boy in Giovanni's place, this ceremony provided special recognition to Kenneth as Giovanni's big brother.

As I told everyone that day, it takes a special child to be a big brother to a disabled child. Kenneth was with me during all the difficult and emotional times and all of the transitions. He was there when Giovanni had seizures. He always helped Giovanni and never showed any jealousy or resentment. Kenneth showed sensitivity and caring beyond what I would expect from a child under the age of six years.

The special gift I gave to Kenneth was a fluffy dog water bottle holder. It had a strap so that he could travel with Kenneth wherever he went. Kenneth named the dog Buddy and he has been Kenneth's favorite toy ever since. Another positive result of acknowledging Kenneth was that it really pumped up his ego and he was even more helpful to me afterwards.

I personally felt that it was important for Kenneth's self-esteem to give him credit for being a great big brother. I am not sure if Jude or his family ever acknowledged Kenneth's contributions to his little brother. I do know that Jude expressed concern that Kenneth's needs were not being met because Giovanni's needs overshadowed Kenneth's needs. Of course, Jude was able to make these comments without ever knowing what truly occurred in my household on a daily basis and how I managed the needs of two children by myself.

Overall, I felt the party was a success. I was disappointed though that Jude left without offering to help clean up or load up presents. Moreover, despite his initial offer to help pay for his son's special party, he later declined because, as he told my dad, he "didn't get to help plan it."

Although I was able to take many pictures of Giovanni with family members, it was difficult to obtain a good picture of Giovanni. Not only was he constantly in motion, but he also did not focus directly at the camera because of his vision. In three years, I had no luck in getting a good portrait of him.

I found a wonderful couple who specialized in children's portraits. Although they were based in Fairfield, James and Doris Casselton drove to Woodland so that Giovanni would be in a comfortable environment. They took the time to talk and bond with him before taking his picture. Consequently, I ended up with not just one, but several very flattering portraits of Giovanni. For the first time in his life, he allowed James to place a hoodie over his head. He usually cried when I even tried to put a hat on his head. It was important for Giovanni to be comfortable within his environment and with visitors, because he responded accordingly.

After the excitement of Giovanni's party, it was time to get him prepared to start school. Before he could start school, he had to go through an initial assessment of his skills. The school psychologist was the primary organizer of this assessment, with input from the schoolteacher, speech-language pathologist, and school nurse. They used a variety of assessment procedures including: multi-disciplinary play-based methods, observation in a natural setting, structured parent interview, the Bayley Scales of Infant and Toddler Development and Social-Emotional and Adaptive Behavior Questionnaire, instruments specific to speech and language evaluation and a record review. The assessment was comprehensive.

Giovanni was evaluated in nine areas to determine his specific needs. First, he was evaluated in pre-academics, which addressed his matching and sorting skills, number and letter skills, and body parts. They determined that Giovanni needed to be observed in a school setting to better determine his skills. The team determined that Giovanni was not yet imitating, but was able to respond to environmental and vocal cues.

Second, Giovanni was evaluated in social and emotional skills, which covered his ability to interact with adults and peers, attachments and separation from caregivers, responding to his environment and appropriate play. The team noted that Giovanni loved to be around people. He generally woke up singing and was happy throughout the day. He loved the rough and tumble play he received from his brother. He loved to be around other children and he laughed and rocked when he was interested in and happy with his environment. According to the pattern of responses I provided on the Bayley III test, Giovanni demonstrated marked delays in his overall social emotional functioning.

The third area in which Giovanni was evaluated was self-help and adaptive behavior. This section covered skills that are needed for daily living such as toileting, feeding, dressing, using communication and social competence. Giovanni was not able to indicate when he needed to use the bathroom or when his diaper was soiled. He needed help with spoon feeding and was not able to eat foods that were too difficult to chew. Basically, he required full assistance with his hygiene needs. He was just beginning to take part in back and forth conversations, though he could not speak clearly. My responses on the Bayley Adaptive Behavior Questionnaire suggested marked global delays overall in the area of self-help and adaptive behavior.

The fourth area in which Giovanni was evaluated was motor development and sensory processing. This assessment area addressed the development of fine and gross motor skills. Fine motor skills were those that used the small muscles of the hands. Gross motor skills were those that used the larger muscle groups of the body. Sensory processing referred to the brain's ability to organize and make sense of different kids of sensory input entering the brain at the same time. Giovanni could not participate in most of the fine motor activities presented during the assessment. He did demonstrate a raking grasp when he reached for objects. In addition, he could roll from supine to prone and back again. He had good abdominal strength which he used to rock and sit up. At this point, he disliked smooth surfaces. Overall, his motor skills were rated significantly delayed.

The fifth area in which Giovanni was evaluated was his problem solving skills, which related to his skills in thinking, learning, memory, using language, attention, judgment, and understanding cause and effect relationships. Since adaptive skills were highly correlated with problem solving skills in young children, his low assessment on adaptive skills led to significant delays in problem solving skills. This did not mean he could not learn, but he would require a high level of support in order to make the best possible progress in school.

The sixth area in which Giovanni was assessed was his receptive language ability, which related to the ability to listen to and comprehend word meanings, word forms, and sentence structures.

Receptive abilities were demonstrated by skills such as object or picture identification, following directions and answering questions. Giovanni appeared to understand his name and was able to turn his head and body towards a preferred activity. However, Giovanni could not show an ability to follow single-action verbal commands. His receptive abilities indicated that he was at a 6-12 month range.

The seventh area in which Giovanni was assessed was his expressive language abilities, which referred to the ability to use language to represent objects and ideas. During the assessment, Giovanni demonstrated use of vowels and a limited range of consonants. Although he had the ability to put two consonant-vowel combinations together such as "Nonna", his abilities were still below the one year old level.

The eighth area of evaluation was pragmatics, which referred to the use of any recognizable language system such as gestures or speech to intentionally communicate. It involved the use of language to regulate social interactions including conversational abilities. Giovanni did not demonstrate any recognizable speech patterns, though, at least during this test, he was not impeded by any outside attempts to assist him with communication.

The ninth area of evaluation was that of articulation or oral motor skills. These skills involved the structure and function of the lips, tongue and jaw as well as the sensory organization and use of these structures to articulate speech sounds. Giovanni showed he could smile, laugh, and cry with adequate muscle movements. He did not have the tone or awareness of oral structure to prevent excessive drool.

In conclusion, the psychologist indicated that Giovanni was globally challenged and would require a high level of support in order to make appropriate progress in school. He would likely require specialized services since he demonstrated severe global delays.

Although it was helpful to see Giovanni's abilities broken down into specific areas, I was depressed when I read it. I always tried to keep a positive outlook about Giovanni's future abilities. However, I could not ignore what was staring me in the face. Giovanni had severe developmental delays. He was three years old, but many of his skills were in the range of six to eighteen months old. Consequently, Giovanni was given the label of severely disabled.

So much for my earlier hope that a "slight" delay of a few months in the beginning would not make a huge difference with the passage of time. It would appear now that he had actually progressed extremely slowly in the past two years. That he had progressed at all was encouraging, given the multiple disabilities that Giovanni had to deal with.

I had spent three years learning all I could about the brain and neurological function. I had researched just about every condition that Giovanni had so that I could become as knowledgeable as possible to be able to help him. It was now time that I needed to learn how to navigate the special education system so that I could be a strong advocate for Giovanni.

For the first three years of his life, Giovanni had received early intervention services through Alta Regional Center. Now that he was turning three years old, he would be transitioning to the county school district for services in the classroom. I needed to attend a final Individualized Family Service Plan meeting to determine if Giovanni would qualify for any ongoing services provided by the regional center. Then I would have a meeting with the school district staff to determine an Individual Education Plan.

The main difference between early intervention services and an IEP is that services in the early intervention program are developmentally based whereas the services provided with an IEP are educationally based.

The school staff ensured that I was informed of all my rights since there were specific statutes and regulations that governed special education. After being referred to a special education program by Alta Regional Center, the assessment team is given fifteen calendar days to meet for the assessment. Giovanni's assessment was completed in the allotted time. After the assessment is completed, the school has sixty calendar days to complete the IEP. Giovanni's IEP was completed well within the required time. The administrator for special education at the Yolo County Office of Education was helpful and addressed Giovanni's needs quickly.

I was fortunate that Giovanni had a proactive teacher and he was attending school in a district that was highly responsive to Giovanni's needs. I found out later that not all school districts took their responsibilities seriously under the Individuals with Disabilities Education Act, known by the acronym IDEA. The states are required to follow rules for identifying, evaluating, and providing services to eligible children between three and twenty-one years old. Federal funds are also provided to the states for early intervention services for children with conditions likely to cause developmental delays. Because of the circumstances around Giovanni's birth, he was identified from infancy as a high-risk child and was provided state services.

Not all conditions, however, will qualify a child for services. A child's disorder must adversely affect the child's educational capacity to the degree that special education is required. Giovanni obviously had impairments that would affect his education. Regardless of whether he had epilepsy or not, he still had visual, speech and motor impairments that would require that he receive special attention.

This statute ensures that all handicapped children receive appropriate education at no additional cost. The statute requires that children be educated in the least restrictive environment, which means they have a right to be included in classrooms with children who do not have disabilities, provided the placement meets the disabled child's educational needs. Even though I hope that Giovanni will someday be mainstreamed into a regular classroom, the fact is that he has multiple disabilities that will likely require him to remain in a special class.

IDEA also requires schools to provide all additional services needed to help children benefit from special education, including transportation, audiology, speech therapy, psychiatric evaluations, physical therapy, occupational therapy, recreation, social work services, counseling, and vision services.

Under the law the Individual Education Plan, or IEP, is a document which is jointly developed by the parents and school personnel. The IEP describes the child's present level of development, short-term and annual goals of special education, specific services, start dates, duration, and goals. This document is legally binding.

During Giovanni's initial IEP, we discussed goals and objectives for his first year. These goals were in many categories including, academic, self-help skills, leisure and recreational skills, communication, motor skills and social and behavioral skills. The primary goals we focused on during that first meeting were academic goals. Since Giovanni was not yet imitating on request to do so, his first goal was to imitate an action on teacher request on four out of five trials. Since Giovanni was not yet consistently making choices, his second goal was to choose a preferred object when given a choice of a preferred object and an undesirable object. These goals would then be evaluated in four to six months.

Furthermore, since Giovanni was no longer eligible for occupational and vision services through the First Steps program, the school district representative agreed to schedule assessments in both of these areas. The IEP provided me with a lot of information to absorb. The first IEP contained eight pages of documentation, which was too much to leave on Jude's voice mail. Based upon his response to date, I did not believe Jude would be interested to know the details. Jude was invited to the IEP, he knew when it was, and knew he could call for the information. He chose none of these options.

On Giovanni's birthday, he was once again ignored by the other family. Neither Jude nor Jude's family called Giovanni on his actual birthday on January 10. I suppose they thought that showing up for the party several days prior relieved them of any other obligation to acknowledge Giovanni's actual birthday. Maybe they thought that Giovanni was only three years old and he was disabled, so therefore he did not know the difference.

Well, Giovanni may not have understood that his father forgot his birthday, but Kenneth sure understood. I am not sure why Jude could not grasp the concept that regardless of what Giovanni thought about him or what his relationship was with Giovanni, his lack of interest in his younger son would most definitely have an effect on his older son.

Perhaps the consequences of this would not be evident until much later, but there would be consequences. I had already concluded that when Kenneth finally confronted his father about his lack of concern for Giovanni, Jude would probably use me as the excuse. After all, he just wanted the divorce. I was the "witch" who stole his children away and moved to the far reaches of civilization in order to keep him away from his children. I suppose he could say that there was no phone or mail service that reached where we lived.

I had no worries, because Kenneth was too smart to be manipulated by his father. He knew which parent he could rely on to be there for him AND his brother.

Even though Jude's family did not call Giovanni on his birthday, Diana wanted to visit him the next day. I dropped him off at the family home in Fairfield. I briefed Diana about Giovanni's issues, particularly the sensory issues, while I gave him his medication. I did my best to sound calm as I entrusted Giovanni's care to Diana.

I admit, I was a little nervous to leave Giovanni with Diana since he was highly sensitive to unfamiliar environments or people. I was concerned that he might be agitated to be left with an aunt he visited so rarely. Knowing Diana's personality, if he did have issues, she would not acknowledge the possibility that he was uncomfortable with her. She would probably blame something else.

When I picked Giovanni up at the end of the day, his grandfather was gone and Diana was alone with him. I gave him his medication and noticed that he was "sparking" quite a bit more than usual.

Diana said he had a few of these episodes today, but she was not concerned because "he didn't turn blue." She also said he had a forty-minute crying spell and she had to take him outside to calm down.

I did not feel it would have been any use to tell her that Giovanni was probably reacting to feeling uncomfortable in his environment. I was afraid she may feel defensive. Therefore, I thanked her for babysitting Giovanni and I lifted him up to get him ready to go home. Almost immediately, he started laughing and giggling. In fact, he giggled all the way home and I did not notice any more myoclonus for two days. If Diana could have seen him, she would have thought he was a different child.

I could understand why Diana may not have believed that this was a sensory reaction to his environment. After all, he was missing his mother and, of course, he would be excited when I returned for him. However, I knew what normal behavior was for Giovanni. Even when I was not around, he was an independent-minded child and usually did not have tantrums just because I was gone. He had spent the night away from me before. He usually responded favorably to lots of affection from my family members, even in my absence.

I had so much information to share about Giovanni in regards to his habits, behaviors, and preferences. My phone calls and messages to Diana went unanswered. Still, if she was interested, all she had to do was ask. Apparently she was content to visit with her nephew without any interest in really getting to know him.

Indeed, Giovanni's expressive speech difficulties made it extremely difficult for anyone to verbally communicate with him. That was why it was so important to understand Giovanni's non-verbal method of communication. It took a lot of patience and many times it was trial and error. However, Giovanni had his ways of letting people know if they interpreted him correctly.

One of the subjects the IEP staff and I discussed in the IEP meeting, as it related to expressive language abilities, was the use of adaptive devices. Giovanni had used what was referred to as a "big mac" in the past, but never used the device consistently. The "big mac" was a large button that contained a voice recording, which Giovanni could use to express a need. Giovanni only needed to press on the button to activate the recording.

One disadvantage of this device was that only one voice message or request could be recorded at a time. For example, I could record "more food please" and place it in front of Giovanni during mealtime. Another disadvantage to using this device was that Giovanni liked to keep pressing the button, not because he needed something, but because he liked to hear my voice. Consequently, I rarely used this particular device with Giovanni.

Another way I tried to communicate with Giovanni was through a unique sign language. Jane, the school speech language patholo-gist, focused on teaching Giovanni his body parts in anticipation of using them as a means of communication. Unfortunately, Giovanni was not very cooperative in touching his body parts on command. However, he could identify many of MY body parts.

After Giovanni's first month of school, he was evaluated by an occupational therapist that provided some recommendations for assisting Giovanni. First, the therapist suggested that when presenting a new activity, I should provide choices between two items. I should talk about each choice while taking his hand and scanning over the item. Then, I should patiently wait for a response such as Giovanni reaching for an item. This would help him to meet his educational goal of making choices.

Second, I should provide simple activities that can produce immediate effects or that have a sensory component, such as a cause and effect toy with lights or sounds, or toys of various textures. She recommended bringing Braille books from home. I could talk about the toy while assisting him to use it.

Third, I could assist Giovanni to touch his food with his hands in preparation for self-feeding skills. This was one area that I was anxious for Giovanni to master. However, I would find that his improvement in this area was slow and gradual.

Fourth, the therapist suggested a few sensory activities. I could help Giovanni stack blocks and have him knock them over. I could place objects of varying weight and texture in his hands as long as tolerable to him. Additionally, I could help him explore the use of switches for cause and effect toys.

Since occupational therapy would only be provided a couple of hours each month, it would be up to my family and to me to follow through with the exercises.

Although Giovanni was receiving some therapies at school, Alta Regional Center still had him as a client, because of his severe developmental disabilities. There were two programs that he qualified for with the regional center. One program that sounded promising to me was respite care. The other program provided a specific amount of funds for diapers.

With respite care, I was allowed a certain amount of hours per calendar quarter in which I could have a family member care for Giovanni in his home so that I could have some time to myself. Giovanni's caseworker, Kristin, advised me that because of his intensive needs, I would qualify for 96 hours. I was excited because that worked out to 13 hours each month. I could not imagine what I would do with so much time!

Because I felt so guilty using Traci so much for childcare so that I could work, I could not bring myself to ask her to watch the boys even more, just so that I could have "me" time. Taking part in the respite care program would enable me to provide Traci with some monetary reimbursement for caring for Giovanni. She wouldn't be paid for Kenneth of course, so I would make sure to take advantage of this program while Kenneth was in school.

I was so grateful for this program, which would allow me to have a break from the boys for just a few hours each month. By this time it was painfully obvious that all of Jude's talk of taking the boys to give me a "break" was just a fabrication; maybe it was Jude's intent but he never took the initiative to make it happen.

As I shared my excitement with Kristin over the potential for 13 hours to myself, she corrected me. I did not qualify for 96 hours of respite care each year. I qualified for 96 hours of respite care each QUARTER. This worked out to 24 hours each month.

I was shocked that I would qualify for so many hours. Kristin assured me it was because of Giovanni's severe disabilities and that he required so much attention for all of his needs. I explained to her that I never considered Giovanni a hardship. He was my son, I loved him, and I did whatever I needed to do to help him. I was playing the cards I had been dealt. I would be doing what I was doing even if there was no respite, though I would gratefully take advantage of the program.

In order to take part in the respite program, I had to attend a seminar, which taught me how to be my own vendor for respite services. I would need to keep records for tax purposes. Traci, or any family member caring for Giovanni as a respite caregiver, would be my employee and I would have to pay payroll taxes at the end of the year.

I suppose I ended up saving the taxpayers some money since I only used 24 hours in respite care services during the seven months that I was a vendor in 2008. Even though I was actually paying Traci for providing care for Giovanni, I still felt guilty asking her to do it for so many hours since she had a toddler of her own.

On the other hand, I took full advantage of the allowance I was given for diapers for Giovanni. Since he was not able to stand on his own, and was only walking short distances with assistance, I knew it would be awhile before he was potty trained. I found that I saved the taxpayers money in this area also as I generally only spent about 25% of what was allotted to me.

Unlike some public agencies, I did not spend the other 75% of the money just to get it in Giovanni's budget the next year.

I was thankful for any assistance that the State could provide since I received nothing from Jude except for the legally required child support.

The concern that I had with respite, however, was that I did want to entrust Giovanni's care to a stranger. Luckily, the program provided the option of "hiring" a family member to provide Giovanni's respite care. This way I was able to have Traci take care of Giovanni so that I truly was able to relax when I did take some time to myself.

I found that I did not need to use the respite program as much as I thought that I would since Giovanni was in school for eight hours a week. With both boys in school, I finally had a few hours truly to myself. Being all alone was so unusual for me that I initially found it difficult to relax. Soon I adjusted and learned to enjoy those hours a week that I had to myself.

Actually, it turned out that I only had about four hours to myself since my schedule for 2008 required me to work two twelve-hour days. I worked Wednesdays and Fridays from 8:00 a.m. until 8:00 p.m. I was fortunate that my parents were willing to drive out to Woodland once a week to care for the boys on Wednesdays. Traci cared for the boys on Fridays.

As I have stated before, my family really did stick together and helped each other. On the other hand, Jude and his family became more and more emotionally distant from the boys, since they only cared for them when it was convenient. Furthermore, no one in Jude's family appeared comfortable with Giovanni, so they were usually only willing to care for Kenneth.

It was too bad that Jude's family were not interested enough to call and inquire about Giovanni. When he started special day school, he started to improve with his motor skills. He was obviously happy to be around other children. Unlike Kenneth, he did not appear to have attachment issues and had no difficulty in being away from me for several hours a day.

With Giovanni in school, I became excited at the prospect of witnessing growth in his motor and cognitive abilities as he was being motivated by his classmates.

Chapter 19

Thankfully, Giovanni made the transition to school without much difficulty. In fact, it was probably more of an adjustment for me than for him. He really thrived among the other children. I probably would have been more stressed if Giovanni was required to ride the bus to school. However, the school was one block away from our home, so I could walk Giovanni to school and drop him off myself.

Although Giovanni appeared content among his peers, I also noticed that he was not as interactive as I had hoped. I believe this was due to his high dosage of Lamictal. Before the end of his first semester, he was up to an all time high of 275 mg a day. The doctor really did not want to increase it much more unless it was an emergency because he was on such a high dose. However, I was beginning to notice that the myoclonus, or "sparks" were not much affected by the medication. Therefore, I assumed that Giovanni was destined to have myoclonus forever, regardless of the medication. As a result, I lowered his dose by 25 mg in order to balance the awful side effects.

Another concern I had during Giovanni's first semester was that he was the most intensive child in the class. He was the only child who was non-ambulatory, which meant he needed someone to care for him constantly. Being unable to walk, combined with his visual impairment and speech delays, required him to have a one-on-one aide.

Fortunately, Giovanni's teacher Belinda agreed that he would benefit from an aide, so she requested one from the school district. I also followed up with a letter of my own to request the aide since Belinda indicated that the district might have a quicker response to a parent. As it turned out, I did not need to worry, as Belinda's request was approved and an aide was assigned to Giovanni.

I believed that an aide for Giovanni would benefit everyone. Not only would Giovanni get the attention he needed, but the other children would receive more attention from the other teachers in the classroom.

In addition to an aide, Giovanni was assigned a vision therapist for consultation. Collette came to Giovanni's class to conduct an assessment and to provide him with some stimulating toys. Collette's evaluation showed that Giovanni's vision had improved over time. The biggest change we noticed was the increase in the length of time that Giovanni exhibited vision. We could tell that he had vision based primarily on his attitude. He was happy and engaged with his environment when he did have vision. When his vision "turned off," he became agitated and withdrawn. Physically, he even appeared "blind" as his eyes showed no focus.

Giovanni seemed to have a preference for the color green, although he did respond favorably to any bright color. He was attracted to light, which would sometimes become a distraction for him. Over time, the novelty of the lights and colors would wear off and he would not be so distracted. Finally, his visual motor skills were delayed as sight and touch occurred as separate functions.

Giovanni reacted positively to Collette, so I hoped that this would translate into his brain becoming more focused on acquiring visual skills.

Overall, the school environment had a positive impact on Giovanni that first semester. The only disappointment was his continued episodes of vomiting every two weeks, which I correlated with the increase in the medication.

Just when I was beginning to accept Giovanni's vomiting episodes as "normal", there was one that caused me great distress. After vomiting several times, over several hours, Giovanni began vomiting blood. I drove him to the clinic to see his pediatrician. I was in tears because he was vomiting blood in the waiting room. I was imagining some awful condition in which Giovanni was bleeding internally.

It turned out that Giovanni was suffering from a Mallory-Weiss tear. The condition was caused by a tear in the mucous membrane of the esophagus, where it connects to the stomach. It was caused by forceful vomiting. The doctor said it would heal on its own within ten days. Even the relatively small amount of blood that Giovanni coughed up, it appeared to be worse than it really was.

One of the emotional setbacks I experienced during this time was accepting the diagnosis of "mental retardation", which was the label that the school psychologist attributed to Giovanni. I did not like the term because "retardation" sounded negative to me. However, "retardation" actually means that there is a slowness or delay in academic progress. It did not necessarily have to mean a lower-than-average IQ.

I was initially upset with the label because of the negative associations I had with it. However, I had to consider the testing process used to assess Giovanni. Giovanni had a visual impairment and expressive speech delays, which obviously would cause him difficulty in any test. Most tests that I have seen, and the tests that were given to Giovanni, did not specifically address his vision issues. Consequently, traditional testing would be highly inaccurate.

I am not sure how anyone could take tests results seriously when a visual impairment strongly affects the results. I had accepted nearly every label given to Giovanni, but I would not accept this one – at least literally. Giovanni's social worker advised me that I could decline to accept this label, but that Giovanni's extended services through the regional center could be affected. It was easier to assign him this "catch-all" label now rather than try to reapply for the services later.

I cried on my friend Lisa's shoulder for a few minutes. Then I decided that I would not allow a label to affect me in this way. After all, this would not be the first label inaccurately attributed to Giovanni.

Giovanni progressed well in school through the spring. He especially enjoyed being outside. Since the special day school was less than a year old, the equipment in the yard was new and there was a nice paved path that circled the equipment. Giovanni enjoyed being wheeled around in his wheelchair.

As the school year progressed, Giovanni's aide, Monica, would get him out of his wheelchair and hold his hands so that he could practice walking. Giovanni was also using a walker at home to help develop his leg muscles. I was happy that he was at least able to stand for a couple of hours. I was excited he was showing an interest in walking, which was nearly always backwards unless someone held on to his hands and assisted his forward movement.

His teacher and aide noticed that Giovanni was moving a lot more on his stomach when he was on the floor. This was an improvement since he usually did not like to be on his stomach because of his sensory issues. I saw this as progress to Giovanni overcoming some of his sensory integration issues.

Another encouraging incident happened during one of Giovanni's episodes of vomiting. One morning, after eating his breakfast and taking his medication, he started vomiting and fell asleep. He awoke several hours later, apparently feeling fine. What was different this time was that there were no "precursor seizures" before the episode. Here was an indication that perhaps his epilepsy was truly under control.

I realized that the remedies that Dr. Kathryn Picoulin had given to Giovanni were really working. His partial seizures had disappeared. However, he was still having "sparks" which Dr. Picoulin believed were not actual seizures. She continued to investigate possible remedies for his myoclonus.

During the spring, Jude contacted me to let me know that he was planning a vacation to Europe. He planned to leave mid-June and return in mid-July. I was disappointed, to say the least, that he intended to leave the country the week after Kenneth got out of school. Furthermore, he intended to be gone for almost a third of the summer.

I anticipated that Kenneth would be disappointed also, since summer time was the only time that Kenneth could spend more than a few hours or a night with his father. Because of Jude's shift work, he did not usually have weekends off to spend with the boys. When Jude did have his days off during the week, he rarely came to visit the boys because it was "too far away."

If Jude was going to take a vacation in the summer, I was supportive of that. However, I believed he should have chosen a destination where he could have taken Kenneth. By now I would not expect Jude to ask to do anything special with Giovanni.

The one time that Jude saw Giovanni in the spring was when Giovanni was sick. We met in Fairfield for a short visit since Jude had "work stuff" that prevented him from taking Kenneth overnight. Jude arrived on his motorcycle and was not talkative during lunch. Although he saw that Giovanni was clearly not feeling well, he did not ask about him at all, nor did he offer to help with feeding him. In fact, he barely even spoke to Kenneth.

It seemed to me that the entire visit was really a waste of time. Jude acted as if he did not really want to be there. Perhaps he was doing it because he felt obligated, since he hardly spent any time with Kenneth over the prior four months. I told him that he was welcome to visit Giovanni at his neurology appointment in San Francisco the following week. I figured that Giovanni would be feeling better by then.

Indeed, Giovanni was feeling better for his appointment. My parents accompanied me again so that I would not have to travel alone. Again, Jude did not attend although it was on his day off.

Dr. Khan was pleased with Giovanni's progress since his last visit. I was excited as I shared with Dr. Khan that Giovanni was more willing to take steps with his walker. He also was willing to stand and walk with assistance. Giovanni's feet were overpronated and externally rotated in their positioning, so the orthotics were having a positive effect on his walking as they kept his feet straight. His muscle tone had improved since the last visit.

As Dr. Khan examined his vision, he noticed that Giovanni was making better eye contact than in prior visits, and was tracking objects. His speech had improved also as he was starting to say "Mama" and "I love you" and was making new guttural sounds. Although he still was lacking in his fine motor skills, Dr. Khan was pleased that he was scooping and grasping. His oral-motor defensiveness had improved since he was now helping to feed himself with a spoon. He was also eating more of a variety of foods, like bananas and cookies (gluten-free), to which he used to have an aversion.

As for his medication, Dr. Khan believed that he had acceptable seizure control with the Lamictal at 250 mg a day. Dr. Khan believed at this point that the "startles" or "sparks" might be stimulus sensitive myolonic seizures. He agreed with me that we did not need to add more medication.

Since my father was always trying to find answers to explain Giovanni's condition, he asked Dr. Khan why Kaiser was not trying any of the new medical procedures used at Stanford Children's Hospital. Dr. Khan noted that Kaiser is doing "what ever is standard of care and considered mainstream." He added that, "There may be research into new and emerging therapies and we could consider them when they become standard of care."

I wondered what "mainstream" really meant and who or what agency determined that a therapy was mainstream. I thought back to when Giovanni was in the hospital after he was born, and how the doctors could not come to a consensus of what was going on with Giovanni. How could any one come to a consensus of what was mainstream? I suppose it was some government agency that needed to give their blessing that a medication or therapy was mainstream in order for the established medical community to accept it as an alternative.

The process of testing new medications and therapies and having them accepted as mainstream might take years. If I did not want Giovanni to wait years for results, I would have to continue to be aggressive in searching out alternatives on my own. I would also have to pay for them on my own since Jude showed no interest for anything beyond traditional therapies covered by insurance.

One of the alternatives that I checked was the research being conducted at the University of California at Davis Mind Institute. This organization was at the forefront in conducting research into the brain. Unfortunately, Giovanni had such a unique set of circumstances with his condition that he did not qualify for study. Most of the studies during that time were focused on autism.

I was not discouraged just because there appeared to be no mainstream therapies for Giovanni to try. I continued to do what I could at home to encourage Giovanni's physical, spiritual, and mental growth. On the days that I worked, I was confident that Giovanni was being challenged by my family while they were taking care of him.

When my parents cared for the boys, they made sure that Giovanni stood for awhile in his walker. This helped him to build up muscle strength. My dad also played many cause-and-effect games that Giovanni really liked. Any time Giovanni heard "one, two, three," he anticipated some type of horseplay with my dad. He also loved the alphabet song. When he was happy and content in his environment, he would sit with one leg crossed over the other. Even though Giovanni could not speak clearly, he communicated well through body language.

When Traci cared for the boys, she made sure that Giovanni did a lot of walking. She usually did not have the walker at her house when she babysat for the boys, so Giovanni did a lot of walking by holding her hands.

Giovanni appeared to be more motivated to do physical work for my mom and for Traci than for me. The biggest motivator of all was his brother Kenneth.

Giovanni would smile from ear to ear when he heard his brother in the room. He was so excited every time Kenneth would show him affection. As Kenneth got older, he was even more patient and understanding with Giovanni's needs than he was when he was younger. I would tell Kenneth how proud I was because he was such a great big brother.

Kenneth was a testament to how accepting and non-judgmental a child could be. One day he overheard me talking to my mom on the phone. I was telling her that I felt sorry for Kenneth because he did not have a typical little brother that he could play with. Kenneth later told me not to feel sorry for him because he loves Giovanni, "Just the way he is."

Giovanni's cousin Marissa was also a powerful motivating force in Giovanni's life. Although she was sixteen months younger than Giovanni, she always took the role of the protective big sister. She had a keen understanding of Giovanni's limitations and was totally accepting of him. She showed patience beyond her years.

With all of the family support, and now support from the school system, Giovanni was making gains in his development. Despite his high levels of medication and periodic episodes of vomiting, Giovanni still made progress with some of his educational goals the first semester. When given the opportunity, Giovanni was beginning to make choices. He was also using new sounds to communicate.

One of the ways that Jane, the speech-language pathologist, tried to get Giovanni to communicate was by identifying body parts. He was cooperative in working hand-over-hand with Jane to identify his body parts. Giovanni declined to cooperate when Jane asked him to identify his own body parts. He continued to show a preference to identify my body parts rather than his own.

This led me to question just how much vision Giovanni truly had. This child could correctly identify my eyes, nose, mouth, ears, head, chin, forehead, and hair. Either Giovanni had some vision to be able to see where these parts were located, or he was incredibly adept at locating the different body parts based on their relative location to my voice.

At any rate, I was excited that he was not only able to follow commands to find the body parts, but he actually knew many of them, which I believed to be a sign of intelligence. Perhaps it was for sensory reasons that he did not want to touch his own body.

Consequently, I used Giovanni's ability to touch my nose as a signal for indicating a choice. I would confirm his need by saying, "Touch my nose if you're hungry," or, "Touch my nose if you want a bath." I would give him a few seconds to respond. He would respond by touching my nose when he heard the choice that he wanted.

The fact that Giovanni was able to understand what I was telling him just proved that his receptive speech abilities were intact. I have no doubt that his delays with expressive speech were causing him frustration.

While Giovanni became periodically frustrated with his difficulty to express himself with words, I became frustrated with his father's inability to use words to communicate with me. Most of the communication that existed between Jude and me were the text messages that we exchanged.

After Kenneth finished school in June, he was looking forward to visiting with his father. However, after only one weekend of visitation, Jude sent me a message that he would be on his vacation from June 19 until July 10. I just could not comprehend a parent giving priority to his own needs and desires over the needs of his children. Kenneth was out of school in the summer and this would be the best time for him and Jude to spend time together. He never told me how to contact him in the event of an emergency with the children and avoided all my texts on the subject.

He did text that his cell phone would be with him and that Kenneth could call him if he wanted to.

In order to help Kenneth get over his disappointment at not being able visit with his father, I signed him up for science camp for a week in June. He really enjoyed the "camp", which was actually just during the day. He liked it, so I signed him up for another camp the following week. By the end of the third week, Kenneth had decided that he really enjoyed the camp so much that he wanted to attend camp the third week.

The third camp was scheduled for the week after Jude returned from Europe. Kenneth was actually disappointed that his dad was returning and interfering with his new summer plans. During one of Jude's rare phone calls during his vacation, he agreed to allow Kenneth to attend the third week of camp.

Giovanni was busy that month with education of his own. He was able to attend summer school for a month. The goal of summer school for the special pre-school was to keep the children progressing forward with their skills. Giovanni enjoyed his month in pre-school.

At least Kenneth had a family vacation to look forward to with Jude and his family. Near the end of July, Jude began exchanging messages with me about what to pack for Kenneth for their family vacation to Virginia. As usual, there was no mention about Giovanni.

Since I knew that Jude's girlfriend Emma would be going on vacation with the family, it appeared to me that the relationship was probably serious. I also knew that Kenneth liked her. Jude never made any comment about whether Emma was curious or wanted to meet Giovanni.

Knowing Jude would never arrange a meeting, I offered to introduce Emma to Giovanni if she was interested. I did not expect any response, but at least I had placed the offer on the table. After all, if this relationship was serious, it was a possibility that Emma would be my children's stepmother. I at least wanted her to know Giovanni. Perhaps she would react opposite of Jude's family and actually embrace Kenneth's brother as she embraced Kenneth.

Much to my surprise, Jude sent a text message back to me indicating, "It would be okay" for Emma to meet Giovanni sometime. The response itself was a shock, though I hardly expected Jude to follow through with it.

At least Emma was interested in meeting Giovanni. The next day when I was in Fairfield, I offered to stop by the family home so that Olivia could visit with Giovanni. She declined because she was too busy packing. I had to assume that if visiting her nephew was a priority, she would stop packing for just a few minutes so she could spend time with him.

Likewise, two days later, when I was again in Fairfield, I asked both Diana and Olivia if they wanted me to stop by with Giovanni. I really was not trying to be pushy. I merely wanted to give Jude's family every opportunity to visit with both their nephews, since distance was the reason they would give for not being able to visit. Since I was in town, it did not require them to sacrifice any time or effort to drive anywhere to see them. Olivia never answered the text message. Diana sent a message that she was working.

A couple of weeks later I found out that Diana had actually left the state to get married. I found this out only after Kenneth returned from vacation. He told me that Diana "...got married and moved away." She did not attend the family vacation. I was so shocked, I did not actually believe Kenneth when he told me. I asked him if he was telling a "tall tale." He said, "No, ask Daddy." Indeed, Diana had been married.

I found it ironic that after Diana made a big deal about buying special clothes for Kenneth to attend Esther's funeral and giving him a special place in the ceremony at her grandmother's service, that she did not even invite him to her wedding.

For Kenneth's part, he did not seem too concerned. When Jude returned Kenneth to me after their vacation, Kenneth was happy to be home. Surprisingly, he also brought along Emma for the ride. I was able to meet Emma and she held Giovanni. Considering she was a stranger, Giovanni reacted positively to her as she held him.

On the other hand, when Jude held him, he started squirming around and trying to get away. I felt that right there Giovanni was making his statement about how he felt about his father. He even felt more comfortable with a complete stranger than with his own father.

Even though Giovanni did not seem to care about his father's sudden interest in him, it did seem to have a positive effect on Kenneth. I believed that Kenneth was perceptive enough to realize that this sudden act of affection was probably just for appearances to impress his girlfriend. This was the first time in months that Jude attempted to show Giovanni any attention. It would also be the last time for at least several months.

Jude did not make any extra attempts during the summer to see either of the boys. Despite all of his prior claims of wanting to spend the day with Giovanni to get to know him better, Jude did not attempt to arrange a day to do so. He did not go out of his way for Kenneth either. He only visited with him on what I assumed were his days off. I say "assume" because Jude was always very vague about his work schedule. With his patterns of information and disinformation, one would assume he was working every day of the week.

When the boys started school again in late August, Jude reverted to his old habits of only calling three or four times during the week to check on Kenneth. He did not attend Kenneth's back-to-school night.

Remembering Jude's claim earlier in the year of not helping with paying for Giovanni's party because he "...didn't get to help plan it," I called Jude early in the fall to start planning for Kenneth's birthday party in October.

Meanwhile, I was becoming extremely frustrated with Giovanni's bi-monthly episodes of vomiting. I am sure he was frustrated also. One day, Giovanni became very defiant when taking his medication, and he spit out one of his tablets. He was becoming increasingly upset with his medication. I wondered if, through his behavior, he was trying to tell me something. Maybe he knew that he did not need such a high dose of medication. I decided to listen to him. I decided to eliminate half of one tablet, which was equal to slightly more than 12 mg.

Amazingly, Giovanni seemed to be happy with that decision, and became much more willing to take his medication. Then, about two weeks later, he decided to spit out a half tablet. I listened to his intuition again and decided not to give him that tablet. I kept him under close observation, watching for any seizures. There were no seizures but the episodes of myoclonic "sparks" continued, with no change on the frequency or severity. In other words, the Lamictal had no effect one way or the other on the myoclonus.

Sure enough, about two weeks later, he spit out the equivalent of about 12 mg of Lamictal. Consequently, I weaned him again. During this time, I also consulted with the neurologist. Deborah told me that, to be safe and avoid major withdrawal symptoms, Giovanni could be weaned by one-half of a tablet, or about 12 ½ mg, every two weeks.

It was about every two weeks that Giovanni would spit out his Lamictal and wean himself off the medication at about 12 mg each time. Ironically, the frequency of the vomiting episodes, which had been occurring every two weeks prior to his withdrawal, suddenly decreased. There was an obvious correlation between the dosage of Lamictal and the frequency of vomiting.

When we attended our family reunion in September, people that remembered how sick he was two years prior made comments how much healthier and alert he appeared to be.

As October approached, I had not heard from Jude as to whether he was willing to help with Kenneth's party. I made plans without him. I let him know when and where it would be and figured that Kenneth would be happy if he just showed up. I sent invitations to Jude's family. Jude's father had another commitment and could not come. Diana and her new husband had other plans also. When Diana got married and moved out of the family home, Olivia also moved out of the family home and purchased a condominium.

Kenneth was excited when Jude arrived at the party with Olivia in her new car. Jude acted like a guest at the party. He came and observed the children play and he talked to me, mostly about his life and all the stressors going on. I felt like he was "crying on my shoulder" like he did when we were married. However, we were not married and it was a little awkward being in the position of confidant again.

Jude did not help with the set up or the clean up. He did not offer to help pay for his son's party. When I brought up the subject, he refused to help pay. He claimed that he "...paid for Kenneth's vaca-tion. That should be enough." I was not going to make an issue of it at Kenneth's party. It was just another sad situation that Kenneth's father was not willing to take an active role in special events and that vacations were considered fulfilled obligations.

Jude's refusal to help with Kenneth's party was not the big shock of the day. The big shock was when Jude admitted to me that he had been off work since June, and that he had just returned to work in October. Additionally, he admitted that his European vacation "fell through" and he never went on vacation.

Again, I cannot imagine why Jude would volunteer to tell me this information unless he believed I would find out in some other way. For a man who was so concerned with appearances, I wondered if Jude even realized how this made him look as a father, that being he spent the entire summer, and beyond, at home without any attempt to see his children?

Although Jude never technically lied, I believed he was dishonest in leading Kenneth and me to believe that he was on vacation and was working four days a week. I had to wonder what he did to occupy all of his time if he was not working. He certainly was not calling Kenneth any more frequently than he ever did. Maybe he was mired in his own depression and did not want Kenneth to witness it.

In a later conversation, Jude explained that he needed to work on his own health and well-being before he could care for his children. That attitude was so frustrating to me. How nice it must have been to be able to "go into hiding" for several months and focus solely on self-improvement, while I did not have that opportunity, since I had two young children that relied solely on me to care for them.

I understood depression. I also understood anger, frustration, regret, and many other emotions. However, as a parent, I believed I needed to address my emotions and find healthy ways to deal with them. Jude, on the other hand, never really took the responsibility for raising children. His first priority was, and always has been, to take care of himself first. Jude's actions over that summer only highlighted his true character.

As I listened to Jude's long story, which sounded like an attempt to gain my sympathy, I could only nod and respond politely. Perhaps Jude had intentionally told me the entire story at the party because he knew that I could not be confrontational in front of the children or other family. However, that would mean that Jude actually had the capacity to plan, which I had never known him to do.

Jude was so engaged in talking to me, that he hardly even acknowledged the boys. He saw Giovanni playing with Traci and remarked that he looked "good" and he seemed happy. He visited with Kenneth for a few minutes and watched him open presents. Overall, I believed that Jude spoke to me more than he visited with Kenneth.

At the party, I gave Jude two weeks notice about Kenneth's parent-teacher conference that I intentionally scheduled on his day off. Jude did not attend that meeting. He never gave me, or Kenneth, any reason for not coming to any meetings. This was usual behavior for Jude where Giovanni was concerned, but Kenneth was the son he favored. I was sad because Kenneth saw how little Jude valued Kenneth's school activities.

Even though Jude did not attend Kenneth's meeting, he did call to say that he wanted to visit Giovanni in his class. I nearly fell over when I heard that! Truthfully, I did not believe that it would actually happen. I anticipated that some personal issue would arise to interfere with Jude actually coming to see Giovanni. However, Jude could at least ease his conscience because he could say that he "offered."

Giovanni's teacher appeared eager to meet Giovanni's father. Giovanni had been in school for almost a year and Jude had never visited the class or attended any of the meetings or assessments. This was the opportunity for Jude to stand up and claim to be "dad" to Giovanni.

Jude always tried to avoid making firm commitments because he did not want to be held accountable when he failed to follow through on them. After nearly four years, Jude had finally committed to a specific time and day to devote solely to Giovanni.

If there was ever any chance of Jude making any kind of sacrifice of time and effort for Giovanni, this would be it.

The day before he was to come to Giovanni's class, Jude called to claim that he was sick and would have to reschedule. Perhaps he really was sick. In light of his dishonesty regarding his availability to the boys the past summer, I was inclined not to believe him. Having been married to him, I knew that he could have had anything from a small stomachache to a major flu. At any rate, I really did not care how sick he was. How could I care if Jude was sick when he disappeared whenever his children were sick?

I did not even concern myself with any possibility that he would "reschedule" because I did not believe it ever would happen. It never has.

During the fall, Traci decided to retire from full time employment in order to stay home and raise her daughter. This also benefited me, as she became a primary caregiver to the boys. She never asked for monetary reimbursement. I repaid her by babysitting my niece so that Traci could have time to do things around the house or attend meetings for her home-based business.

Jude benefited from this arrangement as well, since he did not have to pay for childcare. It would have been nice had he at least thanked Traci, and the rest of my family, for caring for his children when he failed to provide for their care.

Even though Jude failed to take advantage of his chance to see Giovanni, at least Olivia and Grandpa Jude were able to visit with him the week of Thanksgiving. Because of Olivia's work schedule, she was only able to celebrate Thanksgiving the day after. This worked out perfectly for me as I had to work that day. The boys spent the day with Olivia, Grandpa Jude, and their friend Betsy. I believed they also visited with Diana and her husband, but they did not spend much time with them.

I was sure that Jude's family was surprised at how much Giovanni had grown and changed. In fact, Giovanni had withdrawn himself, with my help, off the Lamictal to the level of 187 mg. This was the lowest level of medication that he had ever had. Although there was no sign of seizures, there was still no observable change in the frequency of his "sparks". More importantly, Giovanni had set a record in not having a vomiting episode in over a month. It appeared the current level of his dosage was adequate for him.

In addition, Giovanni was more willing to swallow his Lamictal at the lower dosage. He was cooperative in taking the dose when I mixed it with his cereal.

As a result of having lower levels of medication affecting his brain, Giovanni was improving in all areas during his first semester. He was getting into a crawling position and pushing himself up with his arms. He was able to walk twenty-five steps or more, in a straight line, if someone held his hands in front. He assisted in dressing himself by putting up his arms and putting his legs through his pants. He was also beginning to help feed himself, although he did this more for his teachers at school than for me at home. His diet had more variety as he had become more adept at chewing and more desensitized to the temperature of his food.

I was excited that he was not so sensitive to temperature. He drank cold water and he really enjoyed whipped cream. He appeared to have outgrown many of his tactile sensitivities from when he was younger. My focus at this time was to try and motivate Giovanni to drink from a straw. Unfortunately, he was not interested.

Giovanni was communicating more frequently with touching my nose to indicate his needs. He was reacting more quickly than he used to. I was just starting to potty-train him and he was a more willing participant than Kenneth ever was.

Giovanni was assigned a new physical therapist named Rika who worked with him in the classroom. Sometimes she would have therapy sessions with him at our home. Giovanni responded very positively to Rika. She was exuberant and made lots of different sounds and noises that Giovanni responded to. She focused on training him in transitional movements from his back to a seated position. She also tried to motivate him to get into a crawling position and propel himself forward. He was not ready for that yet. Rika played with Giovanni and helped him improve his fine motor skills with a variety of toys.

As his Lamictal levels decreased, it appeared that his vision was getting better. At any rate, it was more obvious when Giovanni had vision and when he did not. He actually would make eye contact and smile at people. Granted, he still could not speak clearly to say what he was seeing, but whether it was vague shapes or sharp details, it did not seem to matter to him. He was excited just to have his vision.

Dr. Khan had left Kaiser and Dr. Graff had assumed his caseload. Even his new neurologist was pleased with his progress when she saw him in December. I liked Dr. Shayne and Dr. Khan, and I really liked Dr. Graff. Giovanni liked her also and was very active for her during the visit. However, he did not have his vision that day and he did not track objects. Dr. Graff was pleased with his slow but steady progress in all areas.

The primary topic of discussion at this appointment was Giovanni's mycolonus. Since Giovanni was almost four years old, we both felt it was time for him to have an EEG, in order to determine whether his "sparks" were epileptic or non-epileptic myoclonus.

Dr. Graff scheduled Giovanni for a 24-hour EEG during the first week of January 2009. It was about this time that I had decided to write this book about Giovanni. I determined that I would probably cover his life up to his fourth birthday in January.

Giovanni's story began with his birth in January 2005. He had grown and developed slowly and steadily over his first four years. Undoubtedly, he would continue to develop at his own rate. As he did so, I believed he would continue to confound the medical establishment. Four years appeared to me to be a nice round number at which to end the book.

However, just as I was settling into the belief in "slow but steady" progress, events occurred during the first half of 2009 that would drastically change that belief.

Chapter 20

As much as I dreaded the prospect of spending a night in San Francisco, I believed that I was mentally prepared to take Giovanni in for his EEG. My dad came with Giovanni and me to be there for support. Giovanni and I had been through the EEG process twice before since his hospital release. I knew it would be a stressful twenty-four hours.

We arrived at Kaiser just before 10:00 a.m. Giovanni was in a good mood when we arrived. However, that mood changed as the technician attached the electrodes. Giovanni still had sensitivity in his head and did not like anyone to touch him there. He moved around so much, that I had to physically hold him to keep him calm. The entire process was draining for me.

After the EEG began, I was told that Giovanni needed to remain on his back. He also could not do his traditional "bouncing around" since it could tear out the electrodes. There was a television in the room, presumably for the patient to pass the time.

In fact, the technician told me that many older children considered the EEG as a "mini-vacation" since they could spend all day in bed, watching television, or playing videogames. Some patients who had seizures that were induced by stress would actually not have seizures because their EEG was stress-free.

This was not the case for Giovanni.

Because of his visual impairment, he was not able to "watch" television, although at times I believed he was attracted to the movement and colors. He did not have the vision or the motor skills to play video games. His main method of play was through movement, which was severely inhibited.

Giovanni was very unhappy, uncomfortable, and agitated. Thankfully, my father was there to help keep him occupied.

This EEG was not just a matter of keeping Giovanni calm for twenty-four hours. Along with the electrodes to monitor brain activity, there was also a video monitor set up to view Giovanni. I had to monitor his myoclonus. Every time he had a "spark," I had to press a button so that it would be recorded on the video for the neurologist to review.

Knowing that this EEG would be stressful for me, I intentionally made the appointment on Jude's day off. I figured that if he could drive twenty minutes to San Francisco to help for a few hours, this would give my father and me some "downtime" during the day, since I anticipated being up nearly all night.

Jude agreed, since he was working dayshift, he would be able to come up "early" for the EEG. He said he would arrive around 11:00 a.m. and stay until later in the evening. Since San Francisco was so close to his home, he could stay late before he had to go home and get ready for work the next day.

Jude had made this commitment to me about a week before the EEG. I remembered having the conversation with Jude because I had to explain the difference between an IEP and an EEG. He was confused as to what it was he was attending.

It was also only the second time in my recent memory that Jude actually made a commitment to do something.

Because of his past broken commitment, I was skeptical that he would show up. Though I did consider this could be an exception because this was a major procedure that Giovanni was undergoing and I thought that Jude might have finally realized that he needed to be there for something for his son.

As my father and I tried to keep Giovanni calm during the day, 11:00 a.m. came and went. Several hours passed and I had not heard a word from Jude. I sent him text messages that went unanswered.

He called at 3:00 p.m. to say that he was "wiped out" and would be on the way "shortly."

He arrived just before 6:00p.m. He stared at Giovanni, but asked no questions about him. He talked to my father about what was going on at work. He did not even stay around long enough for me to leave the building for a cup of coffee or dinner. Within an hour, Jude claimed that he had to leave "to get ready for work tomorrow."

I am not sure why Jude even bothered to show up. He was seven hours late, showed no interest in Giovanni, and was absolutely no help to me or my dad in giving us a break from monitoring Giovanni.

Giovanni heard Jude's voice, but exhibited no interest or excitement when he was in the room. In contrast, when my father would speak to him, he would smile and react positively, even when he was not feeling physically comfortable.

Giovanni had been confined to bed for over twelve hours by the time it was late enough to try to sleep. Giovanni drifted in and out of sleep. I hardly slept because I was lying right next to him in the hospital bed. My dad hardly slept because he was on a chair.

By the morning, everyone was tired and Giovanni had become highly agitated. His myoclonus was apparently affected quite a bit by the environment, as episodes of "sparking" had become more frequent by morning.

By the time Dr. Graff arrived mid-morning to read the EEG, Giovanni had 19 recorded episodes of myoclonus. Dr. Graff said that Giovanni's myoclonus "...appeared to be" seizure activity. She described that the video showed "a child with almost a flexion spasm, in which arms go up and come inward slightly, his body crunches slightly, lasting about one or two seconds." Additionally, she noted that his spike-wave pattern indicated a genetic susceptibility to seizures. Her recommendation was to slowly increase his Lamictal dose from 187 mg, back to his previous prescribed dose of at least 250mg.

Although I was not entirely surprised by this diagnosis, I was not happy about it. Increasing Giovanni's medication would undoubtedly increase his episodes of stomach upset and vomiting. Furthermore, there was no guarantee that the increase in the medication would have any effect on the myoclonus, especially if this condition was not actually epilepsy.

As we got on the elevator, Giovanni perked up. He listened to the sound of the elevator as we descended. As the doors opened in the lobby, he started grinning, giggling, and said "home." He was so happy to move around again.

While on the way home, Giovanni suffered a partial seizure. I had not witnessed this seizure type in almost 16 months. He had ten seizures of this type over the following week. I knew that he had exactly ten seizures since I had started keeping a seizure journal again. I had no doubt that these seizures were induced by the extreme physical stress to his central nervous system caused by the EEG.

Although I began increasing Giovanni's Lamictal dose immediately after the EEG, I could only increase the dose approximately 12mg per week. The seizures Giovanni had that first week after the EEG could not have been controlled so quickly with such a small dose increase of medication. The occurrence of these seizures stopped as inexplicably as they began. I am convinced that the Lamictal dose played no role in controlling these particular seizures.

Giovanni's fourth birthday was several days after the EEG. He exhibited some seizures and quite a bit of myclonus during that day. We had a family dinner at my parents' house. I had grown tired of trying to organize any activities with Jude's family since they seemed to always be so busy.

I was cynical over the treatment of Giovanni by Jude's family and was not surprised when evening came and no one from Jude's family called to wish Giovanni a "Happy Birthday." Granted, Giovanni probably did not even notice or care since he was not a big part of that family. Kenneth, though, certainly would notice an absence of a phone call since Jude's family always called him on his birthday.

Jude, though out of character, did call that night and asked to speak to Giovanni. He had only asked on one other occasion for me to put Giovanni on the phone. When I put the phone to Giovanni's ear, he paused. Within about thirty seconds, he was pushing the phone away and posing as if he was going to have a seizure. I took the phone and told Jude that Giovanni did not want to listen on the phone right now as he was going to have a seizure.

Giovanni rolled up his eyes and had a very odd-looking myoclonic "spark." It did not even look real to me. When I hung up the phone, he started to smile and giggle. I looked right at him and asked him if he had a seizure to "fake out" his dad. He looked right at me, smiled, and started bouncing back and forth, which was his answer for "yes."

Kenneth witnessed all this and thought it was funny that Giovanni faked a seizure to get off the phone with their dad. When I told Jude about this the next day, he refused to believe that Giovanni had the intelligence or the desire to be able to "fake" a seizure to get what he wanted. Giovanni was certainly acting like a typical four-year-old in his sneaky behavior and using his disability to play on sympathy to get his way.

Giovanni had several more seizures over the next few days. They were obvious non-voluntary seizures, and not the voluntary type that caused him to laugh and giggle.

Dr. Graff agreed that the stress caused by the EEG could have caused the seizures. She believed that it could take up to a week or ten days for Giovanni's body to recover from the stress. Sure enough, within seven days, the seizures had stopped. Furthermore, they ceased immediately. I did not believe that the slight increase in his Lamictal that particular week could have had such a dramatic effect. Therefore, I did not believe that the decrease in his Lamictal was the cause of the seizures that week.

Nevertheless, I continued to increase the Lamictal at 12mg per week.

Just as I suspected, as soon as Giovanni's Lamictal levels increased above about 200mg, he started having vomiting episodes again. I was frustrated since I now knew that the vomiting was a side effect of the Lamictal. Due to Giovanni's reaction after the EEG, I anticipated that the myoclonus was a condition that he was going to have to live with for the rest of his life.

Dr. Kathryn Picoulin was still trying to figure out the origin of the myoclonus. We believed that the major seizures Giovanni had in the past had been cured when the chicken pox virus had been removed from his body.

Consequently, he would be destined to be on high dosages of medication to try to control the myoclonic "seizures." In addition, the Lamictal affected his concentration and he would have to miss school periodically for the several hours that each vomiting episode would last.

At the end of February, both boys and I became sick with a severe cold. Kenneth had it the worst, a high fever that spiked at 104 degrees. Yet, even as sick as he was, he tried to play games. Once, he rolled his eyes back and pretended to be "unresponsive." When he saw my reaction, thinking he was having a fever-induced seizure, he looked at me, laughed, and between coughs, he said, "I'm just playing, Mom."

Meanwhile, Giovanni's temperature remained normal as he spent most of his illness just sleeping. I had to wake him periodically to feed him. Also of note was that as sick as Giovanni was, he exhibited no precursor seizures.

As difficult as it was to be ill with two ill children, I managed to handle things by myself. I left messages for Jude, which went unanswered. Jude's intent may have been to avoid the stressful and unpleasant tasks associated with parenting. What he may not have realized, was that Kenneth was witnessing how Jude prioritized his children in his life.

If a parent cannot even be present to offer comfort to his sick child, or sick children in this case, than how can the children ever grow up to have any respect for that parent?

After Giovanni recovered from his illness, my father suggested I take him to my parents' chiropractor, Dr. Alex Day. My father reminded me of early childhood asthma that both my brother and I experienced and of the immediate correction that resulted from spinal manipulation. I was reluctant at first, primarily because Giovanni was so young and had sensory issues. I was not sure that Giovanni would even sit still long enough for Dr. Day to conduct an exam of his head and spine.

I was surprised, and excited, when Dr. Day happily agreed to examine Giovanni, regardless of his age and issues. Dr. Day explained that Giovanni's Atlas disc was seriously out of alignment in his neck. This could cause problems throughout the central nervous system and also could affect the response of the brain to interruptions in the central nervous system.

Dr. Day also explained that the disc was likely pinching the nerves in the neck, which transmit impulses to the brain. He corrected the alignment of that disc.

When he examined Giovanni's head, he stated that he felt some tension there. He massaged the skull, thereby loosening the sutures in the skull to allow for more movement. As the brain grows, the skull grows also. Giovanni's skull was under a lot of stress. Dr. Day relieved that stress.

Dr. Day was a very friendly, personable man, and I could feel positive energy in his office. If I could feel so at ease so quickly, I am sure Giovanni felt the same. Giovanni really liked Dr. Day and allowed him to adjust his spine and head without too much squirming around.

After several hours, I realized that I had not seen any myoclonic "sparks" since his adjustment.

The next day, when my father called, I told him that I had not seen any "sparks" in almost twenty-four hours. This was a record.

Could it be that the adjustment "cured" the myclonus? For a week, my dad would call every day to see if Giovanni had any "sparks." Each time I would tell him that I had not seen any.

Even as I write this chapter, four months after the chiropractor appointment, I have not seen any further myoclonic sparks— not one. They completely disappeared the day of his chiropractic adjust-ment. The chiropractic adjustment seemed to be the missing piece of the puzzle to correcting Giovanni's condition.

Another positive side effect of the adjustment was that Giovanni was no longer sensitive to touching of his head. I was finally able to wash his hair without him fussing or squirming around. Actually, it turned out that he really liked head massages. He also did not mind getting his hair brushed. However, cutting his hair was another story, though he has reacted more positively to that as well.

Dr. Day told me at a later appointment about a patient that he had that was suffering from epilepsy. She was having grand-mal type seizures. It turned out that she had an abscessed tooth that was putting pressure on the nerve in her jaw. When the tooth was removed, the seizures disappeared.

Through all observable evidence, it would appear that the myoclonus was a nerve issue, which affected the brain. The neurolo-gist was supportive of the option of chiropractic care. Because the myoclonus had disappeared, I decided that I would try lowering Giovanni's dose of Lamictal again.

Within one month of beginning the Lamictal withdrawals, Giovanni had his last episode of vomiting. He has not had one since.

I have noticed that as Giovanni's Lamictal levels have decreased, his ability to sleep longer hours at night has increased. Although he prefers to sleep next to me for several hours each night, he usually starts the night in his own bed. He sleeps up to nine hours at a time. However, if I do not feed him enough before bed, he will get up after several hours stating that he is "hungry." Although he cannot speak clearly, he has his own way of communicating his hunger by stating,

"Hung". I am thankful that he is sleeping more soundly and for more hours, because that means that I get more sleep, too.

Coincidentally, as Giovanni weaned off his medication, it became more evident that he was responding more to vision. He began acting more and more like a typical four-year-old with tantrums to express his frustration and anger at his disabilities.

Giovanni's eyes focused much better than they used to, possibly as a result of the homeopathic remedies that he was taking for it. When his vision was "on", I could tell that his eyes were focused on something. Whenever he had "vision", he would be happy and smiling. I knew that he did not rely on his vision as a primary sense as we do because he would close his eyes to concentrate on input from his other senses.

Even when Giovanni did appear to have vision, I noticed that he used his hands to search the ground in a pattern, much like a blind person would do.

When he had vision, it was difficult to tell what he could actually see. At times, he would roll his eyes up and look at the ceiling. Other times he would look straight ahead. Perhaps he had various types of vision such as central and peripheral. Someday when Giovanni is able to express himself through speech, then he can let us know what he "sees."

As I have lowered Giovanni's Lamictal dosage, his eyes seem to move more, as if they are trying to focus. Kathryn believed this was a positive improvement since his eyes were actually trying to focus rather than remain in a fixed "stare." Also, the movement of the eyes strengthened the ligaments in the eyes.

The worst part of cortical visual impairment is when Giovanni has some vision and then it goes "out." This is like a child having nightmares during the day. It can happen any time and we do not know how long it will last. The cries that Giovanni makes when he is essentially "blind" really are heartbreaking, emotional, and draining.

Giovanni uses his hands to "test" his vision. He waves a hand in the air above his eyes. When there is no vision, his eyes appear "blank" and he screams and cries. When his vision "turns on," I can see him focus on his hand and he starts smiling again.

Since Giovanni's vision is dependent on how his brain is working, it makes sense that when he is tired, he does not have as much vision. When his brain is using "brain power" on another activity, his vision usually suffers. Consequently, when he gets angry and upset when he loses vision, I tell him to "calm down, let your brain rest and your vision will come back." Sometimes he listens to me, and sometimes he does not. Whenever Kenneth tells him to "calm down and your vision will come back," he listens to him and usually quiets down right away.

Although Giovanni's vision is variable on any given day, it does appear that overall his vision has greatly improved and is more consistent.

I have realized how much Giovanni's vision has improved when I offer him choices of toys of different colors. When I ask him to pick a toy with a particular color, he chooses the correct toy. This means that Giovanni can see the color that I am telling him. More importantly, he understands the concept of color.

As Giovanni has become more alert with less medication, he has been responding more actively at school. His teacher reports that he is doing better at making choices. At home, he makes choices by touching my nose when he hears the choice he wants. He is even making the choice to use the toilet, although he still has a way to go to master this skill.

Another skill he is acquiring is the ability to feed himself with a spoon. Although he is lazy at home, I have witnessed that he can use a spoon to feed himself at school. He is not as slow as he used to be. He can now finish the entire snack I pack for him instead of returning home with half of it. His fine motor skills are improving as he is able to chew a variety of foods now. He also can grasp some foods with his fingers, which shows an improvement with his pincer grasp.

One of the tasks that most parents take for granted is their child's ability to feed himself or herself. When Kenneth was younger, I could go on long trips in the car and give him food to snack on while we were driving. Since Giovanni does not have the fine motor skills to feed himself, I need to stop on long trips to feed him. It is now a routine element of our trips to calculate additional time for Giovanni's meal stops.

Giovanni is walking better with assistance. His orthotics help him to walk straight. He is also walking at a quicker pace, which means his brain is not taking so long to process the movements. His speech therapist says that he is walking with assistance to the speech therapy room.

Additionally, Giovanni spends up to an hour or more at a time in his walker. Usually he stands or walks backwards. In August, Giovanni began walking forward in his walker. Coincidentally, he also was laughing and giggling because he had vision. Certainly, vision is a major motivator for movement. Giovanni was motivated by my mother and attempted to walk forward to follow her.

Giovanni continually amazes people around him. He certainly impressed one of the substitute teachers who played his clarinet for the children. The teacher told me after class that Giovanni has a unique ability for music. He said that Giovanni intently listened to the clarinet and tapped his foot to the rhythm. The teacher was amazed at Giovanni's attention span with the music and his ability to keep the rhythm. He suggested that I encourage Giovanni's love for music. This teacher felt he had a special gift for it.

This teacher was no ordinary teacher. He was a retired musician from the San Francisco Symphony Orchestra. I definitely took his comments to heart, as he knew what he was talking about. After speaking with the musical substitute teacher, I purchased a harmonica to play for Giovanni. He listens and smiles when I play it for him. Then, he tries to mimic the notes. Although I am not very proficient at identifying musical notes, I can tell that Giovanni is able to mimic the notes very well.

It is obvious that Giovanni has a great love for music. He definitely shows preferences for certain artists. He enjoys country music, especially female singers. His favorite singer appears to be Andrea Bocelli, the blind opera singer. Giovanni also enjoys rock music with a drum rhythm.

Giovanni concentrates so much on verbal communication that he does not always respond with sign language. He wants to communicate with words and he becomes very frustrated when I do not understand him. He speaks very adamantly in his "language" and scratches his chest in agitation when he is not understood. It is much like speaking to someone who speaks another language. He has his own vocabulary, intonations, and sentence structure. It is obvious to me that he is "speaking." However, I cannot always translate accurately. It helps to observe his body language.

I believe his more consistent vision is probably also helping his speech. In order to attain speech, Giovanni needs to be able to place labels on items in his environment. He needs vision in order to label his environment. Perhaps his speech delays are not related solely to brain injury, but may possibly be related to lack of vision and inability to label the environment.

Very recently, Giovanni was able to complete an entire sentence that was understandable to me. I was taking him out of the hot tub, which he loves, into the house. I told him I would give him a bath. He said, "You give me a bath." This meant that he understood the concept of taking a bath.

Another concept he understands is my concern over "head injuries." A recent trip the department store shows how well Giovanni understands, and how much he plays up his disability.

With Giovanni in his wheelchair, Kenneth was playing games and "driving" him around the store. They took a sharp turn and the wheelchair tipped over. As I rushed to try to catch it, I heard a "thud" as the wheelchair hit the floor. Although the wheelchair has armrests that will likely impact the floor first, I was afraid that Giovanni may still have hit his head on the floor.

I had difficulty hiding my panic when I picked him up. Giovanni started to cry, but immediately stopped when I frantically asked him "are you okay?" and "say something to me." He did not respond. He was totally quiet and began to act disoriented. I told Kenneth I needed to take him home to observe him for signs of a concussion.

However, observing Giovanni for signs of a concussion was a little difficult since his eyes are frequently dilated because of his visual impairment. By the time I got him to the car, he had covered his eyes with his arm so I could not even see them at all.

By now, I was thinking it was very possible he could be faking an injury. Kenneth looked at him and said, very sternly, "Giovanni are you faking?" That is when Giovanni brought his arm down and started laughing. He started bouncing around and giggling.

I learned that Kenneth was not the only one who could sense my panic and play on my sympathy. Giovanni had become very adept at doing the same thing. He knows how to "play up" his disabilities to try to get what he wants.

In many ways Giovanni is a "typical" little boy, but with some very unique needs and abilities.

I tried to share all the positive news with Jude. He did not show any enthusiasm when I spoke to him on the phone. During one of our few phone conversations that addressed Giovanni, I asked Jude if he would be interested in spending some one-on-one time with Giovanni during the summer. Jude claimed that he would take Giovanni if I gave him a checklist on how to give medication and how to feed him. Jude said he still "does not have the proper equipment" to take care of a disabled child. He did not seem interested in obtaining this equipment.

Giovanni did not come with an "owner's manual." I believe that this was just another one of Jude's excuses for refusing to spend time with Giovanni. After 4 ½ years, the excuses never end.

I pointed out to Jude that if he spent more time with Giovanni, then his child support obligation would be reduced. Even THAT did not motivate him to spend time with Giovanni.

If Jude would only spend a little time with Giovanni, he would see how much Giovanni has developed, especially during the first half of 2009.

With all the positive changes Giovanni has gone through this year, I can definitely say that I have reached stage seven of the grief model—hope for the future. Obviously, there are difficult days where I feel sorry for myself, for Giovanni or even for Kenneth. However, Giovanni is such an inspiration to all of us that I can usually pull myself out of my negativity before long.

Giovanni is making great strides every day in proving that his original diagnoses were not entirely accurate. Although he is still severely developmentally disabled, he has made amazing progress. Personally, I believe that alternative medicine has been a primary influence in his development. I also believe that he is flourishing in the care of those who love him and care for him the most—me, Kenneth, Traci, Gina, my parents and my grandmother.

My brother, James, is Giovanni's godfather. James, and his wife Melissa, have helped as much as possible. Because of his active duty military assignments, and the fact that they live 160 miles away, James and Melissa have not been able to be around as much as they would had they lived closer. I should mention, however, that James and Melissa travelled that 320-mile round-trip on an occasion that I was desperate for childcare and Jude failed to return any of my messages.

As an infant, Giovanni was diagnosed with "on-set symptoms of cerebral palsy" and "cortical blindness." Although he has not been diagnosed with cerebral palsy, his CVI diagnosis means that he is "legally blind." His motor planning delays are improving as he is weaned from the Lamictal. His cortical visual impairment has improved to the point that we believe that he has some functional vision the majority of the time. When he loses his vision, he has a very obvious reaction. Those episodes of complete vision loss seem to be decreasing.

Giovanni definitely has speech delays, though based on his responses, the delays are with his expressive language rather than receptive language. In other words, he understands everything that is said to him, but he is not able to respond verbally. I anticipate he will continue to increase his skills to a point where his speech is understandable to everyone around him.

Truly, Giovanni's visual impairment causes him distress. However, I believe that his frustration with his speech delays is overshadowing his frustration with his vision.

Giovanni appears to have outgrown much of the sensory processing difficulties that he had when he was younger. He is no longer sensitive to temperature or taste. In fact, one of his favorite treats is cold whipped cream. As an infant, I could not even imagine the day when Giovanni would not be sensitive to temperature. Most of his sensory issues are a result of his inconsistent and variable vision.

Vision is also a primary motivator in Giovanni's desire to walk. When he can see, he is more excited to move around and explore. His muscles get stronger every day, because of daily exercise in his walker. It is no longer a chore for him. He now has a desire to walk.

Though Giovanni had medical issues early on such as asthma and stomach problems, these were both cured through a combination of diet and reduction in medication.

The label of "mental retardation" just does not seem to fit this child, either. He proves this everyday as he functions and thrives despite some severe physical limitations.

The epilepsy that caused Giovanni so much distraction for the past few years seems to have disappeared. The seizures that he suffered in January were very likely caused by the stress of the EEG. Furthermore, it the nerve issue corrected by chiropractic really caused the myoclonus, then it follows that the 24-hour EEG only exacerbated the nerve issues.

Instead of calling Giovanni's challenges "disabilities", I can call them "differing abilities." Certainly, these differing abilities cause him difficulties and frustration when interacting in this environment. These differing abilities provide him a unique perspective on life. His family, friends, and teachers just need to have patience and understanding, and he will usually respond positively.

Giovanni's differing abilities also give him a unique perspective of the world. He uses his senses differently than most people. Therefore, his relationship to his environment is different from what most people experience. We can call learn lessons about life and how to appreciate it just by observing how Giovanni lives his life.

Chapter 21

O ne of the most difficult tasks in writing this book was deciding when and how to end it. There is so much to be thankful for in how far Giovanni has progressed. When I look back to those first few weeks in the hospital, when the prognosis for his development was grim, I am amazed by his development. Based on his improvement in just the past few months, there is no doubt he has the potential to grow, change and progress even further.

Giovanni has more desire to move around his environment. He is gaining strength in his legs and is able to spend up to two hours in his walker. When he is in his walker, he is now more likely to propel himself forward rather than backward like he used to do. Instead of walking backward or in circles, Giovanni walks with more purpose and is usually drawn to the windows with bright light.

As a result of his progress with is training walker, his physical therapist recommended that he "graduate" to a more mobile, less cumbersome, walker.

Giovanni also is exercising different muscle groups in order to sit up and roll around. He sits with his back straight and does not slouch. He propels himself forward while in a sitting position and tries to crawl. Giovanni has always loved taking a bath while strapped in to his special bath chair. His balance has improved so much, that I can allow him to sit without the strap around his waist and watch him as he balances himself and splashes around.

Taking a bath now serves two purposes. First, Giovanni can splash and play while he gets clean. Second, his constant movement to maintain balance in the moving water provides exercise for his oblique muscles. As Giovanni builds strength in these muscles, he will be able to walk straighter.

I have spent over four years trying to re-wire Giovanni's brain to form neural connections that will improve Giovanni's physical abilities. The brain is remarkable in its ability to re-wire itself and form new memories through repetition. Through the repetition of daily walking, Giovanni has trained his brain to the point of being able to simultaneously walk and speak in his own special language.

Not only does the brain form new connections as it relates to physical abilities, but for mental abilities as well. Giovanni's mental and cognitive growth was evident in our recent trip to Disneyland. Unlike the stressful trip we had four years ago, this trip was fun and exciting as we all witnessed Giovanni's responses to new stimuli. Ironically, like the first trip when Giovanni was weaning off of the Phenobarbital, Giovanni was weaning off of the Lamictal on this trip. Unlike the first trip, Giovanni reacted more positively to having his medication reduced this time.

The rides that Giovanni enjoyed the most were the ones that gave the most vestibular input. Even as I wheeled him around in his wheelchair, he would close his eyes so that he could absorb all the sounds of Disneyland. He had such a good time that he cried when I told him we were going home.

I am convinced that the anti-seizure medication was a primary influence in Giovanni's early brain growth. Although the medication was necessary to bring his seizures under control, it had a negative effect on brain growth. This all translated into slow development, which in turn led to severe developmental delays and extensive sensory processing issues. As I decreased Giovanni's medication dose his sensory processing issues improved. He does not have his fingers in his mouth for sensory input as much as he used to. A major sensory improvement is that he now consistently eats cold foods and recently ate an entire bowl of ice cream.

The side effects of weaning from the Lamictal include headaches and insomnia. Giovanni would become frustrated with the headaches because it would lead to loss of vision. But these episodes are fewer than a few months ago and Giovanni recovers more quickly from them. Most nights, he is now able to sleep straight through for eight or nine hours without sleep disturbances.

One of the most amazing things to happen to Giovanni as I write this chapter is that he has weaned off of his medication. From the time that Giovanni was diagnosed with epilepsy, I had resigned myself to the fact that he would be on medication for his entire life. There are still no signs of seizures. His myoclonus has never returned since Dr. Day adjusted his spine seven months ago. In fact, he has not been ill since that time either.

Since Giovanni has been taking homeopathic remedies recommended to me by Kathryn Picoulin, his eyes focus much better than in the past. Kathryn also stated that he still has double-vision. Overall, thought, it appears that he has some form of vision more often during the day than he ever had before.

Giovanni's vision specialist, Collette, concurred with Kathryn's diagnosis. Collette explained recently that Giovanni has strabismus, which was the first time that I had heard the term. Strabismus means that under normal conditions the eyes are unable to focus in unison, which causes double-vision. Though many medical professionals consider the condition to be lifelong, there are some homeopathic remedies that I will continue to try with Giovanni that may reverse the condition to some degree.

During her visit, Collette witnessed Giovanni's loss of vision and how he reacted to it. I was accustomed to Giovanni's sadness and irritation with his loss of vision. I assumed that his reactions were normal for a child with CVI. According to Collette, many children with CVI who have cognitive delays do not have an obvious reaction to the variation in vision. Giovanni is aware of his environment and cognitively responds to his loss of vision. This is a positive attribute as it supports my belief that Giovanni has cognitive abilities that cannot be measured by traditional testing. Collette also noticed a significant improvement in Giovanni's vision since her last visit three months prior.

Giovanni is trying with much determination to overcome his speech difficulties as well. I can feel the strength of his will as he struggles to form words and get his message across. The more he practices, and struggles, to learn this skill, the more neural connections will be formed in the brain for this task. Although he can use a few hand gestures to communicate some of his needs, he usually prefers to verbalize them. This tendency, I believe, shows his determination and desire to speak with words rather than sign language. As long as he has the determination, I know he will progress.

Since Giovanni started school this semester, his teachers have expressed their amazement at how much he has changed. But he behaves like a typical four-year-old child as he succeeds at tasks at school, while at home he acts like he does not have the ability. At school, he is willing to help feed himself with a special therapeutic spoon. Even though he is more willing to do it for his teachers, but has started to try to feed himself at home, also.

In a recent conversation with Jude, it became clear that he had taken his misconceptions and reiterated them enough, to me and to himself, that they had become his reality. He still places most of the blame on me for moving away and taking the children too far away for him to visit. He also stated his belief that my family and I intentionally took the children away from him in order to push him out of their lives. It appears Jude continues to believe this despite all my assurances to the contrary. It has been these inaccurate interpretations that have formed the basis of his relationship with Giovanni. Since Jude seems intent on continuing with these ideas, his future relationship with Giovanni is unlikely to change.

Additionally, I tried to encourage Jude to provide his input and perspective to this book. I really want to be fair. I am far from perfect and have my faults. Because I am an analytical personality, I find some peace and resolution in analyzing past events and mistakes.

Life is full of learning experiences. Giovanni has taught me that whether a person has a physical impairment or a mental one, there are infinite possibilities for the brain to be reprogrammed to overcome them. Those individuals with the strongest will and the most loving family support are best suited to success.

Jude has declined any opportunity I have given to him to discuss the book. He insists that he does not want to think about the past since he is now in a happy place in his life with his fiancée and his new job. He does not appear to see any benefit to reflecting on the past in order to make better decisions in the future. Whereas I believe in the phrase "those who don't know history are bound to repeat it," I do not believe he has reached that point yet.

Jude seemed willing to provide care for both Kenneth and Giovanni. He expressed his desire to "step up to the plate" and take responsibility for his children. I thought this was a positive step since it was the first time in over four years that he used those words himself. He acknowledged his failure to be involved in his children's life. Now that he is building a new life with a fiancée, he seemed genuine when he told me that he wanted to be a better father to the boys.

Since that conversation, however, Jude has continued to deflect any questions that I have about childcare, or about any other issues that I might be having with the boys that would require any significant thought or compromise. He has reverted back to his prior habit of calling Kenneth only two or three times a week. His proclamation of renewed interest in Giovanni did not last for more than a week. He now declines the opportunity to speak to Giovanni on the phone. Instead, he instructs Kenneth to pass along the message to Giovanni that his dad loves him.

Perhaps Jude has reverted back to his old ways since Emma is no longer a driving influence in his behavior. By the end of summer, their engagement was inexplicably cancelled. Since that time, he has moved on with other women.

In at least the past year, no members of Jude's family have made any phone calls to inquire about Giovanni's progress. Although Jude Sr. and Olivia do not take initiative in making a connection with Giovanni, I am grateful that they still contribute to Kenneth's education and take part in his significant school events. They each spent special time with Kenneth during the summer of 2009. Jude Sr. took Kenneth to a kid's camp for a day. Olivia invited Kenneth to spend a couple of weekends with her, which also happened to assist me with childcare for work.

Diana, however, remains focused on trying to build her marriage. After having visited with Kenneth in April of 2009, she claimed that she wanted to spend more time with him and Giovanni. In the five months since that time, she has made no attempts to visit either of the children. She surprised me with a phone call during the middle of the summer. She told me that she had delivered a child with some of the same issues that Giovanni had at his birth. The similarities caused her to become emotional and she shared her feelings with me about how dire Giovanni's situation was at his birth. According to Diana, she was told we should not expect much progress from Giovanni, as his situation appeared grim.

I explained to Diana that I had survived through the depression and had become a stronger person because of my experience with Giovanni. I also expressed my hope that she would become more involved with Giovanni so that she could witness his incredible spirit. Thus far, I have received no calls. One of the facts I have had to accept is that I cannot force anyone, even family members, to have the desire and the commitment to my children that I have.

Consequently, Jude and his family are missing out on some amazing experiences with Giovanni that not only enrich my life, but inspire Kenneth and my family as well. Because of limitations with his sense of vision, all of his other senses help him to interpret his world. Giovanni interprets the world much differently than we do because of his lack of vision. He responds to the world much differently because of his motor and speech difficulties. I no longer feel sorry for Giovanni, or for myself. I am inspired to "see" the world in a whole new way and take pleasure in the little things.

Giovanni has made such great progress in the past few months, that I am sometimes anxious to witness further improvements. However, I have to remember that Giovanni is developing at his own speed. This is not just based on his physical abilities, but also on his mental abilities and inner strength and will. Since he is more alert than ever, he also understands that he has limitations that other people may not have. Though he may get discouraged, Giovanni is more often happy, content, and interactive.

Giovanni was born with a strong spirit, and that is a big factor in his development. Because of his love for music, his unique ability to mimic tones easier than forming words, and his reliance on his inner strength and intuition, I can say that he progresses forward through life using his own unique rhythm.

Afterword

My family and I have developed a new outlook on life based on our life with Giovanni. We find pleasure in the simple things, much like Giovanni does.

Giovanni is proof that life does not end with a diagnosis. It really is a new beginning. My friend Joe Allio directed me to the Bible scripture James 4:14 (NIV), which states, "Why, you do not even know what will happen tomorrow. What is your life? You are a mist that appears for a little while and then vanishes." A child with special needs gives us the opportunity to slow down and learn to enjoy life every moment.

Besides the Allios, I have met many parents in the past few years that face daily challenges like I do. For some, the road is especially difficult because of disabilities that require extensive medical intervention. Thankfully, Giovanni does not have any chronic illness or disease to complicate the challenges he has because of his brain injury.

The brain is a complex and mysterious organ. It has great potential for growth. In fact, the brain is constantly growing and changing at a great pace for the first several years of life. When the brain is involved, there is always hope of improvement.

We are not mere physical beings; we are also spiritual beings. We are all here on this Earth for a purpose. We are all connected to each other. We each have our own rhythm that contributes to the greater symphony that is humanity. Look beyond the physical, think outside the box, and there you will find hope and light, communication, and intelligence unconfined to the spoken word.

About the Author

Lisa Marie Anderson holds a Bachelor of Arts degree in English from the University of California at Davis, with minors in military science and sociology. She also holds a Master of Arts degree in Education with an emphasis in curriculum and instruction from Chapman University. Lisa is divorced and currently works part time as a police dispatcher. She served for 12 years in the United States Army Reserve and National Guard. Her most notable and proud achievement is full-time mom to Kenneth and Giovanni. She lives with her two sons in Woodland, California, where she is Giovanni's biggest advocate for his multiple disabilities.

Resources

Alta Regional Center
2135 Butano Dr.
Sacramento, CA 95825
916-978-6400
www.altaregional.org

American Foundation for the Blind
11 Penn Plaza Suite 300
New York, NY 10001
800-AFB-LINE
www.afb.org

American Printing House for the Blind
1839 Frankfort Ave.
Louisville, KY 40206-0085
800-223-1839
www.aph.org

Batten Disease Support & Research Association
166 Humphries Dr.
Reynoldsburg, OH 43068
800-448-4510
www.bdsra.org

The Child Trauma Academy
5161 San Felipe St. Suite 320
Houston, TX 77056
866-943-9779
www.childtrauma.org

Dr. Alex Day D.C.
3440 Palmer Dr.
Cameron Park, CA 95682
530-676-8366

Dr. Kathryn Picoulin BSN, ND, PhD
701 High St. Suite 205
Auburn, CA 95603
530-823-5903
http://kathrynpicoulin.com

Hadley School for the Blind
700 Elm St.
Winnetka, IL 60093-2554
800-323-4238
info@hadley.edu

National Federation of the Blind
And National Organization of Parents of Blind Children
1800 Johnson St.
Baltimore, MD 21230
410-649-9314
www.nfb.org

Seedlings Braille Books for Children
POB 51924
Livonia, MI 48151
800-777-8552
info@seedlings.org

Southpaw Enterprises, Inc.
POB 1047
Dayton, OH 45401
800-228-1698
www.southpawenterprises.com

Bibliography

"Building the Legacy of IDEA 2004," (2004). Available from: U.S. Department of Education http://idea.ed.gov.

Balch, James, M.D. and Mark Stengler, N.D.. *Prescription for Natural Cures*. Hoboken: John Wiley & Sons Inc., 2004.

Biel, Lindsey and Nancy Peske. *Raising a Sensory Smart Child*. New York: Penguin Books, 2005.

Devinsky, Orrin, M.D.. *Epilepsy: Patient and Family Guide*. New York: Demos Medical Publishing, 2008.

Harrell, Lois. *Teaching Touch*. Louisville: American Printing House for the Blind, 2002.

Klaus, Marshall M.D. and John Kennell M.D.. "Bonding With Your Newborn," (2008). Available from: Ask Dr. Sears. http://www.askdrsears.com (2009).

Kranowitz, Carol Stock, M.A.. The Out-Of-Sync Child has Fun. New York: Penguin Books, 2003.

Perry, Bruce M.D., Ph.D.. "Protecting the Spirit of Childhood II." Lecture, University of California at Davis, April 1, 2006.

"7 Stages of Grief: Through the Process & Back to Life," (2007). http://www.recover-from-grief.com (2009).

Webster's Ninth New Collegiate Dictionary. Springfield, Massachusetts: Merriam-Webster Inc., 1985.